ERRATUM

The first two paragraphs on page 52 should read as follows:

rational-actor approach in the areas of voting behavior and public choice, and as a technique has spread to other fields of political inquiry. In its essence, it reflects the theoretical approach of contemporary economics and in fact even borrows economic theories for application to political situations (Downs, 1957; Kramer & Hertzberg, 1975).

This rationalistic approach has not been without its critics, and their voices have been growing in number and intensity. In part they have challenged the rationality assumption on the grounds that actors do in fact behave nonrationally and irrationally and that prediction of the behavior of individuals or of aggregates unnecessarily handicaps itself by failing to take such facts into account (Eckstein, 1988; Elster, 1989; Jarvie, 1984; Mansbridge, 1990; Quattrone & Tversky, 1988). In part, however, the rational model has been accused of being overly reductionist in assuming that individual attributes, such as rationality, can explain all behavior. Such a model fails to take into account systematically the institutional and structural context that may determine or, at the very least, actors, severally or as aggregates (Easton, 1990; March & Olsen, 1989). By the beginning of the 1990s, however, it would appear that these increasing reservations about the applicability of the rationality model have not prevented it from carving out a sizeable and, from all appearances, an enduring nitch for itself in the discipline.

DIVIDED KNOWLEDGE

DIVIDED KNOWLEDGE

Across Disciplines, Across Cultures

edited by

David EASTON

Corinne S. SCHELLING

Published in cooperation with the
American Academy of Arts and Sciences

SAGE PUBLICATIONS
The International Professional Publishers
Newbury Park   London   New Delhi

For information address:

SAGE Publications, Inc.
2455 Teller Road
Newbury Park, California 91320

SAGE Publications Ltd.
6 Bonhill Street
London EC2A 4PU
United Kingdom

SAGE Publications India Pvt. Ltd.
M-32 Market
Greater Kailash I
New Delhi 110 048 India

Printed in the United States of America

Library of Congress Cataloging-in-Publication Data

Main entry under title:

Divided knowledge : across disciplines, across cultures / David Easton
  and Corinne S. Schelling, editors.
     p. cm.
  Includes bibliographical references.
  ISBN 0-8039-4038-6. — ISBN 0-8039-4039-4 (pbk.)
   1. Humanities—United States—Congresses. 2. Social sciences—
United States—Congresses. 3. United States—Intellectual
life—20th century—Congresses. 4. Humanities—China—Congresses.
5. Social sciences—China—Congresses. 6. China—Intellectual
life—1976- —Congresses. I. Easton, David, 1917-
II. Schelling, Corinne Saposs.
AZ5076.D58   1991
001.3dc20   90-19482
                                                        CIP

FIRST PRINTING, 1991

Sage Production Editor: Diane S. Foster

Contents

Acknowledgments

On behalf of the American Academy of Arts and Sciences, we would like to express our appreciation to the Chinese Academy of Social Sciences (CASS) for organizing and financing the costs in China of our jointly sponsored May 1988 Beijing symposium, for which the essays in this book were originally prepared. Also, we thank our CASS colleagues for extending such warm hospitality to the members of the U.S. group during our stay in Beijing and elsewhere in China.

Our participation in this joint venture—including our role in planning the symposium, travel to and from China, and preparation of the manuscripts of the U.S. scholars for publication in this book— was made possible by grants to the American Academy from the Ford Foundation, the Andrew Mellon Foundation, and the Research and Planning Committee of the American Academy.

Peter Geithner, the Ford Foundation Representative for China, with his knowledge of Chinese scholarly institutions and his contacts in CASS, was helpful to us in many ways while we were in Beijing, as well as before and after our trip. In the early planning phase of this project, Professor Philip Kuhn of Harvard University was an invaluable adviser. He also served as our interpreter, guide, and link to CASS when we visited Beijing in 1984. In 1988, Professor

1

Thomas Gold of the University of California, Berkeley, with his knowledge of the Chinese language and familiarity with Chinese scholarly institutions, provided invaluable services to our group as translator, guide, and, above all, as colleague.

Many others in the U.S., who know China well, shared with us their insights on and experience with the contemporary Chinese world of scholarship to prepare our group of non-China-specialists to work effectively with our new Chinese colleagues. We want especially to thank Prudence Humphreys, who worked diligently and creatively to ensure that what contributors wrote was properly translated from their machine's language through our editorial process and on to the printer. This turned out to be a challenge that she met with imagination, as well as hard work.

—David Easton
—Corinne S. Schelling

Preface

In 1983 David Easton, vice-president of the American Academy of Arts and Sciences, was invited by the Chinese Academy of Social Sciences (CASS) to lecture to some of its Institutes and to several of the major universities in China. During this visit he spoke with the then-President of CASS, Ma Hong, and others about establishing a continuing scholarly relationship between CASS and the American Academy. The suggestion was warmly received, and in 1984 a planning delegation led by President Herman Feshbach, with Professor Easton, Professor Philip Kuhn of Harvard, and Corinne Schelling, Associate Executive Officer of the American Academy, visited CASS. Our hosts, with whom we worked closely, were Vice-president Ru Xin and then-Deputy Secretary-general, Zhao Fusan. As a result of many working sessions, the two Academies entered into a memorandum of understanding under which mutually agreed-upon programs would be conducted in China and in the United States.

The first of these programs, a survey by leading scholars of recent developments in selected social science and humanistic disciplines in the West, particularly in the United States, took the form of a symposium in Beijing in May 1988. For the Chinese, this theme was of great importance. Especially in the period from the 1950s through the Cultural Revolution of 1966-1976, the country had suffered too much social and political turmoil to rebuild its neglected and often beleaguered ancient scholarly institutions. Indeed for a good part of the twentieth century, ravaged by external wars, the Japanese invasion and occupation, and civil strife, higher education has operated under the most austere and limiting conditions. By the 1970s, however, China was opening its doors to science and technology. Then, in the 1980s, as it began to reconstruct its higher education, China turned to areas that had been recently overlooked and were, in some instances, politically sensitive—the social sciences and the humanities. Knowledge of up-to-date work in these fields, among other things, it was hoped would permit improved understanding of and adjustment to the broad consequences of China's economic reconstruction activities.

As U.S. participants prepared their contributions for the May 1988 Symposium, they were uncertain about the extent to which recent Western developments in the social sciences and humanities had reached their Chinese colleagues. As it turned out, they were pleasantly surprised at how much had got through (despite the doors that had been closed between East and West for so many years and the continuing acute shortage of Western books and periodicals) and at the sophisticated, perceptive critiques of Western scholarship that they heard. At the same time, inevitably there were large gaps in what Chinese scholars had read, and in some cases there was also a philosophical gulf that was often openly discussed.

The May 1988 Symposium consisted of opening and closing plenary sessions with up to 100 participants and informal workshops for each of the selected fields. One U.S. scholar, a major figure who had influenced the field over the past decades, examined each discipline or area of learning. This scholar prepared, for advance distribution, a survey paper, reflecting his own views on developments and future directions of the given field. At the opening plenary session, these papers were presented and responded to by Chinese counterparts (with the help of simultaneous translation). They also were the basis for informal discussion at the disciplinary workshops, which were attended by Chinese scholars, students, and practitioners. In addition, there were many small, informal, and unscheduled discussions among participants from the two countries.

The choice of disciplines or areas of study for the Symposium, as well as of the format of the event, was made through extensive correspondence and direct discussion between the American and the Chinese Academies' planning committees. As is evident from this book, we agreed on five established disciplines—sociology, political science, philosophy, literary theory, and history. Philosophy, literature, and history are areas of traditional strength in China. Political science and sociology until recently had been forbidden areas for study, and thus were in need of considerable renewal. Three interdisciplinary academic fields—public policy, area studies, and business management—that were created in the West specifically to help apply scholarly knowledge and methods to social problems were also included. These interdisciplinary fields were of importance to current Chinese efforts to modernize their society as well as their institutions of higher education.

In our plans, the Symposium had two overarching themes: (a) the specialization or fragmentation of fields of knowledge in the West and consequent efforts to integrate them for application to social problems, a matter of considerable interest to our Chinese colleagues; and (b) the universality or transferability, between national cultures, of knowledge—its concepts, theories, and applications. Both themes, we felt, had particular relevance in a China that, as it was reconstituting its institutions of higher learning as well as restoring its economy, faced difficult choices about how best to organize its scholarship and research. Could China benefit from hearing about our problems as well as our successes?

Because of the events of June 1989, our original plans to publish Chinese commentary on the symposium with the papers have not materialized, although we have tried, especially in Easton's introductory chapter, to give the flavor of informal Chinese comments at the May 1988 meetings. We do not have precise current information about CASS's arrangements to publish the U.S. papers in Chinese in China, as called for in the agreements between the two Academies, but we assume that they are proceeding.

Plans for a second phase of the joint CASS-American Academy program and other activities anticipated in the initial memorandum of understanding await a clarification of scholarly conditions in China.

—David Easton
—Corinne S. Schelling

1

The Division, Integration, and Transfer of Knowledge

DAVID EASTON

Two thousand years of growth in knowledge have left Western scholarship with a host of intractable problems. Many are specific to individual disciplines; some involve the structure of and relationship among the disciplines; others fall into both categories. Perhaps none of these problems has more salience and urgency, or has created more hurdles, than increasing specialization, which affects both the individual disciplines and their inter-relationships. This problem is now widely perceived in both the social sciences and the humanities, two realms of scholarship that in academia are typically kept quite separate from each other—again evidence of specialization, an element of what we refer to as divided knowledge.

AUTHOR'S NOTE: I wish to express my appreciation to the following China-specialist colleagues at the University of California, Irvine, for the careful reading they have been kind enough to give this Chapter: Distinguished Visiting Professor Ping-Ti Ho, Department of History and Social Sciences; and Professors Dorothy Solinger, Department of Politics and Society, and Bin Wong, Department of History. Mr. San-yuan Li at the University of Chicago kept me alert to nuances of meanings so important in intercultural exchanges. Of course, the usual disclaimer applies; they bear no responsibility for the views presented here.

This volume describes and then examines the implications of specialization. Circumstances provided a unique opportunity to consider at the same time recent developments in selected social science *and* humanistic disciplines, as well as the emergence of three fields of learning that were designed specifically to overcome the deficiencies caused by specialization.

How did this unusual opportunity arise? As the preface explains, the essays in this book were commissioned for a joint symposium between the American Academy of Arts and Sciences and The Chinese Academy of Social Sciences in Beijing in May 1988. Moreover, the binational context raised a second major problem long recognized in Western scholarship, that is, the transferability of knowledge from one culture to another—yet another manifestation of divided knowledge. Thus, as it turned out, when a group of scholars from the United States collaborated with a group in the People's Republic of China to design a program reviewing recent developments in selected social science and humanistic disciplines, they created an occasion to consider two major dimensions of the division of knowledge at one time.

As we know from experience, a comparative view may shed new light on a given problem. From the chapters in this volume, we are able to compare disciplines; as a result of the Symposium discussions with our Chinese colleagues, referred to in this essay, we are also able to compare scholarship in national cultures based on different assumptions and perspectives. Thus the project described in the preface has led to a more comprehensive understanding than is usually possible of serious problems in the way we in the West organize knowledge, as well as how others see us. This project has been an example of learning more about oneself by seeing oneself— whether discipline or nation—through the eyes of another.

To our group, three things seemed to distinguish the present effort from other reviews of disciplines. In the first place, it turned out that as planners we crafted better than we knew. Unexpectedly we found that we were creating a setting for a dialogue between social scientists and humanists, an unusual event in the West. What we had only vaguely anticipated at first, but which became apparent as the Beijing symposium progressed, was that the very juxtaposition in one program of the social sciences and humanities that the Chinese simply took for granted, created an unusual opportunity for interdisciplinary exchanges among Western scholars. Despite its name, the Chinese Academy of Social Sciences (CASS) includes all these disciplines that we in the West normally consider to be part of the humanities—history, philosophy, literature, and the like. In the French idiom, CASS might well have been called the Academy of the Humane Sciences. Thus, it was natural for the Chinese to wish to include, in any exchange, disciplines from both the social sciences and the humanities.

What seemed totally ordinary from the history and traditions of the production of knowledge in China was, of course, highly unusual for us. Only as we began to assemble the American group for the symposium did it become apparent that we were inadvertently also creating the setting for a dialogue between the social sciences and the humanities in the West. Aside from any other considerations, Western participants found the symposium an unexpectedly rewarding opportunity to enter into a discourse with each other around common themes, an opportunity, we later agreed, that occurs only too rarely in the West between social scientists and humanists.

In the second place, most reviews of disciplines have been developed largely for American, or, more likely, Western consumption. Certain assumptions could be taken for granted about the intellectual background of the reader, the reservoir of understandings that could be brought to bear on interpreting an analysis, and the accumulated perceptions that could fill any gaps.

Discussions around reviews prepared for non-Western readers could take much less for granted. They would encourage the American participants to return to fundamentals and perhaps open up issues that otherwise would have remained unspoken or unrecognized. Thus we Westerners might come to know our own disciplines better for the very reason that we were seeking to present them to scholars immersed in a radically different culture and tradition. If nothing else, a dialogue with non-Western scholars might appropriately raise a question of paramount importance: To what extent are Western conceptions of science and knowledge culture-bound, products of specific cultural and historical experiences that have only limited relevance for scholars from other cultures and traditions?

In the third place, the time of the symposium, May 1988, was an unusually open moment in the history of education in China. Immediately after the end of the Cultural Revolution, Chinese scholars appeared to be willing to plunge enthusiastically into the task of rebuilding their own social sciences and humanities. Even though they had five thousand years of tradition on which to lean, they were beginning to explore ways in which they might best take advantage of developments in Western culture. Our planned reassessment of Western disciplines could not have occurred at a more favorable moment.

At the time of the symposium, there appeared to be an opportunity for a relatively free exchange of ideas and for the development of educational policies in China to take advantage of such ideas for reconstruction purposes. Since then, of course, circumstances have changed radically in China. The suppression of the democracy movement at Tiananmen Square in June 1989 abruptly shut the window on the new intellectual breezes that were beginning to stir. Whether Tiananmen Square heralds a long intellectual winter no one knows at this moment. We may at least hold out the hope that a country one billion strong, intent on moving into the twenty-first century, is unlikely to be able to isolate itself, intellectually or economically, for long, especially in a world that is already seeing extraordinarily deep and rapid changes in other hitherto nondemocratic countries. Even if the more favorable political climate in which our symposium was held no longer prevails, there is good reason to believe that, if and when that climate returns, the issues raised in the symposium for scholarship will not have disappeared. Indeed, because of the additional delay in addressing them, they may well become more urgent than ever before.

Specialization and Integration

In the West the history of the social sciences and humanities, indeed of all knowledge, with its dedicated search for understanding, is one of increasing specialization and fragmentation. At one time all knowledge about human, social, and physical nature was viewed as one. Scholars continue to refer to such encompassing thinking by Plato and Aristotle as philosophy, as though it were an indivisible unity. Over time, however, this single skein of knowledge divided into two basic strands, initially called natural and moral philosophy. By the seventeenth century the growth in the authority of the physical sciences was such that natural philosophy was transformed into natural science. By the end of the eighteenth century moral philosophy, that is, that branch of knowledge dealing with human relationships, also in hot pursuit of the prestige of science, relabeled itself as moral science. Thus the *The Wealth of Nations* has always been recognized as being as much a dissertation on morality as on the economy, even though in it Adam Smith (1937) began the decisive separation of the study of economics from the main body of moral science.

Shakespeare to the contrary, it is clear that there *is* something in a name. These shifts in identifying labels—from philosophy to natural versus moral philosophy and then to natural versus moral sciences—reflect underlying transformations in the self-image of areas of knowledge, as well as in their methods and perspectives. By the mid-19th century, under the inspiration of Auguste Comte, the founder of sociology, the moral sciences began to assume their modern name as the social sciences. Anthropology and economics had already begun to hive off from the main body of philosophy and moral (that is, social) sciences. Psychology, sociology, and history were not far behind, with political science bringing up the rear. The remainder, philosophy, was left to sort out its own identity, although, as Tilly (this book, Chapter 4) reminds us, history may still be struggling with the same problem.

With increasing acceleration in the 20th century, the social sciences and the humanities began to specialize with a vengeance so that today the basic disciplines have not only clearly identified themselves, but have subdivided internally into many subfields; and often, even within these, specialization continues apace. In proverbial terms, as one of our Chinese scholars phrased it, we seem to be "looking at the sky from the bottom of the well," and historically the wells have been increasing in number and decreasing in diameter.

It is commonplace to observe that the intensity of specialization is so rapid that scholars have difficulty keeping up with the significant literature in their own small niches, let alone with research in even closely adjacent substantive areas within a discipline. And what is true of the social sciences applies with equal validity to other fields of scholarship such as the humanities. Even in area studies, which combines the social and humanistic disciplines and in which we might have expected that explicit efforts to overcome specialization might win out, Lambert (this book, Chapter 7) tells us there has been less success than might have been expected. Area studies, he points out, is just "transdisciplinary," not interdisciplinary. Specialization in the form of factual areal knowledge, linguistic skills, and particular disciplines continues to leave its specific divisive imprints in the field.

In short, true to the Cartesian revolution, with its emphasis on analytic reasoning,[1] we have managed to decompose the world of understanding into a virtually limitless number of fragments. Faithful descendants of Adam Smith as well, we scarcely need to be reminded of the identifiable virtues of specialization. As Max Weber (1946, p. 134-35) once put it, "only by strict specialization can the scientific worker become fully conscious, for once and perhaps never again in his lifetime, that he has achieved something that will endure." The search for understanding seems to have driven Western scholarship into decomposing nature, whether physical or social, into smaller and smaller units on the assumption that when we have understood the smallest unit—the elusive quark of the physical world—we will then be able to reassemble our knowledge for a comprehensive understanding of the whole.

We do not need to address here the issue of whether the Cartesian impulse to analytic decomposition can ever provide satisfactory understanding of the whole or whether in the search for knowledge we may need to begin with the whole entity before we even begin to seek understanding of its parts. Whatever the reader's opinions on that score, the fact is that society confronts us with problems that are, for example, definable as neither political, philosophical, linguistic, economic, nor cultural alone. They may be all of these and more. They are indeed whole multi-faceted problems for which society seeks some kind of resolution or understanding. Poverty, we recognize, is not exclusively an economic problem; there is a culture of poverty, a social structure of poverty, a politics of poverty, and so on. This means that addressing the issue of poverty, however much it may indeed depend on jobs and adequate income, it would be hazardous to seek a solution that takes into account the wisdom derived from any one of these disciplines alone, or even largely, and that ignores understanding that derives from other areas of inquiry.

Herein lies one of the major crises of modern knowledge. It is what I have called the Humpty Dumpty problem. To understand the world it has seemed necessary to analyze it by breaking it into many pieces—the disciplines and their own divisions—in much the way that Humpty Dumpty, now the egg of knowledge, fragmented when he fell off the wall. But to act in the world, to try to address the issues for which the understanding of highly specialized knowledge was presumably sought, we need somehow to reassemble all the pieces. Here is the rub. Try as we may, we have been no more able than all of the king's horses and all of the king's men to put our knowledge together again for coping with the whole real problems of the world.

Understanding that has been acquired through the theoretical and methodological commitments of economics fits only tangentially with knowledge from political science; anthropological perspectives fit uneasily with those from psychology; and the newly conceived applied humanities seem to move in their own idiosyncratic directions. It is commonplace today to point out that disciplinarians find it difficult not only to talk to each other but even to carry on a credible discourse with colleagues in subspecialties within their own disciplines, because the level of development in many areas of inquiry has become so highly differentiated and technical.

A Solution: Interdisciplinary Training

Efforts have been made to overcome these self-created disabilities, some of which are noted in this book in the chapters that follow by Tilly (Chapter 4) and Turner (Chapter 3), with marginal success in the best of cases, a problem recognized long ago (Wirth, 1940). As Turner (1988) has pointed out, disciplines never live in total isolation; they are constantly being influenced by the "points of view and methods of related disciplines" so that at times "the boundaries between disciplines become blurred". Similarly, Tilly (Chapter 4) reflects on the way in which the search for universals has led historians to import the techniques and perspectives of other social sciences, a movement that has, however, sharply divided Western historians.[2] But such ad hoc borrowing among disciplines falls far short of combining them into a theoretical whole, even though such efforts certainly move in that direction.

Interdisciplinary training has been proposed as one way of overcoming the handicaps of specialization. Presumably this is intended to go beyond the mere borrowing or absorption of concepts, theories, and methods that regularly goes on among the disciplines.

Rather it implies the need for training scholars in more than one discipline. With the subdivision of the disciplines into so many specialties, however, it has proved difficult for one person to learn even one discipline comprehensively, let alone two. Learning more than two would be beyond the pale for scholars of all but the most exceptional intelligence. Indeed within single disciplines, as in history (Tilly, Chapter 4) and sociology, internal divisions may create barriers to cooperation that are even more difficult to overcome than those between disciplines.

Nonetheless, in the last several decades fields have grown up based on the premise that training in multiple disciplines will provide for the insights, knowledge, and skills required for coping with various kinds of practical problems facing the world. Public policy, business management, and area studies (viewing certain geographical areas of the world as coherent entities) represent three such fields. Problems addressed by people in these fields appear to elude understanding when approached from the direction of one or another social science or humanistic discipline. They have become focal points for attempts to integrate disciplines in the search for solutions to practical problems.

As the chapters in this volume suggest, at best these interdisciplinary areas have had only limited success in integrating various fields of knowledge. In policy studies, for example, as we learn from the chapter by Fleishman (Chapter 9), there has been a modicum of success in pairing politics with economics or with sociology for limited purposes, or even with ethics in the search for moral guidelines. Although efforts such as these have been synthesized into the newly developing area—one can hardly say discipline—of policy analysis and public management, as Fleishman suggests, the field has been unable to find a systematic way of integrating all or even a reasonable part of the social sciences, let alone relevant humanistic areas, for application to practical social problems. Indeed it appears that the faculty in this relatively new area of inquiry is still dominated by political scientists and economists. This may be appropriate for the issues the field seeks to address: how public decisions are made, what their consequences are, how they are to be assessed, how they might be managed, and the like. To that extent, Fleishman (Chapter 9) suggests, policy analysts are indeed "prescriptive and integrative." But there is little a priori reason for believing that economics and politics with a little salting of ethics, bound together by the concept of public management, will result in a new and coherent body of knowledge. Rather this combination seems to remain just an assembly of large pre-existing bits and pieces, "only a tiny fraction of the contents of the underlying disciplines" (Fleishman, Chapter 9, p. 237).

In short, as Fleishman concludes, policy analysis is still dependent primarily on economics and political science which, we can scarcely believe, exhaust the dimensions relevant for a full understanding of the determinants and consequences of public policies and their strategic implementation. And finally, even if the policy analysis movement meets its most optimistic hopes, as Fleishman seems to believe it will, and out of a selective fusion of parts of a few disciplines becomes a recognized, self-confident, and independent field of inquiry, this would do little more than add one further discipline, albeit a challenging and important one, to the fragmentation and specialization of social knowledge.

Business and management schools, for their part, continue to look like mini-universities within the broader university. They have representatives of most if not all the major disciplines (Cheit, Chapter 8); their students are exposed to the findings and some of the conceptual and theoretical apparatus from these disciplines for management and decision making. But it would be pushing their experience too far to pretend that these schools have come up with an integrative conceptual or theoretical structure that draws knowledge together in some synthetic whole that reflects the business reality with which their graduates must deal. For the most part they are still left to their own devices in drawing on their knowledge from various disciplines as they address problems in business administration and decision making. As Cheit laments, even in what was developed as an integrative field, knowledge "has become highly specialized and fragmented". Indeed, he cites a major 1988 study that concluded that business school curricula lack meaningful integration across functional fields and that called this "one of the most critical issues for business/management schools" (Chapter 8, pp. 210, 217).

Similarly in area studies, a field developed to gather scholars from a range of disciplines, the overwhelming proportion of students are trained primarily in a single discipline (Lambert, Chapter 7) and find themselves limited by their own narrow perspectives as they seek to understand a geographical area. Although at one time history might have offered itself as the integrative discipline, *par excellence*—and there are still advocates of this view—today, as Tilly (Chapter 4) informs us, it can more persuasively lay claim only to drawing events together along space and time dimensions, another form of specialization.

A Solution: Team Work

If the multidisciplinary training of our scholars is not the answer because of its impracticality in the highly specialized world in which we live, frequently the solution of actual social problems has drawn the attention of teams of scholars and practitioners trained in the various disciplines. The assumption is that, if we cannot pack all knowledge into one head, perhaps by bringing many specialized heads together we can achieve essentially the same integrative result through teamwork. To some extent policy analysis, business management, and area studies operate on this premise. Thus in Chapter 7, on area studies, Lambert seems to imply the team nature of the field. He talks of the "blending of disciplinary perspectives" in conferences and symposia and of collaboration around particular research topics, yet cautions us that "the basic reference point for most area specialists is the discipline in which he or she resides, and the long-term tendency is for more and more disciplinary specialization." And he clinches his point by concluding that "the most useful way to think of area studies is not to think of it as an interdisciplinary tradition of scholarship but a set of sub-disciplines"(p. 186).[3]

As promising as a team approach might appear at first glance, unfortunately it runs up against a host of difficulties that are well known to those who have tried working with scholars from a variety of disciplines. People who are trained under different traditions about what constitutes an appropriate question, what kinds of issues are even researchable, what makes for acceptable data as against mere opinion, what is adequate evidence, and when a proposition is to be considered confirmed or not, are not likely to find it simple to work together on a common project. Team members tend to speak in different tongues, often with similar terms for different phenomena and different terms for the same ones. Of course, team participants who have had some interdisciplinary training are more likely to be able to cooperate effectively. However, since education in two disciplines is the great exception—and in more than two, extraordinary—the difficulties of teamwork are not easily overcome in this way.[4]

The hurdles encountered by cooperative teams suggest that this effort to integrate the disciplines for applied purposes may come too late in the educational process, at the end of the road; whereas, if it is to have even a modest chance of success, it may need to be introduced at or close to the beginning. Yet given the Cartesian basis of our understanding of the process of obtaining understanding, that is, through decompositional analysis, we begin our training by moving quickly to specialization.

Thus, at the very outset our Western educational heritage handicaps us by defining our approaches in highly specialized terms, looking at knowledge as though it must come in packages called disciplines. We thereby create the subsequent need for teams to address issues of application. It is this apparent contradiction between disciplinary training as scholars and the demands of society for practical solutions of whole, real-world problems that creates one of the current major dilemmas in social inquiry.

A Solution: General Theory

Another effort to escape from this dilemma has taken the form of the search for general theory as the foundation of understanding, in the social sciences at least. Talcott Parsons long ago proposed the development of a theoretical structure that would provide a common set of concepts for all the social disciplines. General systems theory has moved in the same direction. And, of course, Marxist theory has always laid claim to providing such a body of thought. Most recently comparative historical sociology also has been offering itself as an alternative, overarching theoretical approach with pretensions to universality.

It cannot be denied that if a general theory could be discovered, one that could not be ignored by most social scientists, it would by definition provide a common body of concepts and even of theorems as a starting point for all analysis and application. Such theory would introduce a common language of communication and mutual understanding among the specialized disciplines. This possibility does offer a counsel of hope. To date, however, the few but substantial efforts in this direction have commanded the confidence and commitment of only small segments of the social science or, for that matter, humanistic communities. Whether over time this approach will prove to be a significant path toward the solution of the problems of specialization is not clear, especially as the sentiment favorable to overarching theoretical structures has for the moment at least markedly declined.

In any event, multidisciplinary training, teamwork, and general theory have so far not done the trick. The Humpty Dumpty difficulty in reassembling the whole has seldom been directly confronted, much less overcome.

Specialization in Chinese Scholarship

To what extent might we expect to encounter the same degree of specialization in non-Western societies? If we take China as one example, our symposium experience in 1988 revealed that, at least for scholars in some disciplines, specialization, for the most part, has yet to be seen as the kind of issue it has become in the West. Indeed just the opposite would seem to be the case; increased specialization itself, not integration seems to be the watchword. And the reason for this revealed something of importance about the state of Chinese knowledge in the social sciences and humanities in the 1980s. As new or potential members of the international intellectual community, Chinese scholars were more likely to feel the need for specialized knowledge rather than to complain about the difficulties it creates.[5]

As in the West in earlier periods, before specialization took root, scholars in China often have been broadly educated in many disciplines, cutting across the social sciences and the humanities. They have been exposed to what might be described as multidisciplinary rather than interdisciplinary training in such fields as literature, economics, law, history, and sociology. Furthermore, after 1949 little distinction was made between certain disciplines—political science and sociology, for example. Finally, it is not uncommon to find scholars devoted to the study of the literature of a country who consider themselves students of other disciplines, such as political science and sociology, as well.

For example, under the pressure of necessity, persons with foreign literature and language skills might be assigned to social science institutes to fill gaps in training and research programs simply because of their language competence. As a result, many Chinese scholars have considerable familiarity with what a Western-trained person would consider to be a number of different disciplines. At times they give the appearance of representing the interdisciplinarians often held up as an ideal in the West. In fact, they are likely to have had only limited exposure to a multitude of different areas of knowledge, without the benefit of any theoretical framework for integrating them or specific methodological tools for pursuing research in them.

The outcome in China was somewhat unexpected, however. This diversified background led not to the celebration of multidisciplinary education, with its avoidance of the pitfalls of overspecialization, but rather to the demand for greater specialization. As the comments of Chinese scholars in our various disciplinary workshops during the symposium revealed, they seemed generally to feel less well trained in the concepts, technical skills, and theoretical knowledge in a given area than they would wish, especially in terms of Western disciplinary standards, and in comparison with Western scholars with whom they had become acquainted, either through their writings or in person. For many of the Chinese scholars we met this seemed to indicate that what they required at the moment was a higher degree of technical training in social science tools for acquiring and analyzing data about individual behavior and institutions or, in the humanities, for improving their analytic and critical skills. In short, their desire was for more specialization, not less, for greater reliability in understanding a narrowly defined subject matter rather than for a broader scope.

During the symposium such views were voiced by scholars interested in political science[6] and sociology in particular, as well as by those in the interdisciplinary fields of policy studies, business management, and area studies. On the other hand, the philosophers and scholars in comparative literature we met, who already practiced a high degree of specialization (perhaps because of China's long tradition of scholarship in these disciplines), seemed relatively content with their commitment, even as they sought to improve their familiarity with newer developments in the West.

One might conclude that it is in the nature of research for scholars to turn to decomposition and specialization of their subject matter in order to improve the reliability of their comprehension—that it is a natural part of the logic of inquiry. It may also, however, be premature to draw such an inference from the responses of these Chinese scholars we met.

In the first place, the attractiveness of specialization, in part, might be simply a way of rejecting Marxism, which in itself may be viewed as one kind of holistic approach, especially because, at the time of our symposium, disenchantment with Marxism as a theoretical structure for research appeared to be well advanced. In the second place, it could be that exposure to Western knowledge with its apparent success through increasing specialization has led some East Asian scholars to believe that this is the one and only road to go. They might have wished thereby to preserve the integrity and independence of their disciplines with the not-so-incidental accompanying benefits of enhancing their own professional standing and also, perhaps, improving their chances for jobs and funding in and outside of China.

Once they do go down this road, however, they may well end up where Western knowledge finds itself, namely, confronted with extraordinary difficulties in reassembling that knowledge for application to specific practical social concerns. To the extent that Chinese scholars become aware of integrative problems at the very moment that they set out on this path, they may at least be able to take them into account as their philosophy of education and the reconstruction of their educational programs evolve.

In the third place, if only as an undercurrent during the symposium, some uneasiness with the Western path did reveal itself. In the political science workshop especially, for example, but elsewhere as well, it emerged in the form of what appeared to be a possible "revival" or rethinking of the place of Confucianism in a changing China.[7]

Whether such a revival was under way and if so how widespread it was, even in the case of intellectuals alone, was a matter of some dispute among Chinese scholars in May 1988, as well as among Western sinologists. Nevertheless, to the extent to which there has been a developing reconsideration of Confucian beliefs, it may well derive from a number of sources: the disorientation that appears to have followed the rejection of the values of the Cultural Revolution; the criticism of and general disillusionment with some of the orthodox views of Marxism, without alternative positive values to fill the resulting vacuum in beliefs; uneasiness with the rapid rate of social change and, for newcomers to the city who had been raised in rural traditions, with the somewhat bewildering pace of urban life; and deteriorating confidence in the leadership offered by the Communist Party and officialdom in general, even though after June 4, 1989 official practice no longer permits the new and higher level of social and political criticism so evident in May 1988.

These factors seem to have contributed to dissatisfaction with many other "isms"—Maoism, modernism, existentialism (which early on appealed to some young people)—in addition to Marxism itself, and to a nostalgic return to Confucianism with its stress on harmony, good manners, gentleness, and moderation, a golden age of stability. As elsewhere in the world, in the face of rapid change and incipient doubts about leadership, people tend to look to their traditions for some explanation of what is happening and to search for some security in known values and perspectives. At the symposium this development was at times described as "the Chinese way," reminiscent perhaps of a bland kind of intellectual fundamentalism. Whether this kind of sentiment has survived the suppression of the democracy movement is another matter.

In this vein, the specific relevance to social and humanistic inquiry revealed itself, during the symposium, in occasional admonitions by some Chinese participants that their scholarship ought not succumb to the success of Western technology but ought to let a hundred Chinese flowers bloom and a hundred Chinese schools contend. The paradigms of the West, for social science and humanistic inquiry, it was suggested in more than one disciplinary workshop, may not necessarily be appropriate for China, an issue about indigenization and transferability of knowledge to which I will shortly return. More pointedly, the emphasis of Confucian thought on harmony and wholeness—only one dimension, it might be said, of China's intellectual heritage—might suggest the need for a methodology that would permit, if not require, a holistic approach and thereby avoid at the very outset the problems created by excessive specialization. In other words, there was the hint that built into the very traditions of Chinese scholarship itself, unlike the Cartesian traditions in the West, there may be an imperative that leads away from fragmentation toward a more unified approach in the search for reliable knowledge and understanding. Although no specifics were offered, it was clear from workshop discussions that some Chinese scholars feel that specialization lies uneasily in the traditional Confucian bed of Chinese thinking.

Indeed, in the political science disciplinary workshop, the question was posed as to whether educational policy in China should follow the West in continuing to build specialized, discipline-oriented departments. Should China use as its institutional springboard the point at which the West, after 2,000 years of evolution, now finds itself? Or should China take a new look and build on its own humanistic, holistic past, at least as revealed in the thought of Confucius and Mencius? Would China be able to head off problems in the application of knowledge that may lie down the road if, once it is able to consider again, as it did in the 1980s, the reconstruction of its educational foundations, it stressed multidisciplinary education and research? Although this theme did not loom large in our symposium, it did make its presence felt and offered a means for those who were looking to Confucianism for answers to current problems to link the theme to possible developments in higher education.

Specialization and Application

Recognition of the Humpty Dumpty problem created by the high degree of specialization does not, of course, deny the importance of disciplinary knowledge. The disciplines are invaluable, and undoubtedly inescapable, in that they develop precise skills, concepts, and theories that improve our understanding of various aspects of the world. They provide a solid departure point for linkages to other areas of inquiry. But for the most part they do not do a good job of preparing the way for the application of this knowledge.

However, as Fleishman (see Chapter 9, this book) reminds us, if we can persuade scholars from different disciplines to work together to try to find solutions to specific policy problems, this cooperative effort may help to overcome divisions among them, at least some of the time. Under the best of circumstances, Fleishman suggests, by combining insights and knowledge from a number of disciplines, we may get new and more integrated understanding. To put this in another way, experience shows that some successful attempts at integrating knowledge have been connected, almost of necessity, with attempts to apply discipline-based knowledge to specific problems.

Professionalization

As yet, however, there is no general theory about the best way to integrate the major areas of knowledge in the social sciences, let alone in the humanities. Success, whenever achieved, can be attributed more to trial and error than to any systematic understanding of the requirements for reassembling decomposed, specialized knowledge. Indeed it has been said that one of the most clearly evident generalized processes in the history of the social sciences (and of the humanities as well?) has been the great "inertial strength of institutionalized disciplinary formation" on which, of course, specialization and individuation of the disciplines are built (Stocking & Leary, 1986, p. 57).

Evidence of the continuing strength of the professionalized disciplines easily can be found. In American social science, for example, and in the humanities as well, for that matter, there is little place for the generalist. There are few academic departments to hire such a person, no recognized career paths, and little support for faculty or encouragement for students. Although there is an audience, it is not as numerous, dedicated, or esteemed as professional constituencies—points made, for example, in the chapters that follow by Fleishman, Lambert, and Turner. The Chinese seem to be faced with a similar situation. As they observed in their area studies workshop report, "the requirements for area specialists are very high, almost those for a modern Renaissance man. Yet, in the academic field, they get less recognition than other social scientists."

In conclusion then, if our group's review of selected fields of study in American social science over the last 50 years said anything to our Chinese colleagues at the Beijing symposium, it did at least remind them of possible pitfalls along the path toward specialization. It also suggested that, whenever they do regain the power to reconstruct their higher education, a task they had begun before the suppression of the democracy movement in 1989, they may wish to proceed cautiously in the direction of increased specialization, despite opinions some may hold to the contrary. Before they plunge into emulating American or other Western institutional arrangements for teaching and research, they may wish to consider alternative educational strategies designed to minimize the short-comings of specialization by drawing the disciplines together at the very outset, rather than forcing them further apart. If the experience of the West is any lesson, they may not wish to wait until they are called upon to apply the knowledge gained through research. By then it may be too late. As in the West, the attempt, after the fact, to integrate highly specialized findings in the solution of practical problems may face almost insuperable barriers or may even elude their efforts entirely. Educational inventiveness in this area of Chinese education, attendant to China's own historical experiences, might provide some important leads to the West itself in grappling with this recalcitrant issue of specialization and integration of the disciplines for application to the world's urgent social problems.

Transferability of Knowledge

The second subject illuminated by these overviews of selected disciplines is the transferability of assumptions, methods, concepts, and theories from Western social sciences and humanities to other countries and the associated issue of the globalization as against the *indigenization* of the search for knowledge. Again our experience in China was instructive in looking at these broader aspects of scholarship.

Transferability and globalization raise a host of subsidiary issues critical to the meeting of diverse cultures. Curiously, in our meetings in China they received less attention than might have been expected, especially if we remember Chinese suspicion of things foreign since 1949, particularly those from the United States, but later from the USSR as well, suspicions that were markedly heightened during the Cultural Revolution (and have been in process of revival since June 4, 1989). This parallels the cautious reception given to Western knowledge in numerous other non-Western countries in recent years (Atal, 1981; Kyvik, 1988; Weiner & Huntington, 1987). The low-key response of our Chinese colleagues at the Symposium, however, does not diminish the importance or centrality of the challenges provoked elsewhere by the exchange of knowledge between cultures, nor their relevance for China in the years ahead now that foreign influences are again being officially decried.

Globalization of Society and Knowledge

It is no longer news to point out that the world has been shrinking. Humankind shares a common ecosphere: pollution of the oceans and air and depletion of the ozone layer affect us all in varying degrees. We share a common biosphere: we are all subject, in one way or another, to consequences from the excessive use of pesticides, the presence of acid rain, the depletion of the forests, and the uncontrolled spread of disease. And, if I may coin a word, we share a common sociosphere: we all feel the effects of variations in the state of the world economy, mass migrations of people, rapid and wholesale communications of information, unequal distribution of wealth among nations, and the like. All aspects of life are becoming increasingly globalized (Trent & Lamy, 1984).

Knowledge itself has been on the leading edge of this globalization, especially as less developed countries have experienced increasingly closer contact with advanced industrial societies. Globalization here refers to two tendencies: the diffusion of Western social sciences and humanities (as well as the natural sciences), along with their disciplinary forms of organization, to most regions of the world; and the spread of the view that it is both natural and desirable for knowledge to accumulate, as it were, into one international pool of ideas and methods that is freely accessible to all.

Western social science and humanistic knowledge, the argument runs, presumes that it is built on universalistic criteria. In scientific inquiry about human behavior, for example, it is assumed that the logic, norms, and procedures, based on scientific method as it has evolved over the centuries in the West, are universally applicable and their findings are universally valid. They are represented as discoveries about the way in which the human mind works and, as such, may be imported by any culture that seeks reliable understanding of its own society. Just as the methods of the natural sciences enable the latter to purvey universal truths about their subject matter, so the methods of the social disciplines have implicitly laid claim to being equally appropriate for an understanding of all societies, regardless of time and place. Similarly the humanistic disciplines have on occasion presumed a validity, not only for their theories and methodologies but for their values as well, that transcends Western culture. Miller, for example, describes the older humanism in literature as well as the new criticism of more recent times as claiming to provide "universal values transcending the flux of history" (Chapter 5, p. 128), a claim, however, on which modern literary theory may have begun to cast some doubt.

In short, the Western social sciences and humanities are presumed to offer universalistic criteria of what constitutes reliable knowledge, of the concepts identifying important phenomena, of the methods to be used to acquire and test knowledge, of the theorems that give us explanations and, where relevant, predictive powers, and of the values underlying all knowledge. For the most part, except in special areas of some disciplines, such as philosophy and anthropology (with its theories of cultural relativism), where the issues may be seen as problematic, these assumptions about conceptual and methodological universality tend to be taken for granted in the West. Accordingly there could be little need to question the transferability of the findings and methods of the disciplines to foreign cultures, suitably adapted perhaps, but never requiring fundamental alteration.

Criticism of Universalistic Assumptions

These assumptions have come under attack in recent decades, partly from within the West, but primarily from scholars in cultures that have been importing Western methods and ideas.[8]

There has been a dual focus to the attack: on the culturally-specific character of both substantive findings and methods; and on the need to indigenize both, if non-Western cultures are to obtain a valid and adequate understanding of themselves. The disciplinary workshop on sociology, for example, discussed what it called the "nativization" of sociology, debating the merits of a "sociology with Chinese characteristics [that might] be established on the basis of native cultural conditions instead of copying mechanically Western theories."[9]

Ironically, the revolt against dominance by Western concepts, theories, and methods has its latest roots in a discovery in the West itself.[10] Under the inspiration of phenomenology the West raised a rod for its own back, as it were, in the claim that science may be constitutive of reality, may help to construct the world we see (Berger & Luckman, 1966). In non-Western countries this conception has provided a rational basis for the fear that Western scholarship, imbued with ideological premises alien to non-Western cultures, leads to the misconstruction and, often, distortion in the understanding of these cultures.

This fear is especially understandable when we bear in mind that Western research centers typically overwhelm or dominate the intellectual peripheries.[11] It is popularly estimated that over two-thirds of all research in the social sciences, world-wide, originates in the West. To the extent that non-Western cultures, often even after decolonization, seek to understand themselves through Western eyes, it has been said, they live on a "borrowed consciousness," with ideological blinders provided by others. Imitation of Western scholarship, of high-prestige centers of learning there, serves to destroy the "natural self-awareness" that comes from a consideration of native realities free of outside influence. Non-Western scholars need to "decolonize" their minds and develop their own analytic tools appropriate to a "grass-roots" consciousness of their own culture.[12] Only by invoking indigenous ways of thinking about themselves, it is claimed, can scholars in non-Western cultures hope to gain correct insight and understanding of their own cultures, behavior, and institutions. Of course, this does not address the issue as to whether the result would just be the substitution of one set of ideological blinders for another or how one escapes the limits of one's own culture.[13]

The movement for indigenization of the social sciences and humanities, with its suspicion of and resistance to the importation of Western methods, theories, and concepts, raises complex issues, not all of which need to be elaborated here. In essence, although it is not put in this way, it poses the question as to whether our conceptions of method and of the resulting knowledge itself, as they have evolved over the last two thousand years in the West, are not, after all, just that, namely, products of a unique historical experience. In the extreme view, may they not be the singular outcome of one kind of cultural sequence? Why should we believe, except out of some cultural pride, blindness, or *hubris*, that our experience in the West leads to universal criteria for the production of reliable knowledge but that the divergent experiences of other cultures fall short of offering the same? May not this simply be what it is often seen to be outside the West, an arrogance or imperialism of the idea that has taken the place of (or, in the past, has accomplished) an imperialism of power?

Substantive Universalism

As I have suggested, the argument has two aspects, substantive and methodological. With regard to substance, the point is advanced that many of the concepts generated in the West refer to variable phenomena that may have little counterpart in other civilizations. Accordingly theories based on such concepts need have little relevance or validity elsewhere (Lambert, Chapter 7). Each culture will organize its experiences linguistically and emotionally in its own historic ways; and, insofar as language expresses these variations, terms useful or valid for inquiry in one culture and language may not be so for a different civilization. Much less are they likely to be able to lay claim to universality.

This limited relevance and validity of ideas is true, for example, of the Western concept of authority used to refer to the hierarchical organization of power relationships. As central as this concept is in Western political science (Easton, 1958), it has no counterpart, for example, in the Japanese language. There, presumably because of the specific sensitivity of the culture to the kinds of relationships involved, the idea of authority is decomposed into many aspects with different terms to express each of them. In certain non-Western cultures, even those geographically within the West, as in the case of certain native peoples in the United States, the idea of authority also has little meaning. Among the Fox Indians, for example, traditional culture frowns on anyone who, in Western terms, would seek to use a presumed authority position to utter outright orders or commands to another. Persons are invited to perform what should be considered a duty, not told to do so. Relationships are lateral in character, not hierarchical, even between parent and child or between a political council and the rest of the village or tribe. Authoritative decisions are not made, in the Western sense, and then enforced. Rather, they are arrived at through a consensual process which, at times, may be long and drawn out precisely so that no one will need to be commanded or directed to act (Easton, 1979, pp. 88-89).

An example raised during our symposium in China at the political science workshop discussions made it very clear that certain Western terms could not be taken for granted in China. For example, the notion of *public* administration, which contrasts with *private* administration, has little place in the Chinese lexicon for the study of administration. In Western political science, the public nature of administration usually refers to two things: (a) decisions that affect the public regardless of who makes them (and therefore they may be made by private institutions); (b) decisions that are made by public organs, such as governments, and, therefore, are by their very nature public in character. Since in China, from about the 1950s until recently at least, all economic activity has been conducted by government, all administration, business as well as governmental, has of necessity been public. Our Chinese colleagues thought they would have little use for concepts that drew a central distinction between the public and private aspects of administration and organizational management. For some of them this illustration raised the whole issue of the appropriateness of the transfer of Western models of inquiry for the understanding of Chinese experience.[14]

Even within the mainstream of Western civilization itself we are also familiar with such culturally based conceptual differences. To take a simple homespun example, *la patrie* is a French concept that has no equivalent in any other Western language group. Expression of the underlying ideas and sentiments of this term in other Western subcultures requires a sensitive and extended translation.

Clearly we are already aware of the problems that non-Western cultures would find in any rough-and-ready attempt to apply theories based on culturally specific concepts to other cultures. In anthropology the whole idea of cultural relativism implies as much. It has frequently led to questions as to whether the generalizing theories found in economics, for example, are really as culturally neutral as they appear to be. And when we move into areas of inquiry in which concepts are less generally accepted among their practitioners than in economics, as in political science or sociology, the question of cultural bias, if not ideological commitment, and, therefore, of universal applicability cannot be ignored.

As noted, questioning the universality and transferability of Western-generated concepts and theories is not unfamiliar to Western scholars themselves. Whether in practice Western social sciences and humanities have actually shown the desired degree of sensitivity is another matter that would need to be considered on an empirical basis. But the principle is probably one that would not be denied or ignored by most Western scholars. Concepts need to be attuned to the culture to which they apply, otherwise they would be dealing with non-issues for that culture.[15]

Methodological Universalism

The matter is substantially different, however, with regard not to the content or conceptual structure of knowledge, but to the methods and assumptions in terms of which inquiry is conducted. Scholars in non-Western cultures see the West as claiming, implicitly at least, that our methods represent the way the mind works (Searle, Chapter 6), discovered after two thousand years of effort. Not that our Western understanding of these methods is fixed; we see it as improving with time. But at any moment we have our best notions about the operations of the mind and we tend to regard them as universal criteria, without spatio-temporal restrictions.

Here the critics from outside the West are more insistent. May not Western ways of thinking about a subject matter, our very methods of inquiry, reflect only our own unique historical experience? Are what we call "scientific method," "critical theory," "analytic philosophy," and the like only culturally specific descriptions of ways of thinking? Are positivism, neopositivism, deconstruction, interpretive understanding, and other epistemological postures only parochial Western ways of looking at the world? Or are they ways of thinking that can make genuine claims to universality? If so, can Western producers of knowledge alone claim to have transcended the limits of their own culture and generated universally valid modes of thinking? If so, how then can we account for the fact that there is not a complete consensus, even in the West itself, on the logic of inquiry? Even among those who do happen to agree, if we look behind that agreement we see that it represents only a moment in a long history of changing ideas about the nature of inquiry. That is to say, philosophy of science itself has a history and presumably will continue to have a history of change in the future. At the very least such indeterminacy, the argument would run, does not augur well for claims to universality at any moment of time.

More generally, rather than seeking to discover universally valid ways of thinking about human beings in society, would Western scholars be better advised to assume that each culture, in seeking to understand itself through its own unique intellectual processes, might have a chance of stumbling on some fundamental aspect of thought itself that might elude scholars working within other traditions and cultures? Should diversity be encouraged in place of the adoption of one mode of inquiry imported from the West? If, for example, the Chinese are one day drawn fully into the international intellectual arena, would the clash of different cultural experiences then permit, at some moment, a transcendent point of view, somewhat along the lines contemplated by Mannheim long ago, as he searched for the conditions under which scholars could move beyond the limits imposed by their unique historical roots (Mannheim, 1949)?

This is not to deny the probable existence of universally valid ways of thinking imposed on us by the very nature of the human mind, as implied by Searle (this book, Chapter 6). It is only a questions as to how we go about discovering them and whether the West can make greater claims than other civilizations to having transcended the limits on inquiry imposed by its own cultural traditions and ideological premises. Does Western scholarship need to be more open-minded and less imperialistic about the potential value of modes of thought different from its own in providing new insights into the nature of thought and understanding?

For example, as I have suggested, the specialization of labor, fragmentation of knowledge, and problems of bringing these fragments back together again for purposes of application may be an outcome of Western ways of doing things. The reintegration of certain bodies of specialized knowledge may work on occasion, as Cheit, Fleishman, and Lambert have observed, but by and large it has faced serious difficulties in application. This recognized shortcoming in Western research points up the question as to whether, when looked at autonomously—that is, not through the lenses already colored by experiences of the West, and especially of the United States, but through a vision created by other historical traditions—there is anything in the history of other countries, such as China, that might give us some new insight into ways of rethinking how we go about not only producing knowledge, skills and understanding, but applying them as well? Is it a conceit on the part of American or Western scholars to think that our 2,000 years of thinking have exhausted all possible alternatives and have achieved the ultimate understanding of the way we ought to acquire, analyze, and interpret knowledge, if we are to achieve the highest degree of reliability and applicability? Or does our own thinking itself not caution us to be skeptical of itself—*nosce te ipsum*—especially in the face of the difficulties in application with which it has left us?

Given the context of the symposium in China, the question might be put forward, in a very tentative and exploratory fashion, as to whether Chinese scholars, in borrowing from the West as they must, should be wary of allowing Western scholarship to gradually overwhelm their own ways of thinking. To what extent would they be shortchanging themselves if unsuspectingly this were allowed to happen? Or, to put the matter in a more general way, from the point of view of the difficulties with which Western ways have left us, does the effort to create a shared world intellectual community require an independent assessment of Chinese traditional ways of thinking about man in society? If one of the functions of international conferences such as ours is to facilitate the inclusion of scholarship from one culture into a growing world intellectual community, as part of the globalizing tendencies already under way, clearly this would need to be done in a highly critical spirit. At the very least, this means not the inadvertent acceptance of or immersion in Western epistemology but its critical evaluation in light of possible alternative assumptions present in other ways of thinking about society.

In 1988, before the events in Tiananmen Square, there were already hints that such a critical and comparative assessment in China was in progress or about to begin. For example, a rapporteur at the plenary session at the opening ceremonies of the symposium was concerned that Chinese political science might assume that just because Western political science happened to evolve through several phases (Easton, Chapter 2)—formal, legal (traditional), the behavioral, and the postbehavioral—these exhausted all possible modes of political analysis. In contrast, as noted earlier, he cited the popular injunction to let a hundred flowers bloom and a hundred schools contend. In line with this philosophy, he went on, one could and should expect the testing of any number of alternative approaches in China. One thing was clear: There should be little appetite for accepting American or Western political science as the only basic research paradigm for the study of politics. He proposed that perhaps we should look to older schools of thought in Chinese history such as those of Confucius or Mencius.

This appeal to Confucius was not accidental, of course. It reflected the presence of what appears to be a growing revival of interest in China in Confucian thought, as well as in East Asia more broadly. Here what I have to say about this cultural tradition needs to be carefully separated from its possible political implications for recent events in China. To some degree this reemergence of Confucianism appears to be a basis for arguments against intellectual borrowing from the West as well as against the desirability, if not possibility, of applying scientific methods to the study of human behavior. It is seen as a bulwark of political and intellectual conservatism, if not reaction, as a means of casting suspicion on change. Hence it has little appeal to those who associate increased intellectual and political freedom with the opening up of China to modern Western social sciences and humanities. Many of them are more inclined toward Taoism, another Chinese tradition, that imposes limits on political intervention in the freedom of individuals.

If, however, for the moment we set aside the political role that the incipient revival of Confucianism may be playing and look only at other aspects of its intellectual content, it does provoke a different question. May there indeed be some unique elements in this Chinese cultural tradition that can suggest a way of avoiding some of the problems with which the evolution of Western knowledge has saddled us?

With regard to specialization, for example, there is, in Confucianism, despite its broader negative implications in the matter of political reform, an intriguing holistic element that might offer some insights about ways of approaching the understanding of man in society. Confucianism begins with the whole, rather than with the analytic parts in the intellectual spirit inherited from Descartes. If it is correct to assert that there is a predisposition in Confucian thinking to begin with the whole social entity, a Western scholar can wonder whether this imperative might lead Chinese scholarship— without necessarily encouraging the revival of Confucianism itself—to a different way of absorbing Western epistemology and methodology and toward the avoidance of the very kinds of problems that our own history has bequeathed to us.

It is the discovery of such suggestive opportunities that provides one of the justifications for conferences like the one in Beijing in May 1988. We need not pose the question as to whether there is or can be a unique "Chinese way" of developing social and humanistic knowledge and understanding, a phrasing that, we were cautioned, is often used as a mask to hide and isolate China from liberating external influences. Before the events in Tiananmen Square, the question that could be raised was whether some Chinese should be discouraged from being overly eager to uncritically adopt Western (American?) ways of searching for knowledge or whether they should rather be encouraged, even as they incorporate Western methods and ideas into their own thinking, to mine their own traditions fully for any special contributions they might make toward the improvement of everyone's capacity to produce such knowledge. Of course, with the marked increase in official hostility to Western influences after June 4, 1989, the greater danger is that the door to Western ideas will be tightly shut once again. Nevertheless we may assume that the pressure of world economic and political developments, aside from any internal forces at work, will one day force the door open. In that event, encouraging not just Chinese but other East Asian scholars to bring their own experiences into the world intellectual community, deliberately and self-consciously, could give us new leads for achieving that universally valid way for conducting intellectual inquiry, which has been a more elusive goal of all Western scholarship than we have recognized or may wish to admit.

Notes

1. See Descartes' second methodological maxim: "The second [rule] was to divide each of the difficulties I encountered into as many parts as possible and as might be required for easier solution." *Discourse on Method, Part Two.*

2. In an unpublished report on the history workshop, the Chinese rapporteur wrote that some Chinese scholars agree "with the hope" that "history and sociology, humanistic methods and social scientific methods will eventually be combined into one entity." The report went on to say that "the view of the blurred division between history and the other social science [and humanistic] disciplines reflects the situation in modern Chinese scholarship." But it was also clear that the Chinese scholars were no more unanimous in their opinions about the new interdisciplinary history than are Western scholars.

3. The workshop on political science showed considerable interest in linking the study of politics to other disciplines such as economics, law, and history. With that in mind, the workshop was reminded of a team initiative being undertaken by a number of senior professors at Beijing University who were in the process of setting up the Research Centre for Social Development in Contemporary China, an interdisciplinary research team composed of scholars from economics, politics, law, culture, and education.

4. I should mention, however, that in a personal communication (January 12, 1989) Lambert argues that although "it takes time for individual scholars to tran-

scend—not mix—disciplinary lines and to overcome applied and theoretical divides, the effort is both exciting and intellectually challenging."

5. One might ask whether this is true in other non-Western countries, and indeed in some Western countries and smaller educational institutions in the West?

6. In the political science workshop we learned that political scientists in China were likely to come from diverse educational backgrounds. Many are likely to have had their start not in political science but in such fields as English literature, law, economics, history, or a foreign language. Only after training in one or another of these fields, which themselves might have been very loosely defined and general rather than highly specialized in a Western sense, did they find their way into political science because of a shortage of scholars in that discipline. There they may have had to train themselves on the job, as it were. For some this seemed to indicate that they already had a surfeit of interdisciplinary education. What was lacking in Chinese political science in the 1980s was a higher degree of professional specialized training.

7. Along these lines see, for example, an unpublished memorandum (February 16, 1987) from Professor Tu Wei-ming of the Department of East Asian Languages and Civilization, Harvard University, to the American Academy of Arts and Sciences on "The Post-Confucian States."

8. "the American intellectual style, especially in the social sciences, was increasingly viewed as ethnocentric and irrelevant by indigenous scholars" (Lambert, this book, p. 180).

9. In similar vein the workshop reported that "the nativization of sociological theory never means the complete abolition of existing [Western] theory . . . but the construction of new theoretical paradigms more suited to the native culture."

10. In anthropology, cultural relativism had already at least implied the point.

11. For a suggestion that, on occasion, Western modes of thinking and their products may be "domesticated" by a non-Western host culture, see Stocking and Leary (1986).

12. For these quoted phrases and a discussion of many of these issues as well as reference to some of the literature, see Atal (1981).

13. See footnote 15.

14. It should be pointed out that in the workshop on public policy the matter was viewed very differently. There the Chinese participants felt that despite political and cultural differences they could feel comfortable in applying Western tools of policy analysis in China in such fields, for example, as education and rent control.

15. I have set aside, of course, the issue of the ideological presuppositions that underlie Western views of science and knowledge. They are too involved to address in this brief introduction, but they do challenge the universalistic premises on which much of Western scholarship rests. In fact, in the literature workshop some of our Chinese colleagues made this very point, arguing that literature itself is never neutral. It continues to be an ideological tool even when, as Miller maintains in Chapter 5, it is used as an instrument for unmasking the ideological basis of the literature of others. The very unmasking itself can be interpreted an act to promote an alternative ideological commitment.

References

Atal, Y. (1981). The call for indigenization. *International Social Science Journal, 33,* 189-197.

Berger, P. L., & Luckman, T. (1966). *The social construction of reality.* New York: Anchor Books.

Easton, D. (1958). The perception of political authority and political change. In C. J. Friedrich (Ed.), *Authority* (pp. 176-196). Cambridge, MA: Harvard University Press.

Easton, D. (1965/1979). *A framework for political analysis.* Englewood Cliffs, NJ: Prentice-Hall. Chicago: University of Chicago Press.

Kyvik, S. (1988). Internationality of the social sciences: The Norwegian case. *International Social Science Journal, 39,* 163-172.

Mannheim, K. (1949). *Ideology and utopia.* New York: Harcourt Brace.

Smith, A. (1937). *Inquiry into the nature and causes of the wealth of nations.* New York: Modern Library.

Stocking, G. W., & Leary, D. E. (1986). History of social scientific inquiry. *Items, 40,* 53-57.

Trent, J., & Lamy, P. (1984). *Global crises and the social sciences: North American perspectives.* Ottawa, Canada: University of Ottawa Press/UNESCO.

Turner, R. H. (1988, May) Comments to symposium. Symposium jointly sponsored by the Chinese Academy of Social Sciences and the American Academy of Arts and Sciences, Beijing.

Weber, M., (1946). Science as a vocation. In H. H. Gerth & C. W. Mills (Eds.), *From Max Weber: Essays in sociology* (pp. 129-158). New York: Oxford University Press.

Wirth, L. (1940). Round table discussions: The social sciences, one or many (1940). In L. Wirth (Ed.), *Eleven twenty-six: A decade of social science research* (pp. 113-152). Chicago: University of Chicago Press.

Weiner, M., & Huntington, S. (Eds.), (1987). *Understanding political development.* Boston: Little, Brown.

2

Political Science in the United States

Past and Present

DAVID EASTON

Political science has been defined in many ways—as the study of power, the study of the monopoly of the legitimate use of force, the study of the good life, of the state, and so on. If there is one thing that distinguishes Western political science, it is that it has not yet arrived at a consensus on how to describe its subject matter at the most inclusive level. For reasons that are elaborated at length elsewhere (Easton, 1981a), I have chosen to characterize political science as the study of the way in which decisions for a society are made and considered binding most of the time by most of the people. As political scientists, we are interested in all those actions and institutions in society more or less directly related to the way in which authoritative decisions are made and put into effect, and the consequences they may have (Easton, 1981b). To seek to understand

AUTHOR'S NOTE: This chapter was originally prepared for an audience that had little exposure to U.S. or Western political science. It was based on talks given at the Chinese Academy of Social Sciences and at various universities in China during 1982. It first appeared in the Chinese language in *Political Science and Law* (January, 1984), a journal of the Shanghai Academy of Social Sciences, and was republished in the *International Political Science Review* (1985, 6(1), 133-152). It has been somewhat revised for this book.

political life is to address oneself to the study of the authoritative allocation of values (valued things) for a society.

In effect, this description applies to any and all political systems, whether modern or ancient, large or small, industrialized or agricultural, mass or tribal, and so on. It is probably fair to say that this way of identifying political systems seems to have won the favor of many political scientists over the last quarter of a century. Thereby we are able to distinguish our interests from those of economists, anthropologists, sociologists, and other social scientists.

With this conception of the study of politics, let us now turn to an examination of what has been happening in Western, especially United States, political science during the 20th century. It has passed through four stages. Each of these has been distinctive. Each has been incorporated in and, one hopes, improved upon by each succeeding stage. I shall give the following names to these stages: the formal (legal), the traditional (informal or prebehavioral), the behavioral, and the postbehavioral. I discuss each in turn.

The Formal and Traditional Stages

Toward the latter part of the 19th century, political science started out with the conviction that once the laws governing the distribution of power in a political system have been described, we will have obtained an accurate understanding of how political institutions operate. Students of politics assumed that there was a reasonably close fit between what constitutions and laws said about the rights and privileges people held in various political offices and the way in which they acted in those offices.

Late in the 19th century, Walter Bagehot in Great Britain, followed by Woodrow Wilson in the United States (when he was a student and later a professor), made a major discovery. To everyone's surprise, they found that around the formal structure of political offices and institutions there were all kinds of informal behavior and organizations in which power over decision making might lie. Bagehot, Wilson, and others discovered them in the informal committees of their respective legislatures and in the political parties. Later scholars added interest or pressure groups to a growing list of informal institutions to be taken into account.

These findings introduced a new stage in the development of political science, diverting attention away from the formal, legal structures to the informal practices surrounding them. This change, which had occurred toward the end of the 19th century, was in full swing by the 1920s. People who were trained in the United States from the 1920s to the 1940s were exposed largely to what has come to be called traditional political science, the name for the second distinctive phase of political research in the 20th century. During this period, training included a great deal of attention to the operation of political parties and their effect on Congress or Parliament and to the growth, in the United States, of pressure groups and other types of groups. The latter were drawn to our attention and analyzed in depth, initially by Arthur Bentley (1908/1949), who was ignored at the time, and later, in new ways, by Pendleton Herring (1929) and David Truman (1951).

Methodologically, this traditional period was one in which more attention was paid to mere description and the collection of information about political processes than to overarching theories about how they operated. In fact, however, a latent theory unobtrusively guided research. Even though most of the scholars of that period were not conscious of it, they really saw the political process as a giant mechanism for making decisions. Decisions were, as one scholar, Merle Fainsod (1940), put it, a product of a "parallelogram of forces." This meant that when decisions were to be made, whether at the legislative or administrative levels, they were seen as being subject to a vast array of pressures from social groups—from political parties, from other parts of the bureaucracy itself, from interest groups, from public opinion, and so on. These pressures played against each other, developing a parallelogram of forces that, through bargaining, negotiation, adaptation, compromise, and adjustment (terms commonly used to describe the process), would arrive at some equilibrium point for that time and place. This equilibrium point would yield a particular policy, or the policy could be called the point of equilibrium among the various competing forces pressing against the decision makers. If at some time one of these social forces should change, for example, because of a change in the economic structure, in the social attitudes, or in the occupants of decision-making roles, demands for modification of old policies or for the introduction of new policies might arise. Competition among the various groups for influence over the policy would then begin again, and a new point of equilibrium might be achieved (Easton, 1981a). As I have indicated, for the most part, this equilibrium theory remained only latent in the literature.

The characteristic methods of research during this traditional period were no less informal than their theoretical base. Few special methods were used for the collection of data or for their analysis. Methods were not considered to be problematic, that is, as areas that required special attention or skills. Everyone was equally well equipped to collect and analyze information about politics. As a result, there were no formal or specified methods for testing the reliability of information acquired or of findings and interpretations based upon such information.

In addition, it was often difficult to distinguish whether the research worker was expressing his or her own preferences or was, in fact, describing how institutions operate and how people behave in political life. Statements relating what should be and what is were often almost inextricably intertwined. Facts and values played havoc with each other.

Finally, my own experience as a graduate student reflects the lack of theoretical coherence of traditional political science. At Harvard University, I took many different courses in political science. They covered the history of political thought, municipal or local politics, constitutional law, foreign policy, government regulation of industry, interest or pressure groups, international relations, the governments of specific foreign countries, and law making in Congress. At the end of my graduate training my head was in a whirl. No one had ever tried to help me understand why my interest in politics required me to be exposed to such a wide variety of subject matters aside from the fact that, loosely, they all had to do with something called government. I gained no sense of a basis upon which I could infer that political science formed a coherent body of knowledge. There was no theoretical framework into which, for example, I could place all these courses or by which I could check their relevance.

Political theory might have been the area in which, because of its name, I might have expected to find the opportunity to address this. But theory turned out to be devoted largely to the study of the history of political thought. Such history was, of course, interesting and important in itself, but it did not fulfill what might have been one of the functions of theory in, say, economics, chemistry, or physics, namely, the conceptualization of the discipline in part or as a whole.

The traditional stage then was one in which political science discovered the rich body of informal activities out of which public policy was formed. Yet it was a period during which description was often hard to distinguish from values, when theory did not measure up to the promise implicit in its name, and when method was so taken for granted that it was nonproblematic.

The Behavioral Stage

The formal-legal and traditional periods were the first two phases of recent times. They were displaced by the so-called behavioral revolution in American political science, which rapidly spread to many other parts of the world. This third phase began after World War II although it had its roots in the earlier period. Without question, this is the central transformation that has occurred in Western political science in this century.

Despite the common root in the English terms, behaviorism and behavioralism, the two have little in common and should not be confused. Political science has never been behavioristic, even during the height of its behavioralistic phase. *Behaviorism* refers to a theory in psychology about human behavior and has its origins in the work of J. B. Watson. I know of no political scientist who subscribes to this doctrine. Indeed, I know of no political scientist, although there may be the occasional one, who accepts even the psychological theory of B. F. Skinner, the founder of the "operant conditioning" school of psychology and the modern successor to Watson.

The only real relationship between the terms behaviorism and behavioralism is that both focus on the behavior of human actors as the appropriate source of information about why things happen as they do. Both also assume that a methodology based on that of the natural sciences is inappropriate for the study of human beings. Thus, aside from this acceptance of the individual as the focus of research and of scientific method, there is little resemblance between these tendencies.

Behavioralism in political science had the following major characteristics, which distinguished it from earlier stages in the study of political science (Easton, 1962). Behavioralism, held first, that there are discoverable uniformities in human behavior and, second, that these can be confirmed by empirical tests. Third, behavioralism showed a desire for greater rigor in methods for the acquisition and analysis of data. Methods themselves became problematic. They could no longer be taken for granted. Courses and books on methods for acquiring and analyzing data, once nonexistent, became commonplace. Quantification, whenever possible and plausible, assumed an important place in the discipline. As a result, during the 1950s and 1960s, political science became adept at using a vast array of increasingly sophisticated empirical and quantitative techniques—questionnaires, interviews, sampling, regression analysis, factor analysis, rational modeling, and the like.

Fourth, the behavioral movement committed itself to much greater theoretical sophistication than existed in the past. The search for systematic understanding, grounded in objective observation, led to a marked shift in the meaning of theory as a concept. Traditionally, in the distant past, theory had been philosophical in character, asking questions about the nature of the good life. In more recent times, it had become largely historical, seeking to explicate and account for the emergence of political ideas in past centuries. Behavioral theory, on the other hand, is empirically oriented. It seeks to help us explain, understand, and, if possible, predict the way people behave politically and the way political institutions operate.

A considerable amount of the energies of theoreticians in this period went into the construction of empirically oriented theory at various levels of analysis. So-called middle range theory has sought to build theories about large segments of the discipline, as in the case of power pluralism, which offers a theory of democratic systems, game theory, or public choice theory (Riker & Ordeshook, 1973).

In part, however, theory was of the broadest character, called general theory. This type of theory sought to provide an understanding of political systems at the most inclusive level. Structural-functional theory and systems analysis (Easton, 1981b) represent two major theoretical efforts of such broad scope.

Fifth, many behavioralists felt that the values of the research worker and of society could be largely excluded from the process of inquiry. Ethical evaluation and empirical explanation were viewed as involving two different kinds of statements that clarity required to be kept analytically separate and distinct. Behavioralism adopted the original positivist assumption (as developed by the Vienna Circle of positivists early in this century) that value-free or value-neutral research was possible. Although some of us, including myself (Easton, 1981a, Chapter 9), did not share this point of view, it is nevertheless correct to suggest that it was a dominant one during the height of the behavioral stage. As a result, among the priorities of interesting and acceptable things to do, moral inquiry receded far into the background.

Sixth, behavioralism represented a new-found emphasis on basic or pure theory as against applied research. Its assumption was that the task of the social scientist was to obtain fundamental understanding and explanation. It was felt that only after we have reliable understanding of how political institutions operate and people behave politically would it be possible to apply such knowledge, with confidence, to the solution of urgent social problems. The period of behavioralism, therefore, helped to divert the interests of scholars from social reform and encouraged them to set their sights on the needs of scientific development as a guide to research.

How can we explain the behavioral revolution of the 1950s and 1960s in the United States? It was clearly a product of a number of complex tendencies. It was part of the natural evolution of the discipline. The common sense, proverbial style of traditional political science, with its dependence on historical description and impressionistic analysis, had simply exhausted itself. A developing mass-industrialized society could not cope with its social problems with explanations of the degree of unreliability offered by traditional research. Too many difficulties in understanding political institutions and processes had been left unresolved. The epistemic successes of the natural sciences and of other social sciences, such as psychology and economics, using more rigorous methods of data collection and of analysis, left their impact on political science as well. They suggested alternatives that led political analysis away from "common" sense to "scientific" sense in which theoretical rather than social criteria defined the problems of research and technical skills took the place of mere description and common-sense methods.

In addition, however, there were social forces that encouraged a commitment to the introduction of science into the study of politics.

Early in the cold war period in relations between the United States and the Soviet Union, especially during the Korean War (1950-1953), Senator Joseph McCarthy inaugurated and led a reign of psychological and legal terror against liberals and others in the United States. Scholars were selected as particularly vulnerable targets for attack. McCarthyism succeeded in driving underground an interest in social reform and critical theory.

From this perspective, objective, neutral, or value-free research represented a protective posture for scholars, offering them intellectually legitimate and useful grounds for fleeing from the dangers of open political controversy. This is perhaps an instance in the evolution of knowledge in which inadvertent gains may have been won for the wrong reasons. McCarthyism, of course, had nothing to do with the emergence of behavioralism as a new approach to political research. It represented simply a historical circumstance that drove an interest in social reform underground. In doing so, it led scholars into the politically less dangerous grounds of basic research, an area that, as it turned out, had major benefits to offer for the development of political science.

In addition to McCarthyism, another important social condition contributed significantly to the sustenance of behavioralism. Post-World War II prosperity, with its associated conservatism of the 1950s and the early 1960s, led to the prevalent view that ideology had indeed come to an end in the United States. Rapid economic growth offered material benefits to all segments of the population, even to the poorest. Critical social thought, including critical liberalism itself, seemed to all but disappear in the United States and, with it, all semblance of ideological conflict. Bell (1960) wrote a distinguished book entitled *The End of Ideology* that expressed this conviction.

In retrospect, it is clear that ideology had not disappeared, but only seemed to have ended because mainstream, liberal-conservative ideology was dominant and unchallenged for the moment. There were no major contenders. This situation, of course, changed during the late 1960s with the rise of the civil rights movement on behalf of blacks. But prior to this period, contending ideologies did recede or go underground. This lack of challenge to established ideologies turned the social sciences away from social problems as a source of inspiration for its research toward criteria internal to social theory, derivative from the logic of the development of social science itself. This gave social science the appearance of withdrawing from society into an ivory tower of scientific research, at least if one took the rhetoric of social research at its word.

It is clear that what from a social point of view could be interpreted as a retreat from social responsibility by social scientists, from the point of view of science could be interpreted as a breathing spell free from social involvement. This had the effect of enabling political science to address, in a relatively undisturbed atmosphere, many technical matters that have become central to its development, such as the place of theory in social research, the need for rigorous methods of research, the refinements of techniques for acquiring and analyzing data, the establishment of standards of professionalism among political scientists and social scientists in general, and so on.

In short, we can now recognize the behavioral phase as one in which the social sciences, for whatever historical reasons and fortuitous circumstances, were busy strengthening the scientific bases of their research. The cost was a significant withdrawal from an interest in social criticism and social involvement.

The Postbehavioral Stage

What I have called the postbehavioral revolution—a name now generally used for this next phase—began during the 1960s and is still with us today (Easton, 1969). It represents a deep dissatisfaction with the results of behavioralism but has not led to the abandonment of scientific method in political science. It is, however, leading to a substantial modification of our understanding of the nature of science, and it is a movement that is still evolving.

Why did the postbehavioral movement arise? What were its sources? In the United States, this movement accompanied the so-called counter-cultural revolution, which arose in the West, and touched the East as well, during the later 1960s and early 1970s. It represented a period of worldwide social change. Much of the leadership came from large masses of students congregated in rapidly growing colleges and universities around the world. In the United States, it had its origins in the civil rights movement, especially after the 1954-1955 Supreme Court decisions against educational segregation of blacks, and was accompanied by demands for the improvement of the condition of blacks and other minorities and by widespread protests during the Johnson and Nixon administrations against the Vietnam War. It was most clearly evident in new attitudes toward forms of dress, sexual behavior, the place of women and minorities in society, poverty, respect for the physical environment (pollution, atomic waste, the dangers of nuclear energy), and social inequality. The postbehavioral movement, in its broadest meaning, represented the awakening of the modern world to the dangers of rapid and unregulated industrialization, ethnic and sexual discrimination, worldwide poverty, and nuclear war.

This is not the place to describe this movement in detail. All we need to do is to draw attention to the impact that the counter-cultural revolution of the 1960s and 1970s had on the social sciences in general and on political science in particular. For social scientists, it raised the question as to why we were unable to foresee the kinds of problems, just mentioned, that became salient in this period. In addition, even if the social sciences had foreseen some of these problems, how did it happen that they did nothing about them? It appeared that the social sciences had simply withdrawn into an ivory tower. Questions such as these led to large-scale debates on the nature of our discipline and what it ought to be.

From these debates several things are now clear. The original commitment to science during the behavioral period, that is, during the 1950s and 1960s, has been seriously questioned. Some of the criticisms of scientific method reflect well-known arguments inherited largely from the 19th century: Human behavior is composed of too many complex variables and therefore we are not likely to be able to discover any law-like regularities; unlike atoms, human beings are not determined. They have free will, and therefore their actions can never be predicted even on a probable basis. Even if the methods of the natural sciences have manifested great epistemic success, this is because they deal with inanimate matter. Atoms, however, do not have feelings or intentions, that, by their very nature, are unpredictable or inaccessible to observation or prediction.

Other criticisms of social science were directed to its positivistic claims that behavioral research was value free. As I mentioned earlier, some social scientists had proclaimed the "end of ideology." With the counter-cultural movement came the argument that all social research is, on the contrary, really shot through with ideology.

The point was advanced that the claim that social science was valuationally neutral was possible only because social science had assumed the ideological coloring of the status quo (bourgeois liberalism) and the existing power structure. Its ideological premises were at one with those of the establishment and disappeared into the received views of the day. This claim to false objectivity was seen as serving the interests of the establishment. It seemed to justify or excuse the withdrawal of social scientists from involvement in social issues, to divert social inquiry from urgent social problems, and thereby to allow the status quo to go unchallenged.

This attack on the ideological presuppositions of scientific method in the study of society broadened into a wholesale challenge of the epistemological and ontological bases of social research. In a widely read book, *The Structure of Scientific Revolutions* by T. Kuhn (1962), the view was advanced that all science, natural as well as social, is essentially an irrational process. In this book, scientific change is no longer seen as the product of a gradual accumulation of knowledge and understanding; change now represents only the shift of scientists from acceptance of an existing paradigm or set of ideological and other presuppositions to a new one. The history of science, from this point of view, appears as almost a random shift from one set of premises (paradigms) governing research to another.

Despite the initial impact of this book, it is now realized that this criticism, in denying the possibility of any objective and cumulative knowledge, went far beyond the realm of necessity and plausibility (Suppe, 1977). The criticism did however draw attention to the need to reconsider how we do manage to acquire a valid understanding about the real world despite the fact that research may be saturated with evaluative presuppositions.

I have touched only briefly on the fierce attacks that have been launched against scientific method since the 1970s. They have, however, led to serious reassessments of the original commitment to the positivistic conception of scientific method that was prevalent during the behavioral period of the 1950s and 1960s. We can see the results of this reassessment in the current approaches to political inquiry, which are far more diverse than during the behavioral period. The earlier impressionistic methods have even regained some plausibility, as has the method of interpretive understanding (*verstehen*) put forward at the turn of this century by Max Weber. We have also witnessed the reemergence of proponents of Marxism as an alternative way to develop a social science (Ollman & Vernoff, 1982, Poulantzas, 1973).

Indeed, there are now so many approaches to political research that political science seems to have lost its purpose. During the 1950s and 1960s, in the behavioral phase, there was a messianic spirit and collective effort in the promotion and development of the methods of scientific inquiry even while there continued to be opposition to it. Today there is no longer a single, dominant point of view or one that unmistakably catches the imagination, especially of younger members of the profession. Nor is there even a single defensive adversary. The discipline is fragmented in its method-ological conceptions, even though it is probably fair to say that scientific inquiry still represents the mainstream. However, it is not, as we shall see in a moment, only science in the old positivistic sense. Instead we are adding a new and more relaxed understanding of the nature of science itself.In addition to losing its sense of a dynamic purpose concentrated on the pursuit of scientific validity, political science seems to have lost its core. There was once agreement that political science was a study of values or of the good life. Also, if it will not seem self-serving on my part to say so, there was a dominant point of view. If there was any single comprehensive description of the subject matter of political science it was to be found in the notion that it studied the authoritative allocation of values for a society. This was a conception that I had put forward in 1953, in my book, *The Political System* (Easton, 1981a) and it found widespread acceptance.

Today, however, students are no longer certain what politics is all about. They may be even less concerned than they were in the past. Political science as the study of the state, a conception that, after World War II, had been driven out by the idea of the political system, has now been revived. It has accompanied the reemergence, in U.S. political science at least, of Marxist and quasi-Marxist points of view (Easton, 1981c) and in them, of course, the state is a central concept.

What is being offered today to draw the discipline together, to give it a sense of common purpose, and to provide alternative methods, if any, for inquiry? Here is where the real difficulty arises. As the 1990s begin, political science is still trying to develop a new sense of identity and a new drive or sense of purpose. We are clearly in a transition phase, and it is difficult to predict just where we will end up. We look fragmented and display a great variety of objectives for the very reason that theories, methods, and perspectives are still being questioned, that is, they are in the process of change.

We can get some flavor of the reconstruction taking place by recounting the different interests and approaches of U.S. political science, at least at the present time. Theoretical Marxism, after lying dormant in U.S. social science since the 1940s (even though very much alive in Europe), was reintroduced during the 1970s. However, no single orthodoxy in the Marxist methods or theories has been adopted. The fragmentation of European Marxism is reflected in its American renaissance. We find all schools of Marxism represented—critical theory, humanist, cultural, structural, as well as orthodox. All have had some impact on U.S. political science although structural Marxism, as developed by Althusser and Poulantzas, has probably been the most influential.

What is clear, however, is that in being absorbed into U.S. social research the various schools of Marxism have been attenuated; most inquiry is only quasi-Marxist in character. Even in that form, however, the revival of Marxist thinking has brought to political science a renewed awareness of the importance of history and of the significance of the economy, social classes, and ideology, as well as the total social context (the social formation, as Althusser would phrase it). As of the moment, with the disintegration of the Socialist-bloc countries, the emergence of *perestroika* in the U.S.S.R., and the outbreak of democratic ideologies in Eastern Europe, it is not yet clear what effect these events will have on the plausibility of Marxist theories for future social inquiry.

The mainstream of U.S. political science has, however, moved off in a variety of other directions. The interests of the behavioral period in voting, judicial, legislative, administrative, and executive behavior as well as in interest groups, parties, developing areas, and the like have continued. But during the postbehavioral period new topics of political research have arisen to satisfy the desire to understand the new concerns typical of this period—environmental pollution, ethnic, racial, social and sexual equality, and nuclear war, for example.

In the search for answers to urgent social issues such as these, political science in this period has joined all other social sciences in making an extraordinary commitment of its resources to the application of knowledge. We witness this in the rapid and widespread growth of the so-called policy-analysis movement. Literally hundreds of institutes have arisen not only for the understanding of the way in which policies are formed and implemented, but for the formulation of policy alternatives to help solve the urgent social problems facing all societies at the present time. These institutes ring the changes on all questions of policy creation and execution: What are the policies in various areas? How are they formed? What alternatives are neglected or rejected and why? What are their consequences, direct or indirect? To what extent do they fulfill their ostensible objectives (contributing to the emergence of a vast subfield of policy evaluation)? How does a given set of present policies influence subsequent policies (the feedback process)? Because the effects of policies are felt not only in the political sector but also in most other areas of study, policy institutes typically have been built around interdisciplinary curricula (Fleishman, this book, Chapter 9). In this way policy research has reawakened the hope of an earlier day for integrating the social sciences, at least in the application of its knowledge.

Another shift in interest that is part and parcel of this new policy orientation is reflected in the rebirth of the field of political economy. In the 19th century, as modern political science was evolving, economics and politics had already shown a close and natural affinity, as revealed in the work of John Stuart Mill, which he explicitly called political economy, and of Karl Marx. The revival of this link, beginning in the 1970s is in part attributable, of course, to the revival of Marxist thought. But it has also blossomed independently through efforts to show the numerous relationships between the state of the economy on the one hand and political events and institutions on the other (Frolich & Oppenheimer, 1982; Monroe, 1983). itself.

As I have just noted, political economy is a return to a traditional combination of interests common in the 19th century. But perhaps the most dramatic shift in perspectives has occurred recently in a different area, in what I shall call cognitive political science. The emergence of this approach reflects a movement away from the attempt to understand political phenomena as exclusively a product of nonrational processes, that is, as a product of social forces that influence decisions and actions of political actors and institutions.

The starting assumption of cognitive political science is that there is a strong rational component to political behavior. This can mean one of two things: that human beings do act rationally, or that we can better understand their behavior if we adopt rationality as an assumption.

Whereas the outcome of empirical scientific research consists of generalizations about behavior that are grounded in observations, the products of the cognitive approach are models about how human beings would or should act under varying circumstances if they were to act rationally. The product of inquiry takes the form of rational choice models, game theories, or other kinds of so-called rational-actor models (Downs, 1957; Kramer & Hertzberg, 1975; Riker & Ordeshook, 1973; Taylor, 1975). For some political scientists, these models only tell us how persons might behave if they acted rationally. They are of value insofar as we can compare actual behavior with the model in order to try to account for the deviance from the model. For others, however, these models represent the way in which people actually do behave. The assumption of rationality becomes a reality (Riker & Ordeshook, 1973). For still others, however, rational models represent ways in which people should behave if they are to conform to rational norms, and such norms are assumed to be desirable in themselves. Rational models may, therefore, depict formal calculi of rational behavior, actual strategies of choice, or, preferred strategies, if one values rational behavior.

Not only empirically oriented research but political philosophy also has been a major beneficiary of the rational approach. Rational modeling has breathed new life into political philosophy. During the behavioral period, moral research had all but died out for reasons already mentioned. Values were sometimes thought to be mere expressions of preferences, as in economics to this day. In the current postbehavioral period, renewed efforts are under way to demonstrate that there is a rational basis for moral argument and judgment. Most of the work in this area has been inspired by John Rawls's *A Theory of Justice* (1971), itself influenced by economic modeling and game theory. In this book, the author attempts to develop valid and demonstrable criteria of justice derivable from the assumption of rational action. Using a similar convention about rational behavior, others have turned to the task of developing moral theories about equality, freedom, international justice, legitimacy, and the like (Beitz, 1979; Elster, 1986; Fishkin, 1982; Lehrer & Wagner, 1981).

Political philosophy is not alone in this new approach. It was preceded by and has in turn reinforced the application of the rational-actormpts to develop valid and demonstrable criteria of justice derivable from the assumption of rational action. Using a similar convention about rational behavior, others have turned to the task of developing moral theories about equality, freedom, international justice, legitimacy, and the like (Beitz, 1979; Elster, 1986; Fishkin, 1982; Lehrer & Wagner, 1981).

Political philosophy is not alone in this new approach. It was preceded by and has in turn reinforced the application of the rational-actoron the grounds that actors do in fact behave non-rationally and irrationally and that prediction of the behavior of individuals or of aggregates unnecessarily handicaps itself by failing to take such facts into account (Eckstein, 1988; Elster, 1989; Jarvie, 1984; Mansbridge, 1990; Quattrone & Tversky, 1988). In part, however, the rational model has been accused of being overly reductionist in assuming that individual attributes, such as rationality, can explain all behavior. Such a model fails to take into account systematically the institutional and structural context that may determine, or, at the very least limit, actors, severally or as aggregates (Easton, 1990; March & Olsen, 1989). By the beginning of the 1990s, however, it would appear that these increasing reservations about the applicability of the rationality model have not prevented it from carving out a sizeable and, from all appearances, an enduring niche for itself in the discipline.

In substantive areas such as those just mentioned—policy analysis, political economy, and what I have called cognitive political inquiry (rational modeling and the new political philosophy)—there has been little difficulty in going beyond the range of interests characteristic of the behavioral period and in adding to the latter's methodological perspectives. However, in the matter of actual methods of empirical research and in the fundamental premise that human behavior is subject to scientific inquiry, much less success has been met in finding an alternative, despite the current pervasive criticism of scientific method.

Few people believe any longer in the value neutrality of science. That scientific concepts are value-laden can no longer be denied. But that this does not invalidate the search for objective knowledge and understanding is equally undeniable. How both these statements can be true is still the subject of much debate (Lakatos & Musgrave, 1970; Suppe, 1977).

What, however, do the critics of scientific method offer as an alternative to the methods of science? This is where the real difficulty for the critics arises. The only formal alternative, that is, the only alternative that involves something that looks like a method that can be articulated, formalized, and communicated to succeeding generations is Weberian interpretive (*verstehen*) or empathetic understanding. This method has been and continues to be discussed, and in recent years the interest in the writings of Max Weber has increased enormously. As yet, however, no one has been able to formalize, systemize, or standardize the so-called interpretive method in a way that makes it readily communicable to those who would seek to learn it. Despite this irreducible inexpressibility, strangely enough, many radical critics of conventional social science have adopted this method, implicitly or otherwise. This is especially strange as its inventor, Max Weber, has been called "the Karl Marx of the bourgeoisie."

The Present and the Future

The many often conflicting tendencies in postbehavioral political science in the West make it difficult to draw general conclusions about the state of the discipline. Because political science is still in the process of change, as the 1990s begin we cannot speak of a single, dominant tendency or direction. If there is one, however, we can probably find it in the fact that most leading members of the discipline continue to accept the appropriateness for social inquiry of the scientific methodology found to be so successful in the natural sciences.

It would be misleading, however, to assume that our understanding of scientific method today is the same as it was during the behavioral period. Our conception of science has not stood still; it is itself undergoing change.

We no longer cast ourselves in the image of the positivist ideal of science. An incipient transformation is under way that may well displace that image with a new one. If so, this is probably the most dramatic thing that is happening in the social sciences, though most social scientists may not yet be aware of it.

Positivism as represented in the thinking of the Vienna Circle during the 1920s was largely subsumed, if not consciously

articulated, as behavioralism took shape, especially during the
1950s and 1960s. In this image, the ideal product of scientific inquiry
would be a body of knowledge, based on axioms, with statements
of relationships or generalizations that could be ultimately formalized, especially through the use of mathematics, and that would be
well-grounded in objective observations.

This model is still entertained by many social scientists, especially
those who happen to be in areas where it can be either achieved or
approximated, as, for example, in the areas of public choice and
rational modeling. There, formal mathematization of propositions
works well if only because it is intrinsic to the method of analysis
in those areas. There are vast fields in political science, however,
indeed most of political science to this point, that have not yielded
this kind of intellectual product. Yet these areas of political science
are clearly subject to rigorous inquiry through the use of the normal
rules of logic, through careful acquisition of data consistent with the
canons of science, and through equally sophisticated analysis of
these data. The outcomes, though, do not measure up to the positivistic ideal of an axiomatized and mathematized set of propositions. Does this mean that they are not acceptable as scientific
conclusions?

During the positivistic behavioral phase of political science, the
answer might have been affirmative. Today, under the more relaxed
understanding of science that is growing within philosophy of
science, a different answer can be offered, one that accepts non-
axiomatized and nonmathematical statements as an integral part of
scientific knowledge, even in its ideal form.

Philosophy of science is that special discipline in the West that is
concerned with understanding the nature of science—how it acquires knowledge (epistemology) and the nature of the world we
wish to know and understand (ontology). The findings of philosophy of science itself no less than the findings of any other discipline
are subject to change and, we hope, improvement. Like other fields
of inquiry it grows and changes. Although at one time philosophers of science, under the sway of early positivism, did indeed
conceive of the appropriate outcomes of scientific inquiry in the
manner of the positivists of the Vienna Circle, today, most recent
findings are moving in a far less monolithically mathematical direction. No longer do all philosophers of science see science as re-
stricted to a single kind of formalized product in the image of

classical positivism. In a more skeptical mood, philosophers of science are now beginning to recognize that if we are to understand science we ought not to accept some abstract analysis of the nature of science as an adequate description of the way science operates to acquire valid knowledge. Rather, we are better advised to look at what scientists actually do.

When we do look at the history of scientific practices we find that a larger variety of research products are accepted as useful and necessary than we would have guessed if we had confined ourselves to the positivistic interpretation. Philosophy of science is now discovering that there are many varieties of outcomes with which scientists seem to be satisfied. These outcomes seem to answer the kinds of problems that are being asked in a particular area of science even if the outcomes do not look like the formal or mathematical models of early positivism. For example, systems of classification, taxonomies, conceptual frameworks, and qualitative generalizations about evolutionary processes that do not permit prediction need have little to do with formal models or mathematized propositions. Yet in the various sciences in which they are found, such as botany and biology, they are just as acceptable as final products (Hanson, 1969; Shapere, 1974; Suppe, 1977; Toulmin, 1972).

If this is happening in the natural sciences where the success of their methods cannot be denied, then it ought not to be any less true in the social sciences. In this view, then, systematic classifications of political phenomena, for example, or conceptual frameworks, as developed in my own thinking in systems analysis, would be just as normal a product of scientific inquiry as any generalization about politics or any mathematical model. The only question one must ask is whether, at the time, the intellectual product satisfies the needs of a would-be scientific discipline, such as political science, in terms of rigorous and testable understanding. This is to say, if the knowledge we acquire seems to help us in attaining satisfactory explanation or adequate understanding of an empirically grounded sort, then that is the most that we can ask of the methods of science. The history of inquiry in the natural sciences now seems to reveal that, despite what classical positivism would have us believe, there is no single fixed kind of intellectual product that can be designated as appropriate and necessary to achieve understanding of any given phenomena.

As the 1990s begin, the postbehavioral stage that we have just discussed is still evolving. It will be some time before a definitive statement can be made about how it finally differs from behavioralism and about the new direction in which it may be leading political science. One thing is clear, however. It had its birth in efforts to cope with some of the unresolved problems generated by behavioralism: the indifference to moral judgments, the excessive commitment to formal mathematized statements flowing from the use of scientific method, the focus on theoretical criteria to the neglect of social issues, the preoccupation with social forces as determinants of behavior, overlooking, in the process, important cognitive (rational) elements, and a profound forgetfulness about the history of political systems that helps to shape their present.

In trying to cope with these problems bequeathed by behavioralism, however, we can assume that postbehavioralism is busily generating its own difficulties. Some of these are already obvious; others undoubtedly will emerge as new contemporary explanations exhaust their own potential. For example, in emphasizing the need to apply whatever knowledge we have to the solution of urgent social issues, we have already run into major difficulties in trying to reintegrate the various highly specialized disciplines. Descartes taught us that understanding requires decomposition and analysis of a subject matter. Application of knowledge to the solution of social problems, however, requires the reassembly of the specialized knowledge of the various social sciences. As I discussed in the introduction to this volume, we are still at a loss about how to do this. Application of knowledge has also diverted scarce resources from the continued search for fundamental knowledge so that we are already being called upon to reassess the appropriate division between applied and so-called pure research. Computer technology will clearly change the character of major aspects of research in all the social sciences, including political science, in ways that we can only guess at the present time. And finally, the growing international character of research raises fundamental issues about the universality of concepts in the social sciences as contrasted with the culturally conditioned nature of most thinking about social problems. As I asked in the introduction to this book, can we develop a genuinely transnational social science when different national cultures approach problems of understanding social phenomena in such transparently different ways, often with such different concepts?

To enter into a discussion of the impact of issues such as these on political science would, however, take us too far afield from our present purpose, an analysis of the four basic stages—formal-legal, traditional, behavioral, and postbehavioral—through which political science in the United States has passed in the 20th century. These issues may, however, foreshadow a fifth stage that we have not yet begun to enter.

References

Beitz, C. R. (1979). *Political theory and international relations*. Princeton, NJ: Princeton University Press.

Bell, D. (1960). *The end of ideology: On the exhaustion of political ideas in the fifties*. Glencoe, IL: Free Press.

Bentley A. (1949). *The process of government*. Cambridge, MA: Harvard University Press. (Originally published in 1908)

Downs, A. (1957). *An economic theory of democracy*. New York: Harper.

Easton, D. (1962, October). The current meaning of "behavioralism" in political science. [Monograph]. *Annals of the American Academy of Political and Social Science*, 1-25.

Easton, D. (1969). The new revolution in political sciences. *American Political Science Review, 60*, 1051-1061.

Easton, D. (1981a). *The political system*. New York: Knopf. (Originally published in 1953)

Easton, D. (1981b). *A framework for political analysis*. Chicago: University of Chicago Press. (Originally published in 1965)

Easton, D. (1981c). The political system besieged by the state. *Political Theory, 9*, 303-325.

Easton, D. (1990). *The analysis of political structure*. New York: Routledge

Eckstein, H. (1988). A culturalist theory of political change. *American Political Science Review, 82*, 789-804.

Elster, J. (Ed.). (1986). *Rational choice*. New York: New York University Press.

Elster, J. (1989) *Solomonic judgments: Studies in the limitation of rationality*. New York: Cambridge University Press.

Fainsod, M. (1940). Some reflections on the nature of the regulatory process. In *Public Policy* (pp. 298). Cambridge, MA: Harvard University Press.

Fishkin, J. S. (1982). *The limits of obligation*. New Haven, CT: Yale University Press.

Frolich, N., & Oppenheimer, J. A. (1982). *Modern political economy*. Englewood Cliffs, NJ: Prentice-Hall.

Hanson, N. R. (1969). *Perception and discovery*. San Francisco: Freeman Cooper.

Herring, P. (1929). *Group representation before congress*. Baltimore, MD: Johns Hopkins Press.

Jarvie, I. C. (1984). *Rationality and relativism*. London: Routledge and Kegan Paul.

Kramer, G. H., & Hertzberg, J. (1975). Formal theory. In F. I. Greenstein and N. W. Polsby (Eds.), *Handbook of political science* (Vol. 3, Chap. 7). Reading, MA: Addison-Wesley.

Kuhn, T. (1962). *The structure of scientific revolutions*. Chicago: University of Chicago Press.

Lakatos, I., & Musgrave, A. (1970). *Criticism and the growth of knowledge*. Cambridge: Cambridge University Press.

Lehrer, K., & Wagner, C. (1981). *Rational consensus in science and society*. Dordrecht, Holland: Reidel.

Mansbridge, J. J. (Ed.). (1990). *Beyond self-interest*. Chicago: University of Chicago Press.

March, J. G., & Olsen, J. P. (1989). *Rediscovering institutions: The organizational basis of politics*. New York: The Free Press.

Monroe, K. (1983). *Presidential popularity and the economy*. New York: Praeger.

Ollman, B., & Vernoff, E. (1982). *The left academy: Marxist scholarship on American campuses*. New York: McGraw-Hill.

Poulantzas, N. (1973). *Political power and social classes*. London: New Left Books: Sheed and Ward.

Quattrone, G. A., & Tversky, A. (1988). Contrasting rational and psychological analysis of political choice. *American Political Science Review, 82,* 719-736.

Rawls, J. (1971). *A theory of justice*. Cambridge, MA: Harvard University Press.

Riker, W. H., & Ordeshook, P. C. (1973). *An introduction to positive theory*. Englewood Cliffs, NJ: Prentice-Hall.

Shapere, D. (1974). Discovery, rationality and progress in science. In K. Schaffner and P. Cohen (Eds.), *PSA 1972: Proceedings of 1972 biennial meetings of Philosophy of Science Association* (pp. 407-419). Dordrecht, Holland: Reidel.

Suppe, F. (1977). *The structure of scientific theories*. Urbana: University of Illinois Press.

Taylor, M. (1975). The theory of collective choice. In F. I. Greenstein and N. W. Polsby (Eds.), *Handbook of political choice* (Vol. 3, pp. 413-418). Reading, MA: Addison-Wesley.

Toulmin, S. (1972). *Human understanding*. Princeton, NJ: Princeton University Press.

Truman, D. (1951). *The government process*. New York: Knopf.

3

The Many Faces of American Sociology

A Discipline in Search of Identity

RALPH H. TURNER

The idea of sociology as a field of study emerged in Europe near the middle of the tumultuous 19th century. Reacting to the dissolution of traditional society in a chaotic sequence of revolution, counter-revolution, and international warfare, the French philosopher, Auguste Comte, proposed sociology as the science of human social relationships, employing the positivistic methods of the established sciences. Other scholars, notably Herbert Spencer, Georg Simmel, Emile Durkheim, Ludwig Gumplowicz, Karl Marx, and Max Weber, established the foundations of what has come to be modern sociology. Like Comte, these pioneer sociologists combined the ideal of unbiased scholarship with the goal of developing principles that could be used in solving the major social problems of their times. But their respective sociologies varied from the conflict perspectives of Gumplowicz and Marx to the functionalism of Durkheim and the social Darwinism of Spencer, the microsociology of Simmel, and the interpretative sociology of Weber. This diversity continues to characterize contemporary American sociology.

Sociology was imported into the United States in the mid-1800s, the term first appearing in titles of books published in 1854 and as the title of a university course in 1876 (Martindale, 1976). By a decade later, Lester Ward and William Sumner had emerged as intellectual leaders of reformist and conservative sociological thought, respectively.

The 1890s saw establishment of the leading departments of sociology by Albion Small at the University of Chicago and by Franklin Giddings at Columbia University. The "Chicago School" of sociology, stressing intimate field studies exposing disorganization and conflict in the urban environment, was—for several decades—the paramount center for American sociology.

Giddings, in contrast, adhered strongly to the scientific ideal, promoting statistics as the essential method of sociology and training the first generation of important sociological statisticians.

In the early decades of the 20th century, sociology gained in respectability and, thanks largely to the Chicago tradition and American pragmatism, accumulated a substantial body of empirical research. The relatively collectivistic orientations of such European progenitors as Durkheim and Marx were replaced by individualistic perspectives more in harmony with American culture. The corresponding emphasis on individuals rather than classes as the units in social structure made sociologists' data especially amenable to statistical analysis, so that Giddings's influence was increasingly felt as quantitative methods became a standard component of sociological methodology.

Social reformers found sociological research useful in promoting their reforms. Criminology developed as an established field in sociology and sometimes formed effective liaisons with law enforcement agencies. In the 1920s, the federal government, through the U.S. Department of Agriculture, sponsored a great deal of sociological research in rural communities. Demographers, though not mostly sociologists, were needed in the growing Bureau of the Census. With the coming of the Great Depression of the 1930s, sociology suffered a severe setback because there were few jobs for graduates and little money for research. But a tradition of using sociologists in federal government was established when many were hired to conduct research for agencies of the New Deal. It was a natural step, after the United States entered World War II, to commission sociological research to improve the fighting effectiveness of the armed forces and to help in planning for the period of postwar reconstruction, both at home and abroad.

Sociology After World War II

With the end of World War II, sociology came into its own, not only in educational institutions but for its potential applications in industry, government, and the improvement of family life.[1] Recent volumes of the *Annual Review of Sociology* and such assessments of the field as Short's (1981) *The State of Sociology* and Bottomore, Nowak, and Sokolowska's (1982) *Sociology: The State of the Art* can be compared with baseline works like Bogardus's (1931) *Contemporary Sociology* and Gurvich and Moore's (1945) *Twentieth Century Sociology*, to identify trends over the past 40 to 50 years. Midway through our review period, such works as Robert Faris's (1964) *Handbook of Modern Sociology*, Joseph Gittler's (1957) *Review of Sociology*, Merton, Broom, and Cottrell's (1959) *Sociology Today*, and Lipset and Smelser's (1961) *The Progress of a Decade* provide useful overviews. In addition, we can draw on scattered comparisons of sociologists' stated fields of interest, changes in course offerings in colleges and universities, and changing characteristics of members of the American Sociological Association since World War II.[2]

Changing Fields of Interest

Several marked changes have taken place in the relative popularity of different sociological specialties in the years under review. Community studies are much less prominent today than in the 1940s and 1950s, as interest in both urban and rural sociology and in ecological investigation has declined, and regionalism has almost disappeared from the sociological vocabulary. However, sociologists continue to study a variety of urban phenomena, such as poverty and race relations, without calling their work urban sociology. The once important sociological pronouncements on social ethics for the individual and social progress for the society are now largely forgotten. For at least the first two decades after World War II, marriage and family and demography developed as independent fields with their own professional associations and journals. Demography's methods and frame of reference have, however, been widely diffused through such disparate fields as stratification and even social psychology. The study of minorities, especially important in the first half of this century, lost favor until the 1960s civil rights disturbances in the United States and worldwide ethnic nationalist movements caused a strong resurgence of interest in minorities and in majority-minority relations, albeit with a shift from a microsociological to a macro- sociological perspective.

On the growth side, social stratification and political sociology, unrecognized earlier as sociological specialties, are among the most important contemporary fields. The study of large-scale or formal organizations, such as corporations, was just beginning in the early 1940s, as was the study of occupations and work; these are now prominent specialties in sociology. From limited attention as an aspect of marriage and family, the topic of gender roles (or women's studies) has become a distinct and important field.

Changes in Sociological Method and Theory

Every observer has noted the striking increase in the use of quantification since the prewar era. But it is more accurate to say that both quantitative and qualitative methods have gained in sophistication. Descriptive statistics have given way to measurement of relationships, and such early consensual statistics as coefficients of correlation and chi-squares are being displaced by mathematically more advanced measures. The self-administered questionnaire has been largely replaced by the survey, administered in the interviewee's home or place of work or by telephone. Procedures for sampling, constructing items, arranging the order of questioning, and other technical matters have been greatly refined. Similarly, for qualitative methodology, the once popular "case study" method has been refined to a much more rigorous set of techniques for securing and analyzing data, such as those described by Emerson (1981) and McCall (1984). It is no longer possible for the untrained amateur to conduct research that can stand the test of sociological criticism.[3]

Conceptions of sociological theory likewise have changed. In 1931, Bogardus could organize a review of contemporary sociology around discussions of its most important concepts, writing that "a sociological concept is the abstraction of the meanings of an entire group of specific facts about human interaction. Such concepts, together with their meanings, comprise a unity which is the essence of sociology" (p. 20). Although, in practice, many contemporary theoretical systems are more classificatory than relational, theory today is understood to mean statements concerning the dynamic relationships among variables or events. The shift was initially from concepts to *propositions*, statements of how changes in one or more independent variables affect a dependent variable, and the conditions under which the relationship holds true. More recently, the term theory is applied only to *propositional systems* and *models*, which link together several propositions on the basis of more abstract conceptions of underlying causal principles. To what extent the ideal theory is expressed or expressible in mathematical terms—a new idea to sociologists in the past half century—remains a matter of debate.

The early emphasis on being scientific was reflected in the publication of fewer impressionistic essays and more reports of empirical research in journals. But "mere empiricism" began to get a bad name and the standard became hypothesis testing. Still more recently, the ideal has become the test of hypotheses derived from some general body of theory. Sociology has gone through a cycle from emphasizing theory with little testable empirical basis to an atheoretical empiricism and back to the evaluation of research primarily for its relevance to grand theory. We shall return later to the relationship between theory and research.

As a framework in which to identify *paradigmatic* changes, it will be helpful to consider the kinds of circumstances that have led to change.

Changing Relationships with Other Disciplines

Sociology's changing relationships to other academic fields have paralleled and sometimes preceded changes in subject matter emphasis. In the early 1940s, a separation between sociology and social work was just taking place, as sociology sought to become more of a pure science and social work began looking to other fields, such as psychology and psychiatry, as foundations for practice. Sociologists then looked toward psychology more than to any other discipline, with widespread adoption of behaviorism as the ideal for sociology.

Today, most applied sociologists feel much closer to policy science than to social work. In addition, many sociologists are now employed in professional schools, with medical sociology being the outstanding growth field. To some extent, their problems for investigation are then dictated by the needs of the particular profession. Throughout its history, sociology has always been close to anthropology, and this relationship reached a peak during and immediately after World War II. The early "Chicago School" stressed ethnographic methods in research, and recent resurgent interest in ethnographic research after a period of neglect often draws explicitly on anthropological experience in refining this methodology. Early sociologists borrowed the concept of culture from anthropology, and the late 1940s and 1950s witnessed abortive institutional efforts to develop a unifying theoretical paradigm so as to eliminate the need for separate disciplines of anthropology and sociology. Structure-functionalism, borrowed from anthropology, was the central paradigm in the system developed by Talcott Parsons (1949, 1951), who was America's most prestigious sociological theorist for a quarter of a century. With the reaction against functionalism in the 1970s and 1980s and a growing trend toward explaining culture in terms of social structure, sociologists have increasingly looked to other disciplines, notably political science and economics.

The growing interest in social structure has redirected attention toward the long-neglected concepts of *power* and *conflict,* which became central concerns of the emergent field of political sociology in the 1960s and after. Sociologists have borrowed from political science in their efforts to understand power and as they searched for a genuinely *macro*sociological paradigm. Simultaneously, both macro- and microsociologists frequently turned to economics for models of organizational and individual decision making. The 1970s and 1980s witnessed an unprecedented diffusion of economic models that assume rationality and self-interest into all fields of sociology, where they often replaced earlier models depicting human decision making as irrational and arational.

A final discipline with which sociology has had continuing but changing relationships is history. As scientism and present-time emphases grew, the ties between sociology and history were severely weakened for a decade or two. But the tide was reversed in the 1960s when sociologists began to realize that their failure to predict the upheavals taking place at that time resulted, at least in part, from their shallow understanding of historical processes. Today, many sociologists have learned to use primary as well as secondary historical sources. Political sociology and the sociology of the family are two fields in which historical approaches have been extensively developed.

While relationships with particular fields have ebbed and flowed, the attempt to achieve genuine interdisciplinary collaboration among the social or behavioral sciences has been a constant theme throughout the period we are examining.[4] One of the most important recent manifestations of this theme is the current collaborative work on the *life course*. Life-course specialists study the sequence of events and associated behavioral changes in the lives of individuals, stressing the characteristic series of role transitions that most individuals pass through in a particular social system (Clausen, 1986).

The microsociologists' attention to the life course and the macrosociologists' attention to history should probably be understood as manifestations of a broader trend to take the passage of time seriously in the study of social life. A methodological counterpart is the growing demand for longitudinal studies in which individuals, cohorts, communities, organizations, and societies are studied during a series of time intervals, with change rather than momentary structures the object of investigation.

Critical Historical Events

Critical historical events such as war, economic depression, and the rise of totalitarianism have been a second source of influence on sociological paradigms. Preoccupation with authoritarianism was intense in the sociology of the 1940s and 1950s, reflecting the war against nazism and fascism and the immediate postwar wave of political intolerance. The popularity of functionalism is often attributed to the apparent success and stability of American society in the postwar era from 1940 to 1960. The more critical bent of sociology since 1970, with greater emphasis on conflict than on consensus and stability, is responsive to the national experience of shock and disillusionment following the epidemic of violent racial protest and military involvement in Vietnam. Sociologists also reflected critically on their own failure to predict the decade of turbulence. The burgeoning of historical sociology was one important answer to that question. Following soon after, the growth of women's studies responded to the revitalization of the women's movement in the 1970s.

Intellectual Currents

Often closely related to major events, main intellectual currents in the United States, the Western world, and worldwide constitute a third force for change in sociological paradigms. Evolutionary thought was very influential during the first half of the century, but by midcentury its influence had waned and it was replaced by a more static orientation expressed in such concepts as the psychologist Kurt Lewin's *field theory* and the anthropologist's *anthropological present*. But the past two decades have seen reawakened interest in the possibility of social evolutionary theories as part of the growing interest in historical sociology.

Freudian psychoanalysis and a broader psychiatric perspective were belatedly being taken seriously by more and more sociologists as the postwar era dawned. With this influence came an image of human behavior as irrational and driven by hidden motivations. Sociologists became less interested in social disorganization, viewed as a pathological condition marked by widespread nonconformity to consensual social norms, and more concerned with cultural norms and structural relationships that frustrated and twisted the attitudes of whole classes of people. Most sociologists persisted in explicitly rejecting Freudianism, but few remained uninfluenced in the way they viewed social phenomena.

By the late 1950s and early 1960s, a subjectivist orientation to the world was being imported from Europe in the form of existentialist philosophy and phenomenological social science. These approaches embodied a reaction against "scientism" and strictly quantitative sociology, and gave encouragement to qualitative methods in sociology. *Symbolic interactionism* (Blumer, 1969), which had been reduced to a small and defensive cult at the peak of scientism in the 1950s, attracted new recruits until it came to be acknowledged as the leading paradigm in sociological social psychology. New developments like *ethnomethodology* also appealed to both phenomenologically inclined students and established scholars (Garfinkel, 1967).

While socialism as a political orientation was popular among sociologists during the first half of the century, it was of the typical

American variety that included an explicit repudiation of communism and Marxism. The 1960s witnessed the first serious inroads of Marxist thought into American sociology, although it had been important in European sociologies much earlier. By the 1980s, Marxism was generally accepted as one of the three major paradigms in American sociology (along with structure-functionalism and interactionism).

Combining the influence of events and intellectual currents, we can justifiably speak of *sociological generations*. Students undergoing training and younger academics typically learn the meanings of sociological concepts and principles in the context of the significant events and intellectual currents of the time. As their perspectives on sociology become shaped, they tend to carry them forward throughout their careers. Hence the most productive paradigms in a given period often reflect the socializing impact of events that occurred as much as two decades earlier.

Shifting Support for Research

A fourth type of influence on sociology comes from changing patterns of financial support for research. The general prosperity and the favorable view of social science on the part of liberal federal administrations fostered a steady growth of public funding for research during the 1950s and 1960s. In these halcyon days, the opportunity to conduct significant research became available to most qualified sociologists, the scale and sophistication of research projects grew, and increasing support was available for "basic" or nonapplied research which at other times was considered a luxury.

One response to the student and racial disorders of the 1960s was massive funding for research that might contribute to crime control. While this government research priority did not draw most sociologists away from their major interests, it may have had a substantial effect on paradigms in criminology and the broader study of social control and deviance. In the prewar period, under evolutionary and "applied ethics" thinking, sociologists studied "social pathology." At the end of World War II, the perspective changed to the study of "social disorganization," shifting attention from the individual to societal processes and deflecting moral judgments. But by the early 1950s, social disorganization was being replaced by "deviance," which was viewed as a more measurable and hence more scientific concept. Reflecting cultural relativism and political liberalism, the *labeling* theory of deviance reached a height of popularity. Labeling theory tends to shift responsibility for deviance away from the deviant and to raise questions about the very concepts of crime and other forms of deviance. In contrast, research that did not question the meaning of crime but contributed directly to crime control or measured the relative effectiveness of different kinds of punishment was more easily funded. The eminent criminologist, Donald R. Cressey (1979) complained that, "in fifty years criminology has moved from an abiding concern for sociological theories of crime causation to an overwhelming concern for political control of crime and criminals" (p. 475).

With decreasing federal support for social science research in the 1970s and especially in the 1980s, there is now a greater premium on unequivocally applied research, and basic research is harder to finance. For the sake of economy, there is much more secondary analysis of existing data.

Disciplinary Processes

Developmental and cyclical processes within the discipline itself are a fifth source of changing paradigms. Much change has resulted from progressive refinements of method and theory. Technical limitations of particular statistical techniques, for example, have led to a continuing search for technically more adequate procedures. Paradigms are continually refined on the basis of experience with their use.

Once-popular paradigms fall into disfavor for several reasons. The possibilities for new understandings can be exhausted, so that the old paradigm only produces research that confirms earlier findings. This may have been the fate of once-popular studies of ecology and attitudes. Scholars familiar with a given paradigm often become increasingly aware of the limitations of the paradigm—the kinds of cases that it cannot explain—and search for a new paradigm to fit those cases. An occasional disadvantage of abandoning old paradigms for the sake of new ones, in contrast to continual refinement of old paradigms, is that new paradigms are typically oversimplified until investigators have worked with them for some time.

These internally generated trends are often not linear. The relative emphasis on quantitative and qualitative methods, for example, has been cyclical. The widespread repudiation of Parsonian structure-functionalism of the 1970s has been followed in recent years by a resurgent *neo-Parsonianism*. Many of these trends have approximated a dialectic, though usually without consensus on new syntheses. Neo-Parsonian theory, for example, accepts many of the criticisms of orthodox Parsonian theory and offers revisions while maintaining fundamentals of the original theory. Many versions of neo-Marxist theory have flourished, each addressed to some of the important criticisms of orthodox Marxism. And the stock criticism of symbolic interactionism for ignoring social structure has provoked a widely accepted structural version of symbolic interaction (Stryker, 1980).

Consistent Trends

Considering the variety of circumstances that have influenced both subject matter emphases and paradigmatic preferences, there have been relatively few consistent trends in American sociology. Even the clearest trends have produced reactions.

A trend toward greater methodological sophistication, whether in quantitative or qualitative research, seems clear. Yet there are challenges. No one has yet made a systematic assessment of the accomplishments of newer statistical techniques such as *log linear* analysis, for example, to determine what we have learned that we did not already know before the new techniques were introduced. In qualitative research, methodological rigor probably rules out many erroneous findings and gives us greater confidence in conclusions. But the value of such work still depends principally on the perceptiveness and insightfulness of the investigator.

The increasing demand that empirical research be theoretically relevant is a second trend that has been consistent since the 1940s. The earlier conviction that the accumulation of a vast archive of descriptive studies would serve as a prime resource for the advancement of theory has weakened. Collaboration between a leading theorist, Peter Blau, and an eminent methodologist, Dudley Duncan, produced the landmark study of stratification, *The American Occupational Structure*, in 1967. Major journals today will seldom publish research whose theoretical relevance is not made convincingly explicit. Nevertheless, sociological theories are seldom precise enough to provide clear guidance for designing research, and our most brilliant insights are more often the product of serendipity than of hypothesis confirmation. Furthermore, the growing popularity of *secondary analysis* of data from existing data banks, facilitated by computer methods of data retrieval, has meant that the correspondence between theory and empirical data is too often contrived ex post facto.

A third consistent trend that receives mixed reviews is one toward increasing specialization within the field. In the 1930s and 1940s, the aspiration to be a general sociologist was still realistic. There was a sufficiently common body of core concepts and a small enough body of accumulated research in most fields of sociology that a scholar might make significant contributions to several and speak authoritatively about the field in general. It is difficult to imagine the genius necessary for such accomplishments today. This is, of course, a trend also observed in most of the older scientific and scholarly disciplines. Nevertheless, the trend is troublesome in sociology for at least two reasons. First, pathbreaking ideas within any specialty usually come from cross-referencing ideas from other specialties or disciplines rather than from research that is narrowly focused within the specialty. Second, sociologists have never been able to conceptualize the divisions within their discipline in a sufficiently rational fashion to minimize duplication of effort among specializations. For example, social movements are studied by specialists in collective behavior, political sociology, the sociology of religion, social change, the sociology of sports, and other fields. Social psychologists have complained that much of the best social psychological research is now being done by sociologists who identify themselves with specialties such as sociology of education, sociology of the family, medical sociology, sociology of the life course, sociology of gender roles, and sociology of the emotions, rather than with social psychology. As a result, sociologists often work on similar problems without being aware of each other's research and use different names to describe the same phenomenon.

The fourth consistent trend has been the internationalization of sociology. At the end of World War II, sociology was often referred to as the American social science, and European scholars regularly trekked to American universities to learn the latest methods and theories. However, within a decade or two, sociology had been firmly reestablished in western Europe, followed by developments in eastern Europe, Latin America, and Asia, in such countries as Japan, India, and, most recently, China. Today, American sociologists have at least as much to learn from sociologists in other countries as they have to contribute to them. Furthermore, the need for comparative research in which the supposedly universal dynamics of social systems observed in the United States can be confirmed or modified on the basis of testing in different societies is widely recognized. Unfortunately, accomplishment lags far behind the ideal in this respect. Besides the practical problems of organizing and executing internationally collaborative research, the de-emphasis on foreign language training in American schools and universities has hampered international exchange.

Persistent Issues in American Sociology

Whether we think of trends or oscillations, many of the changes in American sociology are best understood as efforts to deal more effectively with a few recurrent issues.

Technique Versus Insight

One such fundamental issue is the methodological antinomy between technique and insight. Most sociologists today would agree that the early goal of creating a sociology in the pattern of physics or chemistry led to an overemphasis on technique and an unjustified denigration of insight. In 1946, Carl Taylor (1947), who supervised the work of the many rural sociologists employed in the U.S. Department of Agriculture, stated in his presidential address to the American Sociological Association: "I have for a long time worried about the fact that it takes young sociologists from five to ten years to recover from what happens to them in their graduate training" (p. 8). Calling for a reorientation of graduate training, he said that

> if sociology is to develop into a useful discipline it must combine the type of knowledge and understanding which is derived by use of the

most rigid technique of science and the type of knowledge that is known among practical men as common sense. (p. 1)

The publication of Erving Goffman's (1955) initially controversial study, *The Presentation of Self in Everyday Life*, provided an example that stimulated many students and younger faculty to follow what came to be known as *interpretative sociology*. Interpretative sociologists assume that similar words, deeds, and experiences have quite different meanings to different people, and to the same people in different situations. They are critical of survey research in which simple questions and brief answers are assumed to have uniform meanings for all interviewees. The necessary understanding is only obtainable through intimate involvement in the situation and sustained interaction with the subjects under investigation. Investigators must use their own common sense rather than any systematic procedure, such as content analysis, in extracting meanings. For example, a single remark taken from hours of *pro forma* conversation may express most cogently an individual's true feelings. Interpretative sociologists prefer studying a few cases in great depth over more superficial study of large numbers of cases. For a test of validity they may, following Melville Dalton (1959), share their interpretations with their subjects and invite criticism, or they may depend on confirmation from independent investigations by other scholars or wait to see whether their predictions concerning subsequent behavior or events come true.

While Goffman's first work highlighted individual behavior in interpersonal situations, the discovery of informal social structures in apparently anarchistic or chaotic communities became a popular aim. William F. Whyte's 1943 classic, *Street Corner Society*, bringing to life the complex social structure among Italian youth who gathered on a particular corner in Boston, was reissued in 1955 and again in 1981. Gerald Suttles's (1968) examination of territorialism and ethnic relations in a Chicago slum and Elliott Liebow's (1967) study of black "corner boys" won awards as superb examples of participant observer research. Monographs of this genre continue to be published every year, revealing the hidden cultures and social structures of deviant groups, occupational groups, and isolated communities. Unfortunately, little has been done to apply the findings from these accumulated case studies to the improvement of our general theories of culture and social structure.

The rediscovery of interpretative sociology in the 1960s and 1970s did not slow the trend toward refinement of research technique which continues today. The development and dissemination of computer technology has enhanced the opportunities for refinement of technique. Students well trained in quantitative research techniques are still in greater demand than students trained in qualitative, interpretative sociology. But specialists in technique generally acknowledge the importance of interpretative research and accord it a degree of respect seldom granted in the 1940s.

Theory and Empirical Research

A second fundamental issue in sociology is the relationship between theory and empirical research, which in turn is inseparable from the nature of theory. By the beginning of the period under review, the concern to formulate theory in such a way that it could be subjected to empirical testing had already led to a variety of proposals. William Ogburn (1922) proposed his theory of *cultural lag* specifically to illustrate how theory could be formulated with an eye to its empirical application. According to this widely popular theory, social problems resulted when one aspect of culture—usually the material culture—advanced more rapidly than the adaptive culture. Ogburn saw lags as measurable, permitting sound empirical tests of hypotheses derived from the theory. The philosophical school of logical positivism found its counterpart in social science in *operationalism*, the doctrine that concepts should be defined strictly in terms of the operations employed to identify or measure them empirically (Bridgman, 1936). Thus attitudes are what attitude tests measure, rather than "tendencies to act."

Although the insight behind cultural lag theory has become part of accepted sociological wisdom, empirical use of the theory degenerated into merely illustrative studies, and cultural lag theory has fallen out of favor as oversimplified. Operationalism gained little headway since it made meaningful theory impossible and, as George Homans (1986) observed: "All theories of any complexity must contain terms that cannot be defined operationally but only implicitly in the form of propositions" (p. xix).

The most influential solution to the problem of making theory researchable was proposed by the eminent theorist, Robert Merton

(1957). Without denying the ultimate value of highly abstract theorization, he argued that in the current stage of sociological development, the greatest gain would come from working with "theories of the middle range." Most empirical research in the past 30 or 40 years has heeded this advice. Even the ideas of the master grand theorist, Talcott Parsons, that have produced the most empirical research have been his middle-range theories, such as the theory of the sick role and the theory of functional role differentiation in the family.

More inductive is the *grounded theory* approach (Glaser & Strauss, 1967), which is part of the reaction against scientism and widely practiced by interpretative sociologists. Instead of designing research to test hypotheses, the investigator approaches data with minimal preconceptions and attempts to derive theory from the data. Theory becomes established not by testing but inductively as the cumulative product of many researches.

The past decade has witnessed a return to the aim of deriving hypotheses from grand theory. Investigators turn to the great theorists and attempt to devise research that pits Durkheim against Marx or Weber against Marx, for example. Unfortunately, the reasoning that connects the grand theories with research. operations is seldom sufficiently compelling to produce unambiguous results. One consequence is the burgeoning of efforts to revise and refine classic theories so as to relate them more closely to evidence while retaining their essential postulates.

Relating Micro- and Macrosociology

Sociology has always struggled with the problem of how to describe structure and process in large social systems without reducing them to the simple aggregation of actions by individuals. When sociology was transplanted from more collectivistically oriented Europe to individualistic America, such concepts as "group mind" quickly became anathema. Concepts like *attitude* became central in sociology and more sociologists identified themselves with social psychology than any other specialty. Until the late 1960s, macrosociology in the United States dealt largely with the aggregated behavior of individuals.

Merton's (1957) interpretation of Durkheim's analysis of *anomie*, although it was basically individualistic, helped to bring collectivist Durkheim back to respectability. Parsons's (1949) *Structure of Social*

Action had a gradual impact, although it too seemed to make individual behavior the dependent variable in sociology. It was the worldwide youthful unrest of the 1960s that decisively shifted priorities from micro- to macrosociology. In part, communication and diffusion of ideas between American and European youth brought Americans into closer touch with still-collectivistic European ideas. Decades of seemingly fruitless efforts to equalize black and white opportunities through eradicating prejudice gave rise to the idea of *institutional racism*, that discrimination is built into society's institutions regardless of individual attitudes.

Radicalization of students and young academics during the 1960s made Karl Marx required reading and his collectivistic orientation respectable. In addition, the declining dominance of the University of Chicago with its more individualistic sociology and the increasing prominence of two universities—Columbia and Harvard—contributed to a national shift in emphasis from micro- to macrosociology. The popularity of decision-making models assuming rational choice on the basis of self-interest (even though their underlying logic is individualistic) seemed to reduce further the need for the microsociologist's attention to individual attitudes and motives.

If sociology went from a period in which the macro-micro relationship posed little problem because social structures were simply compounded individual behavior to a period in which true sociology was macrosociology with little need for a microsociology, the 1980s brought signs that both macro- and microsociologists are seeking ways to link the two perspectives. James Coleman (1986) recently argued that an adequate macrosociology is not possible until sociologists develop a satisfactory theory of action. Furthermore, it has often been observed that while contemporary sociological theories are mostly formulated at the macrolevel, our most sophisticated research techniques, such as survey research, are better suited to addressing questions about individuals (William Wilson in Short, 1981).

Making Sociology Useful

The dreams of sociology's European founders envisioned an immensely practical science that would supply the key to many of society's intractable problems. Yet the emphasis on making a true science of sociology has often seemed incompatible with a focus on application. Concerned that the balance between pure and applied science in sociology might have swung too far toward the former, Paul Lazarsfeld named "The Uses of Sociology" as his presidential theme for the American Sociological Association in 1962, and he subsequently coedited an influential volume of papers on the subject (Lazarsfeld, Sewell, & Wilensky, 1967).

Perhaps sociology's greatest influence has been through the diffusion of sociological understandings into the general culture. Terms like "role," "mores," and "charisma" have become part of everyday discourse. Appreciation of the significance of poverty and social stigmatization is widespread. Some of this diffusion has occurred through the classroom. But much of it has been facilitated by social reform movements, such as the women's movement and the civil rights movement, which incorporate sociological understandings into their reform messages.

The most common form of applied sociology has been to provide *usable understandings* of social phenomena, either by documenting the significance of a problem whose importance was previously unrecognized or by clarifying the causal dynamics of a problem. Sociological research has been important in revealing the extent of discrimination in employment against racial minorities and women, and in combating the assumption that crime is prevalent only among the lower classes in society by documenting the extent of white-collar crime. The early American sociologist, William I. Thomas (Thomas & Znaniecki, 1927), argued that sociological investigation should provide an alternative to the usually futile "ordering and forbidding" approach to dealing with problems. Instead of passing unenforceable laws against endemic problems and relying primarily on punishment, we should understand the causes of crime, or prejudice, or family breakup, and devise programs on the basis of these understandings.

One of the most dramatically successful applications of sociological understanding contributed crucially to the U.S. Supreme Court decision outlawing racially segregated public education in the United States in 1954. Two landmark studies, *An American Dilemma* (Myrdal, 1944) and the "Coleman Report" (Coleman et al., 1966), helped to establish that the poor quality of their schooling was a primary cause for the limited achievement of blacks and that segregated schools could never provide education of equal quality for Black and White students.

A more ambitious objective in applied research is the development of tools and techniques that can be used by interested parties in addressing their problems. A pioneer in this respect was Ernest Burgess, who devised tests that could be used to predict success and failure of a prisoner on parole (Burgess, 1928) and, later, tests to predict success and failure in marriage (Burgess & Cottrell, 1939; Burgess & Wallin, 1954). In each case, the assumption was that the results of these tests would improve the quality of decision making.

During the period under review, sociologists' enthusiasm for these devices has waned, largely because of the rather superficial and stereotypical nature of the most predictive items. Nevertheless, tests of this kind are widely used as aids in marriage counseling and other types of counseling and planning activity.

Business and industrial firms have made wide use of sociologists as consultants to conduct studies of employee morale and, to a lesser degree, problems in the organization of management. Here, too, tests and various devices have been developed for use by firms. One interesting case is William F. Whyte's (1948) study of the restaurant industry, and the problem of the "crying waitress." He was able to show that much of the interpersonal stress in restaurants arose from a status discrepancy, namely, that waitresses delivered customers' orders to men working in the pantry and kitchen, violating the usual status relationship in which men give orders to women. When an impersonal barrier was placed between the men and the women, by having waitresses simply place their orders on a spindle rather than communicating them personally to the men, the friction was much reduced. Nearly all restaurants in the United States now use a rotary spindle on which waitresses attach their orders, largely as a consequence of Whyte's research.

The use of sociological tools and understandings by business organizations and government gave rise to questions that stimulated a third kind of applied sociology, in which the sociologist becomes an advocate or a critic. Keynoting this approach were Lynd's (1939) *Knowledge for What?*, writings by C. Wright Mills (1959), and an article by Howard S. Becker (1967) entitled "Whose Side Are We On?" As early as 1951, the Society for the Study of Social Problems was established by an initially small group of sociologists "to bridge the gap (which seems to be widening instead of closing) between sociological theory and social problems" (Burgess, 1953, p. 2). The rising tide of criticism against "value-free" sociology crested in the 1960s in consonance with the decade's nationwide protests. Critics charged that most sociological research helped the "establishment" at the expense of the working class, the poor, minorities, and deviants, because sociologists were employed by the establishment, funded by the establishment, and sought to be identified with the establishment. Thus criminologists investigated the causes of crime, rather than asking why particular actions were defined as crime and others were not or why certain culprits were singled out for punishment or for especially severe punishment. The crisis of conscience was brought to a head by the revelation in 1960 that a few sociologists and anthropologists were participating in the planning stages for "Project Camelot." This massive project was sponsored by the U.S. Department of Defense, which often referred to it as a study of insurgency and counterinsurgency (Beals, 1969). Critics accused participating social scientists of lending their support to a thinly veiled effort to stifle justified rebellion and revolution in countries with oppressive governments. The project was quickly aborted in the wake of violent international protest, and the social sciences underwent a period of profound soul searching.

As the 1960s enthusiasm for radical reform of society waned in the 1970s, as investigators became impatient with the uncertainty over whether new understandings would be put to good use, and as disillusionment with many of the tools and techniques invented by sociologists spread, a fourth kind of applied sociology gained in favor and is ascendant today. *Policy research* aims to make a significant impact on society by influencing the formation of policy governing programs that affect thousands or millions of people, rather than by influencing individuals and organizations.

Evaluation research, as one form of policy research, flowered in the 1960s and 1970s in connection with social programs initiated by Presidents Kennedy and Johnson and growing concern over whether expensive social programs really had the intended effects. Sociologists had long engaged in evaluation studies, as, for example, in the many efforts to assess whether capital punishment has any greater deterrent effect on capital crime rates than severe prison sentences (Sellin, 1952, 1980). But evaluation studies were seldom conclusive because of an absence of experimental control of confounding variables.

With more generous funding and methodological sophistication, interdisciplinary teams of social scientists launched a series of large-scale field experiments to measure the effects of innovative social programs, such as Negative Income Tax, Housing Allowance, and Transitional Aid to Released Prisoners.[5] Populations were divided on a random basis into experimental subjects who were covered by the program and control subjects who were not, with comparisons made over a period of from 3 to 5 years. Although much was learned, the difficulties of fully implementing experimental controls in the field made the findings less definitive than hoped (Hunt, 1985). Furthermore, political interest had usually shifted by the time the studies were completed so that the findings were not relevant to current policy decisions. Perhaps most discouraging to liberal-minded investigators, highly vaunted social programs generally turned out to have very little effect (Rossi & Wright, 1984). The reduction in funding for social science research and the policy of cutting back social programs under President Reagan was the final coup de grâce for ambitious field experiments.

Whether or not field experiments on this scale will ever be undertaken again, evaluation researchers agree that social scientists must contribute their advice and research skills when programs are being designed, rather than simply being assigned the task of saying whether a preestablished program works or does not work (Rossi & Wright, 1984). In the meantime, less ambitious evaluation studies continue to be launched, and more and more universities now provide training in this kind of research.

In summary, sociology has been "used" in American society in a variety of ways, and many sociologists have been engaged in the effort to make it more useful. Accomplishments in this respect fall far short of the hopes of sociology's founders, partly because of frequent public resistance to accepting and acting on sociological wisdom, partly because sociologists are seldom able to overcome crucial methodological difficulties, and partly because of the limited development of sound sociological theory. Even more, the most familiar forms of sociological research and theory do not easily lend themselves to practical application. We are best at documenting the existence and scope of a problem or in showing that a program is not working as intended. Our models are more often cross-sectional than longitudinal, and our longitudinal models are primarily deterministic. Longitudinal models that specify critical developments and appropriate interventions are more suitable for providing "treatment" advice, like that of a physician who recognizes symptoms and monitors the course of a disease, with a choice of appropriate interventions under varying developments. Knowledge of causes and correlates is often less useful than this understanding of process and alternatives.

Conclusions

American sociology has undergone a myriad of changes in subject matter, theoretical paradigms, and methodology since the 1930s. Some of the changes have been linear trends, but many have resembled cycles or dialectics more than trends. As a result, sociology today is a much richer and more sophisticated discipline, more critical of its own theories and methods. It is marked by a healthy diversity of viewpoints and a broader perspective that extends over time and across societies.

Nevertheless, several unresolved problems restrict the discipline's accomplishments and usefulness. One severe problem is the great amount of duplicated and wasted effort that results from the difficulty in retrieving the results of relevant prior research and the lack of communication among investigators in different specialties who are working on similar and related problems. Data archives have helped considerably, as have *Sociological Abstracts* and the *Annual Review of Sociology.* But the use of different terminologies and the proliferation of specialty journals and meetings not only fosters wasteful redundancy but deprives investigators of the cross-fertilization so necessary for the generation of new ideas. A surprising homogeneity of problems and subject matter is often masked by the resulting appearance of great diversity.

Another consequence of narrow specialization is often undue focus on trivial issues. Students of vertical mobility have been locked into debates over the relative merit of alternative models whose differences seem unimportant to outsiders; students of social interaction design sophisticated research to choose between theories that are either too vague for precise test or of little consequence. Although Mullins (1973) produced evidence that scholars who address such running issues are cited in sociological literature more often than those who do not, I believe the discipline would benefit from more independently minded scholars willing to disregard trivial controversy and cross the boundaries between specialties in their search for significant problems for research.

A third problem is the recent decline in microsociology and the use of inadequate microsociological assumptions by macrosociologists. Sociologists have often been impatient with having to take account of individuals in the pursuit of principles governing events on a grander scale. There also has been a fear that sociology might be reduced to the mere application of psychological principles. The much advertised discrepancy between "words and deeds" (Deutscher, 1966), or attitudes and actions, has also raised doubts about the usefulness of information concerning attitudes and other subjective variables. Yet it seems clear to me that macrosociologists will soon exhaust the limited increments of understanding derivable on the basis of the half-truths in rational decision models. There is urgent need for a microsociology whose problems and parameters are defined with a clear eye to the explanatory needs of macrosociology.

A final problem, cited repeatedly by different scholars in connection with sociology as a whole or specialized fields within sociology, is the lack of a unifying theoretical paradigm. Such a paradigm would focus research efforts and make findings cumulative. It is difficult to imagine a single paradigm applying to the range of problems and levels of analysis in sociology. Perhaps exchange theory comes closest to meeting the requirements of a general paradigm, but it sheds little light on the nature of values that give meaning to social orders and individual social experience.

The difficulty may be that we are looking for too much when we seek a unifying paradigm. It is my experience that nearly every sociological theory or model becomes ridiculous when its implications are pursued to the limit. For example, the brilliant insight of labeling theory is lost when it becomes a substitute for understanding why people commit deviant acts in the first place, and both Freud's and Marx's insights became dangerous half-truths when converted into schemes for the reform of individuals or societies.

Perhaps a less elegant model of society could serve as a unifying paradigm (Turner, 1980, 1988), if we would but settle for a less tidy and less deterministic system of sociological principles. Society might be viewed as a loosely bonded and inefficiently functioning monopoly, with accommodation rather than either conflict or consensus the governing principle. Courses of action in society could be seen as reflecting a constant tension between instrumental and expressive orientations and between social bonding and individuated self-interest.

Notes

1. For a more extended history of sociology before World War II, see Faris (1967) and Martindale (1976). For three decades after the war, see Coser (1976).

2. Cf. Brown and Gilmartin (1969), Simpson (1961), and Riley (1960). Staff of the American Sociological Association and Leo P. Chall, editor of *Sociological Abstracts,* also provided helpful detailed information.

3. For an enlightening account of social science research, detailing its practical difficulties through case studies of especially important research projects, cf. Hunt (1985).

4. One of the most impressive efforts to think through the interrelationships among disciplines was the project that brought together the anthropologists John Gillin and A. Irving Hallowell, the psychologists Theodore M. Newcomb and M. Brewster Smith, and the sociologists Howard Becker and Talcott Parsons—all leaders in their respective disciplines. Cf. Gillin (1954).

5. Negative Income Tax was a proposal for government to guarantee a set standard of income for a family by providing cash supplements whenever family income fell below that standard. Housing Allowance programs would provide income supplements to families in substandard housing for the purpose of bringing their housing up to standard. Transitional Aid to Released Prisoners provided limited unemployment compensation for a set number of months after an inmate was released from prison.

References

Beals, R. (1969). *Politics of social research: An inquiry into the ethics and responsibilities of social scientists.* Chicago: Aldine.

Becker, H. S. (1967). Whose side are we on? *Social Problems, 14,* 239-247.

Blau, P. M., & Duncan, O. D. (1967) *The American occupational structure.* New York: Wiley.

Blumer, H. (1969). *Symbolic interaction: Perspective and method.* Englewood Cliffs, NJ: Prentice-Hall.

Bogardus, E. S. (1931). *Contemporary sociology.* Los Angeles: University of Southern California Press.

Bottomore, T., Nowak, S., & Sokolowska, M. (Eds.). (1982). *Sociology: The state of the art.* London and Beverly Hills, CA: Sage.

Bridgman, P. W. (1936). *The nature of physical theory.* Princeton, NJ: Princeton University Press.

Brown, J. S., & Gilmartin, B. G. (1969). Sociology today: Lacunae, emphases, and surfeits. *American Sociologist, 4,* 283-291.

Burgess, E. (1928). Factors determining success or failure on parole. *Journal of Criminal Law, 19,* pt. 2, 239-306.

Burgess, E. (1953). The aims of the Society for the Study of Social Problems. *Social Problems, 1,* 2-3.

Burgess, E., & Cottrell, L. S., Jr. (1939). *Predicting success or failure in marriage.* New York: Prentice-Hall.

Burgess, E., & Wallin, P. (1954). *Courtship, engagement, and marriage.* Philadelphia: J. B. Lippincott.

Clausen, J. A. (1986). *The life course: A sociological perspective.* Englewood Cliffs, NJ: Prentice-Hall.

Coleman, J. S. (1986). Social theory, social research, and a theory of action. *American Journal of Sociology, 91,* 1309-1335.

Coleman, J. S., Campbell, E. Q., Hobson, C. J., McPartland, J., Mood, A. M., Weinfeld, F. D., & York, R. L. (1966). *Equality of educational opportunity.* Washington, DC: U.S. Government Printing Office.

Coser, L. A. (1976). Sociological theory from the Chicago dominance to 1965. In A. Inkeles, J. Coleman, & N. Smelser (Eds.), *Annual review of sociology* (Vol. 2, pp. 145-160). Palo Alto, CA: Annual Reviews, Inc.

Cressey, D. R. (1979). Fifty years of criminology: From sociological theory to political control. *Pacific Sociological Review, 22,* 457-480.

Dalton, M. (1959). *Men who manage: Fusions of feeling and theory in administration.* New York: Wiley.

Deutscher, I. (1966). Words and deeds: Social science and social policy. *Social Problems, 13,* 235-254.

Emerson, R. M. (1981). Observational field work. In R. H. Turner & J. F. Short, Jr. (Eds.), *Annual review of sociology* (Vol. 7, pp. 351-378). Palo Alto, CA: Annual Reviews, Inc.

Faris, R.E.L. (Ed.). (1964). *Handbook of modern sociology.* Chicago: Rand McNally.

Faris, R.E.L. (1967). *Chicago sociology: 1920-1932.* San Francisco: Chandler.

Garfinkel, H. (1967). *Studies in ethnomethodology.* Englewood Cliffs, NJ: Prentice-Hall.

Gillin, J. (Ed.). (1954). *For a science of social man: Convergences in anthropology, psychology, and sociology.* New York: Macmillan.

Gittler, J. B. (Ed.). (1957). *Review of sociology: Analysis of a decade.* New York: Wiley.

Glaser, B. G., & Strauss, A. (1967). *The discovery of grounded theory: Strategies of qualitative research.* Chicago: Aldine.

Goffman, E. (1955). *The presentation of self in everyday life.* Garden City, NY: Doubleday.

Gurvich, G., & Moore, W. E. (Eds.). (1945). *Twentieth century sociology*. New York: Philosophical Library.

Homans, G. C. (1986). Fifty years of sociology. In R. H. Turner & J. F. Short, Jr. (Eds.), *Annual review of sociology* (Vol. 12, pp. xiii-xxx). Palo Alto, CA: Annual Reviews, Inc.

Hunt, M. (1985). *Profiles of social research: The scientific study of human interactions*. New York: Russell Sage.

Lazarsfeld, P. F., Sewell, W. H., & Wilensky, H. L. (Eds.). (1967). *The uses of sociology*. New York: Basic Books.

Liebow, E. (1967). *Tally's corner: A study of negro streetcorner men*. Boston: Little, Brown.

Lipset, S. M., & Smelser, N. J. (Eds.). (1961). *Sociology: The progress of a decade*. Englewood Cliffs, NJ: Prentice-Hall.

Lynd, R. S. (1939). *Knowledge for what? The place of social science in American culture*. Princeton, NJ: Princeton University Press.

Martindale, D. (1976). American sociology before World War II. In A. Inkeles, J. Coleman, & N. Smelser (Eds.), *Annual review of sociology* (Vol. 2, pp. 121-143). Palo Alto, CA: Annual Reviews, Inc.

McCall, G. J. (1984). Systematic field observation. In R. H. Turner & J. F. Short, Jr. (Eds.), *Annual review of sociology* (Vol. 10, pp. 263-282). Palo Alto, CA: Annual Reviews, Inc.

Merton, R. K. (1957). *Social theory and social structure*. New York: Free Press.

Merton, R. K., Broom, L. K., & Cottrell, L. S., Jr. (Eds.). (1959). *Sociology today: Problems and prospects*. New York: Basic Books.

Mills, C. W. (1959). *The sociological imagination*. New York: Oxford University Press.

Mullins, N. C. (1973). *Theories and theory groups in contemporary American sociology*. New York: Harper & Row.

Myrdal, G. (1944). *An American dilemma: The negro problem and modern democracy*. New York: Harper & Row.

Ogburn, W. F. (1922). *Social change: With respect to culture and original nature*. New York: Viking.

Parsons, T. (1949). *The structure of social action: A study in social theory with special reference to a group of recent European writers*. New York: Free Press.

Parsons, T. (1951). *The social system*. New York: Free Press.

Riley, M. W. (1960). Membership of the American Sociological Association: 1950-1959. *American Sociological Review, 25*, 914-926.

Rossi, P. H., & Wright, J. D. (1984). Evaluation research: An assessment. In R. H. Turner & J. F. Short, Jr. (Eds.), *Annual review of sociology* (Vol. 10, pp. 331-352). Palo Alto, CA: Annual Reviews, Inc.

Sellin, T. (Ed). (1952). Murder and the penalty of death. *Annals of the American Academy of Political and Social Science, Vol. 284*. Philadelphia: American Academy of Political and Social Science.

Sellin, T. (1980). *The penalty of death*. Beverly Hills, CA: Sage.

Short, J. F., Jr. (Ed.). (1981). *The state of sociology: Problems and prospects*. Beverly Hills, CA and London: Sage.

Simpson, R. L. (1961). Expanding and declining fields in American sociology. *American Sociological Review, 26*, 458-466.

Stryker, S. (1980). *Symbolic interactionism: A social structural version*. Menlo Park, CA: Benjamin/Cummings.

Suttles, G. D. (1968). *The social order of the slum: Ethnicity and territory in the inner city.* Chicago: University of Chicago Press.

Taylor, C. C. (1947). Sociology and common sense. *American Sociological Review, 12,* 1-9.

Thomas, W. I., & Znaniecki, F. 91927). *The Polish peasant in Europe and America* (Vol. 1). New York: Alfred A. Knopf.

Turner, R. H. (1980). The forgotten paradigm? *Contemporary Sociology, 9,* 609-612.

Turner, R. H. (1988). Personality in society: Social psychology's contribution to sociology. *Social Psychology Quarterly, 51,* 1-10.

Whyte, W. F. (1948). *Human relations in the restaurant industry.* New York: McGraw-Hill.

Whyte, W. F. (1943, 1955). *Street corner society: The social structure of an Italian slum.* Chicago: University of Chicago Press.

4

How (and What) Are Historians Doing?

CHARLES TILLY

Why We Study History

Why should anyone care what happened in the past? Isn't the present unique and the future unknowable? If so, why not concentrate on the present? Let us leave aside the moral, political, psychic, and aesthetic value of knowing that we now live in only one of many possible worlds and of having some sense of roots; those are valuable reasons for studying history, but they are not essential. The crucial answer is simple and compelling: All reliable knowledge of human affairs rests on events that are already history. To the extent that the social structures and processes we wish to understand endure or take a long time to unfold, historical knowledge becomes increasingly valuable. To the degree that social processes are path-dependent—to the extent that the prior sequence of events constrains what happens at a given point in time—historical knowledge of sequences becomes essential. Historical verification is vital in any analysis of large-scale social change; anyone who wants to understand warmaking, capital accumulation, population growth, international migration, military rule, and any number of other crucial phenomena of the contemporary world had better take history seriously. History provides a key to the present and a guide to the future.

History as a phenomenon and history as a specialized inquiry, however, are two quite different things. History as the set of connections among human activities in time and space certainly concerns specialized historians, but it also plays a significant part in the analyses by geographers, economists, anthropologists, philosophers, and many other skilled observers of human affairs. What sets off the study of history as a specialized discipline?

Any intellectual discipline worth mentioning unites four elements: (1) a set of self-identified practitioners; (2) a series of questions the practitioners regard as important and answerable; (3) a body of evidence they consider relevant to answering the questions; and (4) an ensemble of legitimated practices that extract acceptable answers from the evidence. To the extent that they establish an academic base, most disciplines add a fifth element: an institutional structure consisting of associations, meetings, journals, publication series, and incentives to do good work. As pursued in Western countries, the subdisciplines of professional history (e.g., Eastern European diplomatic history, American intellectual history, and modern African history) clearly pass these tests. History in general, over the West as a whole, has more trouble qualifying; salient questions, relevant evidence, and legitimated practices vary significantly from country to country, period to period, and subject to subject. We might best think of history in general as a federation of overlapping disciplines.

Throughout the West, the study of history occupies some common ground. As practiced in Western countries today, history stands out from other organized inquiries by virtue of:

1. Its insistence on time and place as fundamental principles of variation—the prevailing idea being that social processes in, say, contemporary China occur differently than related social processes in medieval Europe

2. The corresponding time-place subdivision of its practitioners, with most historians concentrating on one part of the world, however large, during one historical period, however long

3. The anchoring of most of its dominant questions in national politics, with great attention accorded new answers to old questions or new challenges to old answers, and consequent variation in the major questions being asked by historians of different countries

4. The vagueness of its distinction between professionals and amateurs, with the skilled synthesizer and storyteller who attracts a large public often commanding respect from the specialists

5. Its heavy reliance on documentary evidence and its consequent concentration on the literate world

6. Its emphasis on practices that involve (a) identification of crucial actors, (b) imputation of attitudes and motives to those actors, (c) validation of those imputations by means of texts, and (d) presentation of the outcome as narrative.

I do not claim that every history and every historian in the West exhibits all these characteristics all of the time; some well-established branches of history fail to conform to one or another of these principles. I claim only that they are salient traits of most Western historical practice, that, on the average, they set historians off from other students of human affairs, and that historians whose work does not fit these standards have more trouble making other historians understand what they are about. Let us examine each of these characteristics in turn.

1. *Time and Place as Fundamental Variables*

Although they rarely make the assertion explicit, most historians assume that *where* and *when* a social process—the formation of a friendship, the outbreak of revolution, the disintegration of a community, or something else—occurs significantly affects *how* it occurs. All important social processes, in this view, are path-dependent; what happened last year significantly constrains what can happen this year and what will happen next year. Thus Italian industrialization followed a different path from British industrialization in part precisely because Britain started industrializing earlier; Britain both provided a model and shaped the world market for Italy's industrial products. Within Italy, furthermore, the extensive prior development of small-scale industry in the hinterlands of such commercial cities as Milan significantly affected the opportunities for 19th- and 20th-century industrial concentration.

A fortiori, according to standard historical reasoning, urbanization, militarization, and commercialization are not the same processes when they occur within feudal and capitalist regions or periods. Two methodological injunctions follow: First, never interpret an action until you have placed it in its time and place setting; and second, use the greatest caution in making generalizations and comparisons over disparate blocks of time and place.

2. Time-Place Specialization

With spectacular exceptions, such as William McNeill, professional historians nearly always specialize in one or two combinations of place and time. Even Fernand Braudel (1979), who defined European history very broadly and roamed easily over five or six centuries, ultimately concentrated his research and writing on southern and western Europe during the 16th to 18th centuries. Most historians content themselves with a much smaller range, arguing that learning the languages, sources, historiography, and social context for the competent study of one or two countries over a century or so taxes human stamina, memory, and ingenuity. A few historical fields, it is true, shrug off time and space limits to deal with specialized phenomena, such as science, population change, coinage, or kinship. In those fields, discussions often move quickly from one time-space division to another. But even there, individual researchers commonly specialize in a single area of the world during a single block of time. And historical fields defined by phenomena rather than by time and place provide the primary identifications of no more than a small minority of practicing historians.

3. Questions Rooted in National Politics

Even if they point to more exceptions than I have allowed, few historians will dispute my first two statements as broad generalizations about historical practice. Many more will challenge the third, on the grounds that historians pursue their own questions, that much of history does not concern sharply defined questions but efforts to recapture certain situations, mentalities, events, or actions, and that many kinds of history have little or nothing to do with national politics. Nevertheless, I claim that within each major time-place block of historical research, specialists (a) implicitly recognize a few questions as crucial; (b) reward each other for putting new questions on the agenda, for proposing persuasive new answers to established questions, and for challenging established answers to the standard questions; and (c) draw their dominant questions from problems on the national political agenda either of the nation under study or the nation to which they belong, or both.

Historians of the United States, for example, ask recurrently whether a distinctive mentality and social structure was formed in the North American colonies and subsequently guided American life, whether the American war for independence from Great Britain involved a social revolution, whether the Civil War marked the inevitable struggle between two different forms of American civilization, whether slavery and its aftermath made the experience of blacks entirely different from that of their fellow Americans, whether mass immigration changed the structure of economic opportunity and the possibilities for a militant labor movement, and whether the United States became an exploiter on the European model as it rose to world power. These and perhaps a dozen more questions constitute the general agenda of American history. Teaching, research, and writing center on more concrete versions of these questions. Historians gain recognition by challenging old answers to them, proposing new answers to them, or (best of all) putting new questions on the agenda. Historians, finally, recognize the relevance of new work to the extent that it addresses these questions.

As I have summarized them, to be sure, the questions are all too broad and vague for precise answers; they require explication, refinement, subdivision, and translation into terms of more or less, when and where, under what conditions. Yet they all remain on the agenda of national politics, shaping debate, identifying relevant analogies to contemporary problems, and suggesting solutions to national ills. Historians of one nationality who study the history of another nation thus become ambivalent, sometimes responding to the agenda set by the object country's nationals and sometimes interpreting that country's history in terms that their own compatriots will understand.

4. Amateurs and Professionals

Although the Western world contains 40,000 or 50,000 professional historians—people who not only have doctoral degrees in history or their equivalents but also spend the major part of their time teaching, writing, or doing research on history—a number of nonprofessionals make significant contributions to historical research. Some are novelists, essayists, and other kinds of writers who occasionally undertake historical writing, some are public figures who write memoirs or reflections, while others are people who make their livings in other ways but spend time digging in old books, newspaper files, private papers, and local archives for material that will appear in lectures, films, pamphlets, books, and articles for specialized historical periodicals. Without much hesitation, professionals use the best of those nonprofessional works for reference. They do not assume that only the anointed can do valid history.

Professionals and nonprofessionals alike value good historical writing that appeals to the general reading public. As compared with most other academic fields, historians do not make an especially sharp distinction between the contributions of professionals and nonprofessionals. Let me not exaggerate: Publications in internationally esteemed journals and by well-known presses clearly command greater respect among historians than do articles in local historical journals. The historical works that attract the largest lay audiences often do not meet professional standards, and many professionals feel envious ambivalence when nonprofessionals, however expert, write widely selling historical works. Nevertheless, history stands out from other social science disciplines in the relative interpenetration of professional and amateur efforts.

5. Documentary Evidence

Written material provides the vast majority of recognized historical evidence. For very recent history, interviews, films, and tapes begin to supply important evidence. At the far reaches of history, nonwritten artifacts start to matter seriously as evidence. But between those limits, written documents constitute the historian's stock in trade, the ability to locate and read relevant documents makes up a significant part of the trade's secrets, and members of the trade recognize the skillful deployment of documents as good craftsmanship. Historians share with linguists and literary critics a great concern for texts, but the historian's texts often include such dull, routine documents as tax rolls and administrative correspondence. Indeed, in many kinds of history (certainly in those I practice), one of the active researcher's primary qualifications is the ability to sit still and stay awake while going through mounds of papers having little intrinsic interest, and either accumulating bits and pieces of information that will eventually fit into a larger design or searching for the one text that will make a big difference.

6. *Actors, Motives, and Narratives*

Any student of human behavior balances between treating people as objects of external forces or as motivated actors. By and large, Western historians assume that they are describing the actions of motivated actors—individuals, families, classes, nations, or others—and that they can therefore reasonably arrange those actions in narratives—coherent sequences of motivated actions. Historians justify the imputation of attitudes and motives to actors by means of texts that presumably reflect those attitudes and motives. The narrative mode is by no means the only possible way to present history. One could, for instance, trace simultaneous connections among many actors and show how they changed, or follow the unfolding of complex processes, such as proletarianization and capital formation. Historians sometimes do these other things, of course. But on the whole, they do not recognize the enterprise as history unless it eventually yields, or at least informs, motivated narratives. Most historical writing, furthermore, consists of creating motivated narratives from documents that do not contain narratives and provide only sketchy indications of motives.

The education of professional historians reflects these six characteristics. Speaking very generally, a historical graduate education in Western countries falls into four phases. First comes a general synthetic survey of the histories of different areas and periods, spiced with occasional looks at exemplary or controversial works. Next, closer examination of current historiography is conducted, with particular attention to substantive and methodological controversies. Third, the student is initiated in the use of documents, often in the form of a master's thesis or its equivalent. Finally, one or two doctoral dissertations establish the initiate's ability make original contributions to knowledge in some particular field of history. (Where the full state-recognized doctoral dissertation makes the scholar a candidate for major professorships, as in most Germanic countries, the second dissertation is supposed to be a major work and typically appears after years and years of teaching and research.) The dissertation sets the standard for the historical monograph: a focused problem, a well identified set of primary sources, exhaustive coverage of the existing literature and available sources, and a careful statement of the ways in which the research alters previous understanding of the problem. In general, professional historians feel that only mature scholars who have already crafted a monograph or two can (or should) bring off broader syntheses.

The six traits of Western history-writing mentioned earlier mark out a distinctive enterprise. Whether they are advantages or disadvantages depends on the task at hand. A discipline organized in this way is unlikely to discover principles that apply across large ranges of space and time, to make much headway analyzing processes that leave few written traces, or to have great success dealing with social changes that operate through the cumulation of diverse actions by millions of actors. But it is likely to do very well in helping literate people appreciate the problems of their counterparts in distant places and times. For many historians, that establishment of sympathetic understanding is the hallmark of well-crafted history. For some, indeed, it constitutes the only valid ground of historical knowledge.

History as an organized discipline shares a number of traits with folk history, the ways that ordinary people reconstruct the past. In the West, for the most part, people take history as a set of stories about individuals who act for well-defined motives with clear consequences. At a scale larger than the storyteller's own milieu, powerful and famous individuals occupy a large part of the story, just as their motives, actions, and consequences provide a major basis for moral and political reasoning; Stalin, Churchill, de Gaulle, and Roosevelt become emblems and explanations of a whole era. Folk history rarely concerns superhuman forces, complex social processes, or ordinary people—except as objects or distant causes of history, or at the point of contact between the teller's own life and certifiably great events or persons. History written by specialists gains popular appeal to the extent that it conforms to these standards.

Peculiarities of Social and Economic History

Within such a discipline, the sorts of social and economic history that have taken shape since World War II occupy a peculiar position.

On one hand, they became auxiliaries to the pursuit of the standard big questions: What accounts for the rise and fall of ancient empires? To what extent did the growth of large-scale industry mark off a new stage of world history? What caused the great revolutions of our era? Did the major world religions shape distinctively different ways of political, economic, and social life? On the other hand, their practitioners soon began to identify actors who did not appear in the standard playbill, turned away from the construction of motivated narratives, borrowed extensively from the adjacent social sciences, and started to ask eccentric questions such as: Under what conditions have sustained declines in fertility occurred? Have family forms and sentiments changed fundamentally in the era of capitalism? When and how do industrial economies stagnate? These deviations generated plenty of excitement but made it more difficult to integrate the analyses of social and economic history into attempts to answer the grand old questions.

Consider the case of European social history, the historical field that I know best. Some of postwar history's greatest achievements occurred in European social history: the revision of our ideas concerning population change, the discovery of human faces in revolutionary crowds, the charting of historical variants in family life, and the identification of mobility, complexity, and variety in what had been considered a vast, immobile, and undifferentiated European peasantry. Consequently, some of the discipline's sharper controversies also broke out on the terrain of European social history: whether the typical concerns of European social historians actually blinded them to politics, whether classes form in direct response to changes in the organization of production, whether the old extended family is a myth, whether cottage industry marked a (or *the*) standard path to capital-concentrated production, and so on. The controversies have drawn even more attention to the difficulties of integrating conclusions from European social history into general histories of Europe.

On the whole, European social history, as practiced in Western countries since 1945, has centered on one enterprise: reconstructing ordinary people's experience of large structural changes. In general, that has meant tracing the impact of capitalism (however defined) and changes in the character of national states on day-to-day behavior. Studies of migration, urbanization, family life, standards of living, social movements, and most other old reliables of European social history fit the description. Disputes within the field, by and large, concern (a) the means of detecting ordinary people's experience and of describing large structural changes, (b) the actual assessment of that experience, and (c) the identity, character, and causal priority of the relevant structural changes. Social historians contend rather little about whether they ought to be linking big changes and small-scale experiences.

Much of recent European social history emits a populist tone. Its writers rail against histories of kings and generals, insist on the intrinsic value of knowing how relatively powerless people lived in the past, claim that synthetic histories commonly misconstrue the character of the masses, and argue for a significant cumulative effect of ordinary people's action on national events, such as revolutions and onsets of economic growth. "History from below" is the cry.

Populism complements the central method of social history: collective biography. The painstaking accumulation of uniformly described individual events or lives into collective portraits, as in political prosopography, family reconstitution, and analyses of social mobility, takes its justification from the belief that the aggregates so constructed will provide a more telling portrayal of popular experience than would the recapitulation of general impressions, observers' commentaries, or convenient examples. It also establishes much of the common ground between social history and sociology, political science, and economics. In those disciplines, researchers likewise often build up evidence about aggregates from uniform observations of many individual units.

Within the area occupied by collective biography, social historians are most likely to adopt formal methods of measurement and analysis: fragmentation of individual characteristics into variables, quantification of those variables, formal modeling of the processes and structures under study, and rigorous comparison of observations with the models, frequently by means of statistical procedures. Where observations are uniform, instances numerous, models complex but explicit, and characteristics of the instances meaningfully quantifiable, formal methods permit social historians to wring more reliable information from their evidence than they could possibly manage by informal means.

There, however, acute controversy begins. First, despite the readily available example of survey research, historians have not been nearly as assiduous and successful at measuring attitudes, orientations, and mentalities as they have at quantifying births, deaths, and marriages. A major object of study and a major mode of explanation in history therefore remain relatively inaccessible to formalization. Second, historians tend to ground their pressing questions in times and places whereas social scientists tend to root them in structures and processes; to the extent that social historians adopt social scientific approaches to their material, they separate themselves from the questions that animate other historical work. Which set of questions should take priority? Third, the models and arguments that social historians borrow from adjacent social sciences often fit their historical applications badly—assuming independence of observations, being indifferent to the order in which events occur, calling for the recurrence of identical sequences, and so on.

Alas, historians could not deal with these disparities between social history and other histories by shrugging them off as simply another way of learning about human action. For the social scientific approaches, if valid, challenged the very means by which conventional historians moved from elites to masses, from leaders to followers, from kings to their kingdoms, by treating the larger body as a more or less unitary actor or set of actors and imputing to the actor(s) coherent motives, attitudes, or mentalities. If collective effects occur chiefly not through the aggregation of individual mentalities but through the compounding of social relations and resources—which is the premise of most social scientific work—then historians who want to move validly beyond this level of the single individual have no choice but to analyze that compounding. If they do so, they are undertaking a version of social science.

Lest anyone take me for a social science imperialist, let me state clearly that my hope for the social sciences is that they will all become more historical and that sociology, in particular, will dissolve into history. But that is not the issue here. We are examining the choices that confront present-day Western historians as they now practice their craft.

Alternative Histories

The division between social scientific and other kinds of history reflects a much broader division within Western historical thinking.

The division ultimately depends on philosophical choices which we might define provisionally as a series of alternatives:

1. History's dominant phenomena are (a) large social processes or (b) individual experiences.
2. Historical analysis centers on (a) systematic observation of human action or (b) interpretation of motives and meanings.
3. History and the social sciences are (a) the same enterprise or (b) quite distinct.
4. Historical writing should stress (a) explanation or (b) narrative.

Beneath these choices lie deep questions of ontology and epistemology: Is the social world orderly? To what degree and in what ways is it knowable? Does the capacity to reflect and react to reflection distinguish humans from all other animals and thereby render the assumptions and procedures of the natural sciences inapplicable to human history?

Rather than a strict dichotomy, to be sure, each of these pairs represents the poles of a continuum; the many historians who say "Let's look at the intersection between individual experiences and large social processes" or "Let's combine explanation with narrative" aim at the middle of those continua. Very few historians station themselves precisely at either pole of any continuum.

Nevertheless, the choice of a position within any continuum entails (however unconsciously) profound philosophical choices. In general, historians choose similar positions within each of the continua, and on the whole historians place themselves closer to the second choice in each continuum—closer to interpretation, individual experience, distinctness, and narrative—than do social scientists, psychologists, biologists, and other students of human behavior. Without too much violence to the complexity of historical practice, we might therefore combine the four continua into one, whose extremes bear the labels "social scientific" and "humanistic."

A second division comes immediately to mind. Historians vary enormously in the scales at which they typically work: from the individual person to the whole human race. Although logically independent, the continua small-scale/large-scale and social scientific/humanistic correlate weakly; to a certain degree, historians who choose the humanistic end of the one range also tend to choose the individual end of the other. Still, those relatively humanistic

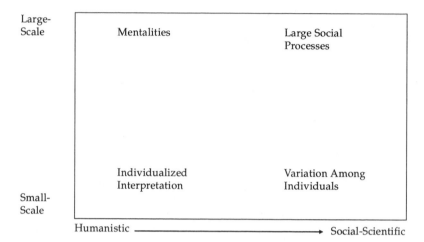

Figure 4.1. Two dimensional representation of variations in historical approaches.

historians who emphasize mentalities and culture—their number has increased in recent years—frequently work at the scale of the region, the nation, or even the continent. Many relatively social scientific historians, moreover, work by aggregating individual observations into distributions and then adopt quite individualistic explanations of the distributions they find. Thus a rough two-dimensional representation of variations in historical approaches looks like Figure 4.1.

The distinctions make a difference. Gertrude Himmelfarb, historian of England and astringent critic of what she calls the "new history," draws her sharpest line between the diagram's lower left-hand corner and all the rest:

> Thus the new history tends to be analytic rather than narrative, thematic rather than chronological. It relies more upon statistical tables, oral interviews, sociological models, and psychoanalytic theories than upon constitutions, treaties, parliamentary debates, or party manifestoes. Where the old history concerned itself with regimes and administrations, legislation and politics, diplomacy and foreign policy, wars and revolutions, the new focuses on social groups and social problems, factories and farms, cities and villages, work and play, family and sex,

birth and death, childhood and old age, crime and insanity. Where the old features kings, presidents, politicians, leaders, political theorists, the new takes as its subjects the "anonymous masses." The old is "history from above," "elitist history," as is now said, the new is "history from below," "populist history." (Himmelfarb, 1987, p. 14)

Himmelfarb argues that these new histories have no capacity to deal with politics and suggests that without politics history has no coherent frame. By *politics*, she appears to mean national politics, the politics of states rather than of such groupings as local communities, lineages, or ethnic blocs. "After several decades of the new history," she continues,

we can better appreciate what we are in danger of losing if we abandon the old. We will lose not only the unifying theme that has given coherence to history, not only the notable events, individuals, and institutions that have constituted our historical memory and our heritage, not only the narrative that has made history readable and memorable—not only, in short, a meaningful past—but also a conception of man as a rational, political animal. And that loss will be even more difficult to sustain, for it involves a radical redefinition of human nature. (p. 25)

She regrets, it seems, the loss of the liaison between professional history and folk history.

Furthermore, in the lower left-hand corner of the diagram, Himmelfarb is not delighted with all the company she finds. Some historians who work humanistically at the small scale—as we shall see—show a disinterest in national politics and have a weakness for the interpretation of ordinary people's experiences. Himmelfarb wants politics, especially national and international politics, to retain its priority throughout history. As for the other corners, she regards the histories of mentalities, of large-scale processes, and of individual-to-individual variation, to the extent that they become the dominant historical concerns, as threats to the very enterprise of history.

A few years earlier, E.J. Hobsbawm (1980) replied to a similar indictment, less shrilly stated, from Lawrence Stone, a pioneer of the "new history" who had become disillusioned with what he regarded as its excesses (not fast enough, however, to escape the wrath of Himmelfarb, who holds Stone's work up as a salient example of history's decay). "In short," declared Hobsbawn,

> those historians who continue to believe in the possibility of generalizing about human societies and their development, continue to be interested in "the big *why* questions", though they may sometimes focus on different ones from those on which they concentrated twenty or thirty years ago. There is really no evidence that such historians . . . have abandoned "the attempt to produce a coherent . . . explanation of change in the past." (p. 4; internal quotations from Stone, 1979).

The contrasting positions make it clear what is at issue: not only taste and political preference (although both have their weight) but the very explanatory schemes and central questions of historical research.

In case it is not already obvious, perhaps I should declare frankly that my own preferences and most of my own work lie on the right-hand side of the diagram. But I greatly enjoy, and profit from, the best contributions on the diagram's left-hand side; the following discussion, whatever else it does, should prove that. The point of this essay, in any case, is not to argue for the superiority of one kind of history or another but to identify alternative forms of historical practice, discuss their requirements, assumptions and consequences, and clarify the choices that Western historians are actually making.

Around the Four Corners

Let us explore the two-dimensional variation by reviewing some exemplary historical works—books that almost all historians will agree are excellent but that take very different approaches to their subjects. To see historical craftsmanship at work, let us concentrate on monographs rather than syntheses. To increase comparability and keep me on relatively certain ground, let us examine four outstanding works in western European and North American history: books by Carlo Ginzburg, E. P. Thompson, E. A. Wrigley and R. S. Schofield, and finally Olivier Zunz. The four do not constitute a representative sample of recent historical work—what four could? But they do provide relatively pure examples of monographs in each of the diagram's four corners, and thus mark out the space within which most historical work goes on.

Ginzburg's Sixteenth-Century Miller

Carlo Ginzburg's (1980) *The Cheese and the Worms* places itself firmly in the lower left-hand corner of our diagram: small-scale and humanistic, seeking to interpret an individual's experience. In 1584 and again in 1599, the Roman Inquisition tried and convicted Domenico Scandella, a miller from Montereale in northeastern Italy, for heresy; the first time he went to jail, the second time to the stake for burning. From the trial records, a few other local sources, and an enormous knowledge of 16th-century Italian popular culture, Ginzburg constructs a credible account of both an extraordinary person and of the cultural world in which he lived.

Scandella did not join some existing heretical sect but fashioned his own cosmogony from experience, inclination, and fragments of oral and written tradition. He believed, for example, that the world, including God, had emerged from a primitive chaos; the image of worms generating spontaneously in cheese—whence the book's title—often served him as a metaphor for that original creation. He denied many Catholic orthodoxies in favor of his own view that Christ was human and the Catholic Church a tool of greedy priests and monks. He not only believed these things but told many other people about them. The church's hierarchy could not forgive Scandella for teaching others such heresies, even after he had gone to prison for them.

Ginzburg places the text of Scandella's interrogation at the center of his book, but uses it as a prism. He looks through the prism at different angles, seeking to ask how a 16th-century village miller could have arrived at his astonishing worldview. In the search for sources of Scandella's beliefs, Ginzburg undertook a close reading of all the books with which the miller's testimony reveals him to have been familiar. The same method took Ginzburg to books and booklets that Scandella probably did not know to see whether his heterodox ideas were circulating more widely in the Italy of his time. "Naturally," says Ginzburg in one instance,

there's no reason to suppose that [Scandella] was familiar with the
Ragioni del perdonare. In sixteenth-century Italy, however, in the most
heterogeneous circles a tendency existed ... to reduce religion to nothing more than worldly reality—to a moral or political bond. This
tendency found different modes of expression, based on very different
premises. However, even in this instance, it may be possible to discern
a partial convergence between the most progressive circles among the
educated classes and popular groups with radical leanings. (p. 41)

Then, like a detective tracking his suspect, Ginzburg begins searching for the traces of an oral tradition on which Scandella might have
drawn. First he shows that the heretic systematically recast the texts
he mentioned as his sources in favor of consistent ideas about the
nature of God and man. Then Ginzburg assembles fragments of
evidence, including the existence of another heretical miller, for the
activity of a loosely connected network through which independent, rural people might have circulated the radical egalitarian ideas
for which Scandella died.

That search leads Ginzburg to his more general argument. Little
by little, he raises doubts that the rural heresies radiated downward
from elite thinkers, such as Martin Luther, and tenders, ever so
delicately, the counterhypothesis that both peasant heresies and
literary heterodoxies drew on a widely circulated, constantly evolving, popular oral tradition. "It is this tradition, deeply rooted in the
European countryside," Ginzburg writes at one point, "that explains the tenacious persistence of a peasant religion intolerant of
dogma and ritual, tied to the cycles of nature, and fundamentally
pre-Christian" (p. 112).

Ginzburg proves neither the existence of such a coherent tradition
nor the derivation of Scandella's extraordinary beliefs from it; although Ginzburg's scholarly notes establishes his wide awareness
of parallels and connections, his method excludes the possibility of
proof in any strong sense of the word. But his patient, subtle gloss-
ing of the texts concerning the village miller eventually expands a
reader's awareness of popular creativity and of intellectual traditions that moved in partial independence of elite culture.

More conventional biographies belong in the same small-scale
interpretive category as Ginzburg's essay; some of them (for example, Harvey Goldberg's [1962] still-stunning appreciation of Jean
Jaurès) likewise help us understand their subject and the subject's

milieu simultaneously. Richard Cobb's (1986) incomparable blends of reminiscence, biography, and *pointilliste* history belong in the class as well. Alain Lottin's (1968) portrait of 17th-century Lille through the journal of an artisan offers an example of a less daring, but very rich, approach to the subject. At a slightly larger scale, Emmanuel Le Roy Ladurie's (1975) reconstruction of the life of a 14th- century Pyrenean village from another set of Inquisition proceedings, Franco Ramella's (1984) treatment of the struggles of Biella's 19th-century wool workers, and Dirk Hoerder's (1977) portrayal of popular involvement in Massachusetts' portion of the American Revolution all display the power of small-scale interpretive studies to recapture the actual terms in which ordinary people experienced great issues and events.

Thinking small, then, does not necessarily mean thinking unambitiously. As Lucette Valensi and Nathan Wachtel (1976) said of Le Roy Ladurie's *Montaillou:*

> Individual destinies are situated where they intersect with each other: the *domus,* the region, the intellectual universe—the environment, the "mental equipment" of the time: but while Lucien Febvre did portraits of illustrious persons, Le Roy Ladurie reconstructs obscure lives and plunges us into the everyday life of the past. The attempt to totalize history encounters history's traditional calling, the study of those things that only happened once: the particular touches the general, reappearing in all its inexhaustible richness. (p. 8)

The general, in this view, is ineffably complex; interpretation of life at the small scale provides the principal path to historical knowledge.

Thompson's English Working Class

Those who work in the upper left-hand corner—the large-scale and humanistic corner—of our diagram agree on the complexity of collective life but argue that a historian can nevertheless identify and interpret patterns concerning whole peoples. In that corner, E. P. Thompson's work has been a beacon to historians. Thompson's *The Making of the English Working Class,* published in 1963, immediately stimulated the greatest tribute to a historical work: a combination of delighted praise, angry criticism, and eager emulation. Soon after the book's appearance, many bright young scholars of different lands had formed the ambition to write "The History of the _ Working Class" on the model of Thompson's classic.

No one who reads the book will have trouble understanding why. *The Making* combines scintillating history with vigorous polemic. It stalks two different preys: the capitalist interpretation of economic history and econo- mistic Marxism. "In this tradition," says Thompson of the latter,

> the very simplified notion of the creation of the working class was that of a determined process: steam power plus the factory system equals the working class. Some kind of raw material, like peasants "flocking to factories," was then processed into so many yards of class-conscious proletarians. I was polemicizing against this notion in order to show the existing plebeian consciousness refracted by new experiences in social being, which experiences were handled in cultural ways by the people, thus giving rise to a transformed consciousness. (In Abelove et al., 1983, p. 7)

Assuming, rather than establishing, a common experience throughout England, Thompson traces transformations in class action and consciousness between 1790 and 1832. "This book," says Thompson (1963, p. 11), "can be seen as a biography of the English working class from its adolescence until its early manhood. In the years between 1780 and 1832 most English working people came to feel an identity of interests as between themselves, and as against their rulers and employers." Thompson insists on this sense of class not as a thing or a position but as a dynamic relationship to antagonists. The *making* of the English working class, in his account, consisted of bringing to full consciousness that dynamic relationship of workers to employers and rulers, with the accompanying realization that workers had the power to act against their exploiters.

Rather than a chronological narrative, Thompson's 800-page book contains 16 closely linked essays grouped into four sets: 18th-century traditions bearing on England's Jacobin movement of the 1790s; workers' experiences with industrialization; popular radicalism from the early 19th century to the 1830s; and class and politics in the 1820s and 1830s. Within individual chapters, however, Thompson blends narratives of particular struggles and movements with analyses of the ideas that informed them: Jacobinism, working-class religious movements, Luddism, agricultural labor-ers' revolts, strikes, and demands for Parliamentary reform. He takes his account up through the mobilization that brought the Parliamentary Reform of 1832 without offering a sustained analysis of that mobilization—or of its aftermath, when workers who had joined with artisans, shopkeepers, and capitalists to demand broad-ened representation faced the fact that many of their allies had gained the franchise while they had not. At that moment, Thompson suggests the English working class came close to shared conscious-ness and revolutionary intent.

Thompson's pages overflow with stories, argumentative asides, and quotations from relevant texts—especially the texts. In the vein of literary history, Thompson made two great innovations. The first was to broaden the notion of texts from written books and pam-phlets to include not only poems, songs, and broadsheets but ora-tions, utterances, rallying cries, visual symbols, and ritual acts. He sees a few great texts—especially those of John Bunyan, Thomas Paine, William Cobbett, and Robert Owen—as fundamental sources and expressions of working-class ideas. But he regards the more fragmentary and less literary sources as crucial for establishing how workers actually articulated the great ideas and (like Ginzburg, 1980) holds open the possibility that the great authors actually crystallized well-established popular traditions.

Thompson's second innovation was in piecing together the whole range of texts as a literary historian might, grouping them into families identified by similar themes, matching working-class shouts and threatening letters with well-known essays, interpreting the fragments in terms of the master texts and the master texts in the light of the fragments. He uses this method, among other things, to determine which thinkers and activists came closest to the genu-ine temper of workers; thus he argues that the great organizer Francis Place, for all his effectiveness in creating associations and lobbying Parliament, represented working-class views far less well than Thomas Hodgskin or John Gast (Thompson, 1963, p. 521).

By this weaving together of diverse texts, Thompson arrives at an interpretation of changes in working-class consciousness over the course of successive struggles from the 1780s to the 1830s. The basic transformation in that period, declares Thompson, is the formation of "the working class." This is revealed, first, in the growth of class-consciousness: the consciousness of an identity of interests as between all these diverse groups of working people and as against the interests of other classes. And, second, in the growth of corresponding forms of political and industrial organisation. By 1832 there were strongly-based and self-conscious working-class institutions—trade unions, friendly societies, educational and religious movements, political organisations, periodicals—working-class intellectual traditions, working-class community patterns, and a working-class structure of feeling. (p. 194)

The same transformation, in Thompson's account, took English workers from John Bunyan to Bronterre O'Brien, from defense of the old moral economy to demands for power in the industrial economy, from scattered attacks on local enemies to mass movements, and from Luddism to Chartism.

E. P. Thompson's analysis shares with Carlo Ginzburg's the effort to construct a worldview from the incomplete evidence supplied by texts. But Thompson operates on a much larger scale and looks much more deliberately for signs of change; his subject includes all English workers (not to mention their allies and enemies) over half a century. He preserves the unity of his subject and holds to an interpretive mode by taking all fragments as variations on the same theme: the emergence of a widely shared consciousness, a strongly connected organization, and intimate links between organization and consciousness.

Although Thompson wrote one of the most influential historical works of the past 30 years, he does not stand alone in his corner. John Brewer (1976) used similar materials and methods (and a different theoretical perspective) to examine British popular politics in the decades before the beginning of Thompson's book. Natalie Zemon Davis (1975) used small events to illuminate large themes of popular culture in 16th-century France, and Eugene Genovese (1974) inquired into the lives and beliefs of black American slaves. More than anything else, the idea of partly autonomous, widely shared popular orientations—whether called mentalities, culture, or something else —has animated work in the upper left-hand corner of our diagram.

Wrigley and Schofield's English Population

Demographic history locates chiefly in the upper right-hand corner of our diagram, stressing social science and the large scale. That certainly applies to E. A. Wrigley and R. S. Schofield's (1981) *The Population History of England, 1541-1871: A Reconstruction.* In the 1960s, both French and English demographers began to realize that the registers of baptisms, burials, and marriages long maintained by Christian churches would, under some conditions, yield reliable estimates of changes in the fertility, mortality, and nuptiality of the populations attached to those churches. In different ways, French and English research groups began the massive task of using those sources systematically to reconstruct vital trends before the age of regular national censuses, which began at the outset of the 19th century. The Cambridge Group for the History of Population and Social Structure took a threefold approach: extensive studies of household composition and other characteristics of local populations using whatever sources were available; derivation of refined estimates of vital rates by means of genealogies compiled from parish registers and similar records; and estimates of national vital rates by aggregation of births, deaths, and marriages from a sample of parish registers.

The Population History of England draws on the first two but concentrates on the third. Bulky and technical, its style stands about as far from *The Cheese and the Worms* and *The Making of the English Working Class* as one could imagine. More than half of the book's nearly 800 pages go into methodological discussions. The pages swarm with numbers, tables, and graphs. Yet the book generates excitement in its own way. For the Cambridge Group's research transforms our understanding of population change in England —and, by extension, in other parts of Europe—before 1800.

Wrigley, Schofield, and their collaborators wrought their revolution by means of wide-ranging organization and a series of technical innovations. Their organization included the recruitment of volunteers throughout England who abstracted information about baptisms, burials, and marriages from more than 400 sets of local registers from as early as continuous series existed, and then shipped the information to Cambridge in standard format for computerization, tests for reliability, and aggregation into national estimates of annual numbers of births, deaths, and marriages. The central technical innovation was "back projection," the use of birth and death series to move back, 5 years at a time, from the sizes and age structures of populations enumerated in 19th-century censuses to best estimates of population sizes and age structures before that time. After making allowances for immigration and emigration, they essentially subtracted the children born in a given 5-year interval from the population in the previous interval, added the persons who died in the same 5-year interval to the population in the previous interval, then cycled through the series again and again until they had consistent demographic histories of the 5-year cohorts that entered the English population from 1541 onward. After years of compilation, testing, and refinement, the estimates of total population made it possible to compute birth, death, and marriage rates back to 1541.

The results are remarkable. They reveal 16th- and 17th-century populations (a) in which large numbers of people never married; (b) which never suffered the great waves of death once believed to be the inevitable consequences of periodic harvest failures under pre-industrial conditions; (c) which recovered very rapidly from the losses that were brought on by subsistence crises because marriage and marital fertility rose rapidly; (d) in which illegitimate births and marriages rose and fell together instead of varying in opposite directions; and (e) which experienced a substantial rise in fertility (much more important than the conventionally expected decline in mortality) during the rapid population growth of the 18th century.

The resulting portrait of English population dynamics shows how much Malthus underestimated the effectiveness of the "preventive check" (abstinence from marriage and sex) in his own country and how much England escaped from "Malthusian" vulnerability to harvest fluctuations during the commercialization, proletarianization, and agricultural expansion of the 18th century. Explanations of these changes remain controversial (see Goldstone, 1986; Levine, 1984, 1987; Lindert, 1983; Weir, 1984a, 1984b; Wrigley, 1987). Still, the Cambridge Group's research has set what has to be explained on an entirely new plane.

As the nearly instantaneous response to the Wrigley and Schofield findings indicates, they made a difference far outside the zone of strictly demographic concerns. The total population figures supply denominators for a whole series of crucial per capita measures, such as personal income and agricultural productivity, and thus affect both the periodizing and overall characterization of British economic growth. The rising nuptiality and fertility of the 18th-century call for a much more active account of people's involvement in rapid population growth than did the old notion of declining death rates and "population pressure." And the high rates of celibacy in earlier centuries—long suspected but now confirmed—help explain the large role of unmarried "servants" in English agriculture and manufacturing before the era of capital concentration.

Wrigley, Schofield, and the Cambridge Group carried out one of the largest enterprises in the upper right-hand corner of our diagram, but not the only one. Philip Curtin's (1984) studies of the slave trade and of long-distance exchange in general, Robert Fogel and Stanley Engerman's (1974) econometric analyses of production under slavery in the United States, Jan de Vries' (1984) portrayal of European urbanization, Peter Lindert and Jeffery Williamson's (1983) analyses of changes in income and labor force during English industrialization, and Michael Schwartz's (1976) examination of smallholders' politics in the United States all exemplify the use of social- scientific approaches to investigate history on the large scale.

Zunz's Detroit

Olivier Zunz's (1982) study of Detroit's changing social geography from 1880 to 1920 does not operate on the small scale—a single individual and his environment—of *The Cheese and the Worms*, but it does use evidence on individuals and households to build up a picture of alterations in the city as a whole. Over the 40-year period that Zunz studies, Detroit went from a city of small machine shops and mixed trades to the factory-dominated metropolis of the automobile industry. But it remained a fairly low-density city with much of its housing stock in buildings lodging one, two, or three families rather than dozens or hundreds. To trace alterations in the city's fine spatial structure, Zunz sampled the household-by-household manuscript records of the 1880, 1900, and 1920 United States censuses, using the block cluster (four sides of one block and the adjacent sides of two blocks across the street) as his sampling unit (see Figure 4.2).

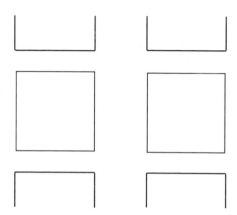

Figure 4.2. Diagram of block-cluster sampling unit.

(It helped, of course, that most of Detroit was laid out in rectangular blocks between rectilinear streets). This meticulous effort gave him observations on the households who were likely to see and interact with each other from day to day. (Research in Detroit's local records confirmed that plenty of social life did proceed at the scale of the block front.) As a complement to the large file on households, Zunz compiled evidence on land use and building type in each block cluster. Thus he had extraordinarily fine evidence concerning who lived where, in whose company, and in what physical surroundings.

In the Detroit of 1880, Zunz discovered well-defined patterns of clustering by national origin, but at this small scale rather than in the form of major segments of the city settled by Germans, Irish, Blacks, Yankees, or others. In that city of fragmented capital, migrants clustered near their places of work, which were often ethnic enterprises. They created ethnic neighborhoods by helping each other find housing close at hand, by sharing dwellings, and by establishing local stores that catered to their own countrymen. The Detroit of 1900 displayed similar patterns, although the arrival of many Poles and Russian Jews altered significantly who lived and worked where.

The year 1920, however, marked a fundamental change. During the previous two decades, the automobile industry had exploded and become the city's dominant economic activity. By then, automobile manufacturers, especially Henry Ford, had installed assembly lines in large factories employing hundreds of workers. The reorganization of production transformed Detroit's labor force, especially by expanding the number of machine tenders working under relatively strict time-discipline. In the process, thousands of migrants, black and white, came to Detroit from the American South.

The city's residential geography shifted accordingly. From a city of small-scale clustering by national origin, with pockets of high-income housing, Detroit became an exemplary case of large-scale segregation by class and race, with national origin operating chiefly within the limits set by class divisions. Two factors converged to produce that result: the change in employment, which made it impossible for workers' households to cluster around ethnically defined workplaces; and developers' deliberate construction of housing for separate markets defined by class and income. Thus the concentration of capital promoted the concentration of social classes.

Ever prudent, Zunz states the results of his study more cautiously than I have. As Zunz summarizes his findings:

> In nineteenth century Detroit . . . industrial geography allowed the immigrant working classes access to jobs without disrupting their neighborhoods. The factories progressively encircled the city, and immigrant neighborhoods found themselves at the focal point of industries. The location of these communities, near no particular factory but not too distant from any, was an asset to family economy; men and women, parents and children went off to work in different directions. It was not until 1920 that cohesive socio-ethnic neighborhoods, well adapted to the new urban and suburban subdivisions of residences and large factories, replaced the nineteenth-century ethnic neighborhoods. (p. 343)

For some decades, then, Detroit hosted what Zunz calls a "dual opportunity structure," one set of channels feeding people of a given national origin into firms run by people from the same background and the other set taking them into the bureaucratized world of industrial employment. Eventually, the first set shriveled as the second expanded, and ethnic firms survived only in enclaves. As a result, daily routines, everyday social relations, opportunities for social mobility, and the quality of life changed drastically. Zunz's study shows us the making of a class-based world built around jobs in big industry.

Zunz's *Changing Face of Inequality* presents the standard technique of social history, collective biography, in unfamiliar garb. Although the conventional individuals and households appear in his analysis, Zunz focuses his effort on arbitrarily defined block clusters, whose virtue is that they are arbitrary but uniform, and therefore allows him to make comparable observations in different parts of the city and at different points in time—comparable, that is, from the viewpoint of a systematic observer. A whole generation of American urban historians (e.g., Katz, 1975, Thernstrom, 1964) assumed the possibility of systematic observation without agonizing over exactly what meaning their subjects attached to class position, mobility, or work experience. Historians who do collective biographies of officeholders, political conflicts, or organizations likewise sidestep the problem of subjective comparability by assuming partial equivalence of uniformly observed events. So far, neither they nor their many critics have clarified the grounds for justifying or denying the validity of their assumptions.

Comparisons and Conclusions

The monographs by Ginzburg, Thompson, Wrigley and Schofield, and Zunz fall far short of representing the full variety of Western historical work. Nevertheless, they provide relatively sharp examples of four distinctly different genres of historical research. Since none of the authors stays strictly in the corner assigned to him, we might represent the location as shown in Figure 4.3.

Ginzburg aims primarily at the smallest scale possible—a single individual—but moves repeatedly up the scale to offer interpretations of 16th- century mentalities in general. Wrigley and Schofield, in sharp contrast, reach down to the level of parishes for important parts of their evidence but concentrate the bulk of their effort on a national population; they do so, furthermore, in impeccably social scientific terms. Zunz alternates between the levels of his block clusters and the city as a whole but occasionally deals with individuals, and in his more synthetic moments associates changes in Detroit with transformations of the whole American economy. He, like Wrigley and Schofield, conceives of his task as the systematic

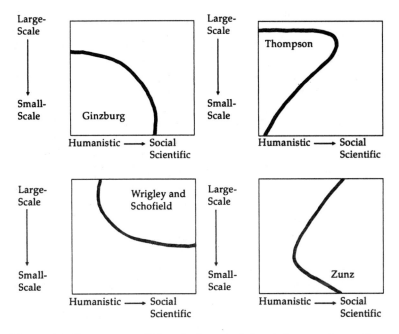

Figure 4.3. Four genres of historical research located on continua of scale and humanistic/social-scientific orientation.

explanation of variation, although his variation occurs in both time and space. Thompson frequently turns to observations of individuals and small groups on his way to building an interpretation of changing outlooks at a national scale.

Other historians occupy more of a middle ground. Rudolf Braun (1960) combines simple demographic descriptions with a close reading of sermons and other direct testimonies as he reconstructs change in the hinterland of Zurich during the rise and fall of cottage industry. Keith Wrightson and David Levine (1981) take one Essex village as their object, using detailed evidence of long-term demographic change as a base for identifying transformations of social structure, but turn quickly to information bearing on the texture of local life. Tamara Hareven (1982) confronts interviews of former mill workers with materials drawn from censuses and similar sources on the way to recapturing experience in a New England textile town. Herbert Gutman (1976) blends a poetic sense of 19th-century black experience with robust numbers describing shifts in black household composition. The remarkable contributions of Emmanuel Le Roy Ladurie (1966, 1975), Catharina Lis (1986), Ewa Morawska (1985), Jean-Claude Perrot (1975), Michelle Perrot (1974), Jane and Peter Schneider (1976), Rebecca Scott (1985), Laurence Stone (1977), William Taylor (1979), and Katherine Verdery (1983) all demonstrate the practical possibility of combining interpretation and systematic analysis of variation.

Nevertheless, the choices are real and pressing. Suppose we accept in full the premises of interpretive history at the small scale, thereby making Ginzburg's modus operandi (if not his subject matter) the center of historical practice. Then the claims of social scientific history at the large scale will seem foolish and distasteful. Suppose, on the other hand, we surmount the epistemological and ontological barriers to believing large-scale social- scientific history feasible. Then interpretation will recede from the center to the close periphery of historical practice.

All in all, the choice of scales appears to be less daunting than the choice of historical philosophies. As the authors we have reviewed demonstrate, a skilled historian can move gracefully from the individual to the group to the nation without losing grip on a historical problem. Despite Gertrude Himmelfarb's fears, a political focus and a concern with mentalities can complement each other very nicely; E. P. Thompson's histories display that complementarity from beginning to end. The hard choices separate the endeavors which I have, all too simply, labeled "humanistic" and "social- scientific."

It is tempting to take a flatly pragmatic view of the choices: Let's do all kinds of history, and see which of them yield the best results. But the debate about which is "best" ultimately goes beyond taste or practical experience to questions about the character and accessibility of social reality. The philosophical problems will not wait forever.

Are historians, like migrant birds, condemned forever to oscillate between two poles? Is any synthesis of humanistic and social scientific approaches to history possible in principle? Yes, it is. Let us leave aside uneasy compromises: a gesture to each side, including Ginzburgian glosses of Zunzian findings and Wrigfield-style "verifications" of Thompsonian interpretations. A resolution to the difficulty will arrive under one of four conditions:

1. A discovery that reliable knowledge of human action is impossible, in which case both enterprises collapse

2. Proof that individual experiences are coherent and intelligible but large social processes are not, which condemns social science

3. Contrary proof that subjectivity is never reliably accessible but recurrent patterns of human action are, which scuttles humanistic history

4. Successful aggregation of reliably known individual experiences into collective action and durable social relations—which, if accomplished, will transform all the social sciences, as well as history.

I never said the task was modest—or easy.

References

Abelove, H., Blackmar, B., Dimock, P., & Schneer, J. (Eds.). (1983). *Visions of history.* New York: Pantheon.

Braudel, F. (1979). *Civilisation matérielle, économie et capitalisme, XVe-XVIIIe siècle,* 3 vols. Paris: Armand Colin.

Braun, R. (1960). *Industrialisierung und Volksleben.* Zurich: Rentsch.

Brewer, J. (1976). *Party ideology and popular politics at the accession of George III.* Cambridge: Cambridge University Press.

Cobb, R. (1986). *People and places.* Oxford: Oxford University Press.

Curtin, P. (1984). *Cross-cultural trade in world history.* Cambridge: Cambridge University Press.

Davis, N. Z. (1975). *Society and culture in early modern France.* Stanford, CA: Stanford University Press.

De Vries, J. (1984). *European urbanization, 1500-1800.* Cambridge, MA: Harvard University Press.

Fogel, R. W., & Engerman, S. L. (1974), *Time on the cross,* 2 vols. Boston: Little, Brown.

Genovese, E. D. (1974). *Roll, Jordan, roll: The world the slaves made.* New York: Pantheon.

Ginzburg, C. (1980). *The cheese and the worms: The cosmos of a sixteenth-century miller.* Baltimore, MD: Johns Hopkins University Press.

Goldberg, H. (1962). *The life of Jean Jaurès.* Madison: University of Wisconsin Press.

Goldstone, J. A. (1986). The demographic revolution in England: A re-examination. *Population Studies, 49,* 5-33.

Gutman, H. G. (1976). *The black family in slavery and freedom, 1750-1925.* New York: Pantheon.

Hareven, T. K. (1982) *Family time and industrial time: The relationship between family and work in a New England industrial community.* Cambridge: Cambridge University Press.

Himmelfarb, G. (1987). *The new history and the old: Critical essays and reappraisals.* Cambridge, MA: Harvard University Press.

Hobsbawn, E. J. (1980). The revival of narrative: Some comments. *Past & Present, 86,* 3-8.

Hoerder, D. (1977). *Crowd action in revolutionary Massachusetts, 1765-1780.* New York: Academic Press.

Katz, M. B. (1975) *The people of Hamilton, Canada West: Family and class in a mid-nineteenth-century city.* Cambridge, MA: Harvard University Press.

Le Roy Ladurie, E. (1966). *Les paysans de Languedoc,* 2 vols. Paris: SEVPEN.

Le Roy Ladurie, E. (1975). *Montaillou, village occitan de 1294 à 1324.* Paris: Gallimard.

Levine, D. (1984). Production, reproduction, and the proletarian family in England, 1500-1851. In D. Levine (Ed.), *Proletarianization and family history.* Orlando, FL: Academic Press.

Levine, D. (1987). *Reproducing families.* Cambridge: Cambridge University Press.

Lindert, P. H. (1983). English living standards, population growth, and Wrigley-Schofield. *Explorations in Economic History, 20,* 131-155.

Lindert, P. H., & Williamson, J. G. (1983). Reinterpreting Britain's social tables, 1688-1913. *Explorations in Economic History, 20,* 94-109.

Lis, C. (1986). *Social change and the labouring poor: Antwerp, 1770-1860.* New Haven, CT: Yale University Press.

Lottin, A. (1968) *Vie et mentalité d'un lillois sous Louis XIV.* Lille: Raoust.

Morawska, E. (1985). *For bread with butter: Life-worlds of East Central Europeans in Johns- town, Pennsylvania, 1890-1940.* Cambridge: Cambridge University Press.

Perrot, J.-C. (1975). *Genèse d'une ville moderne: Caen au XVIIIe siécle,* 2 vols. Paris: Mouton.

Perrot, M. (1974). *Les ouvriers en grève: France, 1871-1890,* 2 vols. Paris: Mouton.

Ramella, F. (1984). *Terra e telai. Sistemi di parentala e manifattura nel Biellese dell'Ottocento.* Turin: Einaudi.

Schneider, J., & Peter, S., (1976). *Culture and political economy in western Sicily.* New York: Academic Press.

Schwartz, M. (1976). *Radical protest and social structure: The southern farmers' alliance and cotton tenancy, 1880-1890.* New York: Academic Press.

Scott, R. J. (1985). *Slave emancipation in Cuba: The transition to free labor, 1860-1899.* Princeton, NJ: Princeton University Press.

Stone, L. (1977). *The family, sex and marriage in England, 1500-1800.* New York: Harper & Row.

Stone, L. (1979). The revival of narrative: Reflections on a new old history. *Past & Present, 86,* 3-24.

Taylor, W. B. (1979). *Drinking, homicide, and rebellion in colonial Mexican villages.* Stanford, CA: Stanford University Press.

Thernstrom, S. (1964). *Poverty and progress.* Cambridge, MA: Harvard University Press.

Thompson, E. P. (1963). *The making of the English working class.* London: Gollancz.

Valensi, L., & Wachtel, N. (1976). L'historien errant. *L'Arc, 65,* 3-9.

Verdery, K. (1983). *Transylvanian villagers: Three centuries of political, economic and ethnic change.* Berkeley: University of California Press.

Weir, D. R. (1984a). Rather never than late: Celibacy and age at marriage in English cohort fertility, 1541-1871. *Journal of Family History, 9,* 340-354.

Weir, D. R. (1984b). Life under pressure: France and England, 1670-1870. *Journal of Economic History, 44,* 27-47.

Wrightson, K., & Levine, D. 91981). *Poverty and piety in an English village: Terling, 1525-1700.* New York: Academic Press.

Wrigley, E. A. (1987). *People, cities and wealth: The transformation of traditional society.* Oxford: Blackwell.

Wrigley, E. A., & Schofield, R. S. (1981). *The population history of England, 1541-1871: A reconstruction.* Cambridge, MA: Harvard University Press.

Zunz, O. (1982). *The changing face of inequality: urbanization, industrial development, and immigrants in Detroit, 1880-1920.* Chicago: University of Chicago Press.

5

The Role of Theory in the Development of Literary Studies in the United States

J. HILLIS MILLER

This is a brief account of the origins and subsequent development of literary studies in the United States since the creation of departments of English and of other modern languages during the last quarter of the 19th century. I shall focus especially on the changing role of literary theory in this development and on the theories explicit and implicit in the actual practices of literary study. Let me begin by making two general points:

1. Because the United States is a large democratic country with a relatively small degree of centralization or prescriptive governmental control over education, and because one of our most precious freedoms is the freedom of the teacher in the classroom, any attempt, such as this one, to make an orderly narrative out of the development of literary studies in America will necessarily ignore many regional and local differences and many cases of brilliant, effective, but in one way or another idiosyncratic, teaching of literature or writing about literature in the United States. The institutionalization of literary studies in America, the organization of departments, the setting of curriculum, degree requirements, and so on, has been to

a considerable degree individual and ad hoc, and therefore different from one college or university to another. An example is a form of literary study, practiced mostly at The Johns Hopkins University during the 1940s and 1950s, that was strongly influenced by the "history of ideas" of two philosophers, A. O. Lovejoy and George Boas. Another example is the work of the so-called Chicago Aristoteleans active in the 1940s and 1950s at the University of Chicago under the leadership of R. S. Crane. This mode of literary study is still influential here and there in the work of younger scholars and teachers. Although both of these forms of literary study produced brilliant results, they were relatively local phenomena. They do not fit very well into the developmental paradigm I shall propose. That paradigm is roughly and on the whole true, but a closer look at the texture or grain of the phenomena in question would reveal many irregularities and anomalies that cannot be fully described and accounted for here.

2. In my account, the role of theory in American literary study is emphasized. All literary study is at least implicitly theoretical. From the beginning of literary studies in the United States there has been a fair amount of theoretical reflection about the actual practices of teaching and scholarship, their nature and goals. On the other hand, one feature of literary study in the United States has been a strong anti-theoretical bias. This has been partly an attempt to suggest that whatever is being done goes without saying and does not need overt theoretical justification and partly a pragmatic American suspicion of the abstractions of theory. Theory, we Americans tend to think, comes between the reader and direct experience of literature. One useful way to tell the story of literary study in America is to focus on the changing role, over the years, of overt theoretical or methodological reflection.

Literary studies in the United States have had a threefold and to a considerable degree contradictory historical origin. Such studies are, first, an outgrowth of the training of students in composition, oratory, and forensic rhetoric for the purpose of teaching them to write and speak well in professional and public life. Second, such studies are an adaptation to the study of vernacular literatures of the tradition of scientific philology developed originally for the investigation of the Bible and of the "classics" of Greek and Latin literature. Third, they are a development of the humanism especially associated with the 19th-century English poet and critic, Matthew

Arnold. Such humanism justifies the study of literature by seeing it as a culturing acculturating power in education, making available knowledge of "the best that is known and thought in the world." The purpose of imparting this knowledge is to make students better persons and better citizens.

It is difficult to reconcile completely these three presuppositions about the nature and purpose of literary study. The historical development of literary studies in the United States, as I shall show, has therefore been marked by the fissures among these presuppositions, as now one, now another, or a combination of all three presuppositions has been dominant. These fissures, however, have rarely been acknowledged openly, although, as Gerald Graff (1987) has argued, recognition of them not only is an important historical insight but would have great heuristic value in teaching. In this chapter my contention is that all three of these theoretical justifications for the study of literature are still strongly active and operative today, that they remain still irreconcilable with one another, and that, in spite of their cogency and plausibility, in spite of the fact that so many intelligent people of goodwill have held one or another or some combination of them, they are not wholly appropriate for present circumstances in the United States.

In the place of these three rationales, in my conclusion, I shall suggest another justification, another definition of the social, cultural, and personal function of literary study in the United States today. Literary study of certain kinds, I shall argue, is a powerful and indispensable means of the critique of ideology. To put it another way, literary study is a means of using the mind to protect us against the mind itself and against the baneful effects that confusing linguistic with natural reality can have in the real world. The great 20th-century American poet Wallace Stevens puts this in the following way: "If the mind is the most terrible force in the world, it is also the only force that defends us against terror. Or, the mind is the most terrible force in the world principally in this, that it is the only force that can defend us against itself" (Stevens, 1957, p. 174). Stevens goes on to say that "The poet represents the mind in the act of defending us against itself." If this is true of poetry, the study of poetry can also be such a self-defense. It can extend and cooperate with the work of the poet. Before discussing 20th century developments and the present situation, however, I shall first say something more about each of the three historical origins or roots of American literary study.

Until the development of graduate education in the United States in the late decades of the 19th century and the concurrent development of departments of English and other European languages and literatures, the study of literature in American colleges was primarily an ancillary part of the education of young men, primarily white affluent young men, in speaking and writing well in preparation for public life and the professions. This included the inculcation of Christian morals, often most explicitly in a required senior course in moral philosophy, as well as in required chapel attendance.

Training in Greek and Latin languages, not in vernacular literature, was the central feature of the humanities curriculum in American colleges until the last decades of the 19th century. That training inevitably involved some reading of works of literature in those languages. The interpretation of these works that went on in the classroom, however, when it went on at all, would probably strike most people today as exceedingly unsophisticated. The teaching was mostly rote drill in getting the translations, grammar, and syntax right, with occasional pauses to see the stories as moral exempla. In fact there seems to have been precious little of that, perhaps because the morality was taken for granted, as apparently were answers to all these questions about meaning that we have come to raise.

The implicit theory behind all these years of training in the minutiae of Greek and Latin grammar and syntax is so patently absurd that one is surprised that it was expressed as often as it was. The assumption was that all that hard labor of memorizing vocabulary and paradigms was good moral discipline, and, beyond that, that the spiritual essence of Greek and Roman culture was somehow embodied in the grammar, syntax, and etymologies of those languages, so that the classical spirit would be absorbed by the rote learning of linguistic minutiae. It is all very well to say that this is absurd, but does not some such belief still lurk in the minds of those who justify some kinds of language study as "good mental training" and as somehow morally uplifting? Graff (1987) quotes a splendid attack on these assumptions by Charles Francis Adams in a Harvard Phi Beta Kappa address of 1883. Adams called these assumptions "the great-impalpable-essence-and-precious-residuum theory" of classical study, defining that theory as the assumption that "a knowledge of Greek grammar, and the having puzzled through the Anabasis and three books of the Iliad, infuses into the boy's nature the imperceptible spirit of Greek literature, which will appear in the results of his subsequent work, just as manure, spread upon a field, appears in the crop which that field bears" (Graff, 1987, p. 30).[1] All that drillwork in Greek and Latin, then, presupposed a theory of *Bildung* or the education of the mind and character of young American upper-class males in preparation for professional and public life.

As scholars have begun recently to demonstrate (Frantzen and Venegoni, 1986), the high value put on the study of Anglo-Saxon or Old English, when departments of English were established, was to a considerable degree based on a variant of this theory, namely the notion that the study of Old English grammar would lead students to absorb the roots of the Germanic or Aryan or Indo-European way of thinking, including the political principles that were the foundation of American democracy.

The second branch of the trifurcated root of American literary study is the establishment in the late 19th century in the United States of research universities modeled on the German university with its concept of universal *Wissenschaft* or scientific, verifiable knowledge. The founding in 1876 of the Johns Hopkins University by Daniel Coit Gilman initiated this development and began serious graduate education in the United States. As Jacques Derrida has persuasively argued (1983, 1984), the founding of the University of Berlin in the early 19th century followed by the gradual reshaping of all universities in the West on that model was the deliberate institutionalization of the university's mission as the universal accounting for everything according to the Leibnizian principle of reason. This is the presupposition that everything has its reason, or, to put it in more exactly Leibnizian terms, "for any true proposition, reason can be rendered: *Omnis veritatis reddi ratio potest.*"

Everything can be accounted for and should be accounted for—by the university. This obligation to account for everything tended to be tied to the nationalistic aspirations of the universities. Each great research university tended to think of itself as serving one particular nation state in its aim for dominance, and as a part of this nationalism, increasing importance was given to the study of the nation's vernacular literature. The modern research university is where this vast enterprise of inventory, investigation, and explanation takes place. This occurs most evidently in the sciences. Or, to put it another way, the gradual transformation in the 19th century of all the universities in the West, including those in the United States, into the great modern research-oriented technoscientific servants of society, government, and industry we know today took place as the institution of the principle of reason. It was a response to the obligation to account for everything, to give everything its reason, to explain everything by its cause. No doubt Leibniz would be surprised, and perhaps dismayed, to see the historical course his principle of reason has taken.

One region of this enormous collective work of the new research university was the obligation to account for the language and literature of all countries and historical periods. The names for this branch of the universal accounting for were "scholarship," "research," and, especially, "philology." When philology was introduced into American universities in the late 19th century, at the same time as departments of vernacular languages were established, a procedure and rationale for the study of vernacular literature quite different from the older notion of the cultivation of the gentleman were instituted. The new commitment to the principle of a universal accounting justified, as one part of the new research university, a vast collective scholarly enterprise of editing, annotating, collating, establishing of texts, biography, bibliography, source study, dictionary and concordance making, etymological research, discovery and verification of historical and linguistic facts, and the writing of literary and intellectual history. The models for this development of English, Germanic, and romance philology (the main forms) were the disciplines of Biblical scholarship and classical philology, which were highly developed, especially in Germany and England, in the 19th century and then appropriated in the United States. Although the theory of *Bildung,* which I have already mentioned, was present as a justification for this work, as well as humanistic theory, which I have not yet discussed, philology was also more centrally justified in terms of a theory of "value-free" research, the assumption that it is good, in fact it is an obligation, for the university to assemble in a knowable and retrievable form information about everything whatsoever. This must be done simply because it is knowable, because it can be compiled, recorded, and stored in the library archives, and just in case someone needs to use it later on. Values as such, on the other hand, are not amenable to such study and compilation; therefore they have no place in it. The assimilation and storage of facts was implicitly the highest value, the *raison d'être* of the university professor.

The ideology behind this enormous enterprise is the assumption that the establishment of facts and of the explanatory causes about anything whatever is a good in itself. But though a distinguished philologist like James Wilson Bright of the Johns Hopkins University, in his presidential address of 1902 before the Modern Language Association, could assert that "the philological strength and sanity of a nation is the measure of its intellectual and spiritual vitality," and that the philologist must participate in "the work of guiding the destinies of the country," he was utterly unable, as Gerald Graff observes, to give any reasonable explanation of just how the philologist—as philologist—was going to guide America's destiny (Graff 1987, p. 114). As has been pointed out over and over through the decades by the humanistic critics of "philology," the fact is that the positivistic or scientific ideal of literary study has no intrinsic way of determining any social or personal use that may be made of its results, despite the vague assumption that to get the facts right is an ethical good. The philological ideal, as such, is as nearly without persuasive cogency in its claims for the cultural use of such study as is the notion that the study of the minutiae of Greek, Latin, Old English, or Middle High German grammar is good in itself. The cogent justification of the social and personal utility of literary study therefore has to come from some other source, for example in present-day justifications of the study of "minor" works or works hitherto excluded from the canon on the grounds that they are an indispensable means of understanding our cultural history or in resisting the ideological presuppositions built into the choice of works in the traditional canons of the national literatures.

Among other such justifications the one stemming from the humanism of Matthew Arnold (1822-1888), the third fork in the trifurcated root of literary studies in the United States, has had the most shaping influence. The ideas about the social function of literary study that Arnold expresses were widely diffused in the 19th century and have a complex history in our own century. The American version of these ideas, moreover, had many other sources beside Matthew Arnold, for example, Carlyle and Ruskin, Arnold's contemporaries in England, and America's own Ralph Waldo Emerson. This humanism has a complicated history before Arnold, a history that goes back, to name one important genetic line, through the concept of *Bildung* in Goethe and Schiller, along with other German romantic writers (strong influences on Arnold), through Renaissance humanism, to the idea of *Paideia* in the Greeks. Nevertheless, Arnold's particular way of formulating the claim that the study of literature plays a fundamental role in the cultural formation of the citizen has had enormous influence on literary study in the United States. Arnold twice visited the United States on lecture tours, in 1883-1884 and again in 1886. His admirable series of essays and books on culture and on the function of literary study perhaps best formulates these humanistic presuppositions about literary study. These assumptions were institutionalized in the teaching and writing of the long line of distinguished humanist professors, or as Graff calls them, "generalists" (1987, pp. 81-97), who taught in the early 20th century in American colleges and universities: William Lyon Phelps of Yale; Bliss Perry of Williams, Princeton, and Harvard; Robert Morss Lovett of the University of Chicago; Irving Babbitt of Harvard; Stuart P. Sherman of Illinois; and Lionel Trilling of Columbia, among many others. Trilling was the youngest of these humanist teachers. His superb book on Matthew Arnold (1939) can be taken as a kind of summing up of the ideals of Arnoldian literary culture as they were embodied in one way or another in the teaching of literature in hundreds of American colleges and universities during the first half of the 20th century. These ideals also provided college and university presidents, commencement speakers, and department chairmen with their defense of the social utility of literary study.

In essays like "The Study of Poetry" and "The Function of Criticism at the Present Time," as well as in his influential book of cultural criticism, *Culture and Anarchy,* Arnold proposed the notion that Western literature from the Greeks on down to Goethe and Wordsworth is the storage house of "the best that has been thought and said in the world." Arnold presupposed that he and his readers lived in a bad time, a time when the influence of traditional religion was waning and a time when commercialism, anarchic individualism, industrialization, and the rise of a Philistine middle class were weakening culture and making genuine education difficult. Only study of the classics of our tradition could save our culture. How often similar ideas about twentieth-century American culture have been expressed in our own century by teachers of literature and by administrators, as well as by politicians who concern themselves with education! And how often the study of the great works of literature of the past, from the Greeks on down, has been put forward as the sovereign antidote to our cultural sickness! The study of literature, the argument goes, alone can maintain culture in such bad times, or, as Lionel Trilling put this, "great works of art and thought have a decisive part in shaping the life of a polity" (quoted in Graff, 1987, p. 85).

With the assumptions eloquently expressed by Arnold so deeply embedded in their thinking about teaching and scholarship in the humanities that they were hardly aware of them as assumptions open to criticism, in the decades from 1890 to the 1940s professors of literature in the United States set about to create and maintain the departments, curricula, and programs in teaching and research in vernacular literature that are to a considerable degree still intact today, especially in departments of English. The institutionalization of Arnoldian humanism in American departments of English has meant the following: a commitment to "coverage" of all English literature from *Beowulf* to at least Hardy or Kipling, more recently including coverage of literature down to the present day, with American literature now also included; a primary focus on a list of canonical works, almost exclusively by male writers, (Chaucer, Spenser, Shakespeare, Donne, Milton, Pope, Johnson, Wordsworth, Keats, Shelley, Tennyson, Browning, Dickens, and the Victorian prose writers: Arnold, Huxley, Newman, Ruskin), a canon that is a relatively recent invention and that was established at the same moment in history that the departments of English were instituted; and emphasis on a thematic rather than formal or even historically relativistic reading of these writers. What was stressed was their expression of timeless and universal values, virtues, and ideals.

When the so-called "New Criticism" entered American literary study in the 1940s, that study was still dominated by an uneasy mixture of the three sets of presuppositions I have described. The New Criticism rapidly took over the curricula and procedures of teaching in English departments almost everywhere in the United States, although as a strong overlay superimposed on the old "scholarly" ideals, rather than as the complete displacement of those ideals. The New Criticism dominated American literary study for the next twenty years, displacing or redefining all three of the assumptions about literary study that had presided over the first fifty years of its development. The story of the New Criticism, its assumptions, practices, and main figures, has been told often, most authoritatively and fully by Murray Krieger (Krieger, 1956), and most recently in the chapter on the subject in Vincent Leitch's recent book (1988). Here I shall only name the chief critics, name one landmark book, identify the main assumptions of the New Critics, and suggest some reasons why the New Criticism was so successful in transforming literary study in America.

The immediate precursors of the American New Critics were I. A. Richards, William Empson, and T. S. Eliot, in England, and the great American critic Kenneth Burke, who transcends any school or movement. The major critics involved in the development and institutionalizing of the New Criticism in American colleges and universities were John Crowe Ransom, Allen Tate, R. P. Blackmur, Cleanth Brooks, Robert Penn Warren, René Wellek, and W. K. Wimsatt. The one book most responsible for the triumphant institutionalization of the New Criticism was the introductory textbook by Brooks and Warren, *Understanding Poetry* (1938, 2nd ed., 1950), which made available in teachable form the basic assumptions about reading literature that the New Critics were exemplifying in their various books, for example Cleanth Brooks in *The Well Wrought Urn* (1947). But for every student who read *The Well Wrought Urn* hundreds used *Understanding Poetry* as a basic textbook.

The New Critics focused primarily on lyric poetry, especially modern poetry and metaphysical poetry. Poems by Donne or Eliot were taken as paradigmatic of literature in general. The "close reading" of poems was assumed to be the main business of literary study. The poem was read more or less in detachment from its historical and social context. The assumption was that no special knowledge beyond what could be found in the dictionary, especially in the *Oxford English Dictionary*, was necessary to read a poem. A good poem was assumed to be, as Leitch puts it, "an autonomous, ahistorical, spatial object." (1988, p. 35). A good poem, moreover, was assumed to be an "organic unity" bringing disparate materials together in a complex ironic harmony of opposites in tension. Metaphor was assumed to be the fundamental trope of poetry and therefore of literature in general. Metaphor was seen as the basic way in which heterogeneous materials could be yoked together. The reading of poetry was assumed to be a good in itself, an end in itself; and at the same time, somewhat implicitly and covertly, it was assumed that reading poems has personal and social utility by providing models for the kind of reconciliation of competing needs, desires, or values necessary for successful living in the real world of 20th-century America. Or as Graff has put this, reading poems provides a non-conceptual "embodied" knowledge of universal values transcending the flux of history.

The New Criticism was so successful in part because it made possible the teaching of poetry to the new kinds of young people who were getting a college and university education in America, especially after the return of veterans from service in World War II. These were middle- and working-class Americans without wide historical or cultural knowledge, students who were more or less starting from scratch in freshman or sophomore college courses in literature. For the most part they were ignorant of the Bible, classical mythology, and all the other sorts of knowledge that previously had been taken for granted in readers of poetry. *Understanding Poetry* made possible the teaching of literature in a democratic country committed as no great nation had ever been before to mass higher education, the offering of a college or university degree to more or less anybody. At the same time *Understanding Poetry*, in its choice of poems to be read and in what was said of them in the commentaries in the book, more or less covertly smuggled in some presuppositions borrowed from T. S. Eliot and from the Southern American heritage of many of the New Critics. These presuppositions were conservative politically, religiously, and culturally. The choice of poems in *Understanding Poetry*, for example, was a choice made primarily from the traditional canon established in the earlier decades of the century. Even the denigration of the English Romantics, although taken straight from Eliot, echoed similar reservations about Shelley, for example, in Matthew Arnold. The metaphysical poets were prized, at least implicitly, for their expression of a certain kind of traditional Christian vision of human life.

The next and so far final phase in the development of literary study in the United States up to present time was the gradual importation and domestication of continental literary theories that began in the 1950s. This importation occurred at the same time that the myth criticism of a Canadian scholar, Northrop Frye, was exerting a strong influence in the United States. The wide appeal of Frye's all-inclusive systematic typology of literature in his *Anatomy of Criticism* (1957) was evidence that teachers and students of literature were beginning to feel a need for an explicit theory of literature, a need not satisfied by the New Criticism.

By the mid-1960s, partly as a result of political events like the Vietnam War, student activism, women's liberation, and the Civil Rights movement, conventional approaches to literary studies seemed increasingly irrelevant. Those who deplore the gradual triumph of the new theoretical approaches should remember that they were a response to a widely felt sense of the detachment of literary studies from social or personal usefulness. Theoretical work imported from Europe responded to that need for "relevance." First existentialism and phenomenology began to be assimilated as the basis of a new kind of literary criticism, and then in the 1960s structuralism, Lacanian psychoanalysis, newer kinds of Marxist criticism, and so-called "deconstruction" were brought in. It is convenient to date the start of the second, more radical, wave of this primarily French invasion as 1966, the date of a structuralist symposium held at The Johns Hopkins University and sponsored by the Ford Foundation. Papers from this symposium were published in *The Languages of Criticism and the Sciences of Man* (Macksey and Donato, 1970). This symposium was one of the earliest and most influential of the multitude of international conferences on literary theory that now have become commonplace almost everywhere in the world. The Hopkins symposium brought Jacques Lacan and Jacques Derrida to the United States to present papers for the first time (Derrida had studied for a year at Harvard in the 1950s), along with representatives of a somewhat older generation of phenomenological critics like Georges Poulet and Marxist critics like Lucien Goldmann and the classicist Jean-Paul Vernant. American literary study since then has been increasingly dominated by these imported theories and by the assumption of a need to base literary study on explicit theoretical reflection. This invasion of literary study by "theory" is a major example of the breaking open of a discipline's traditional boundaries that is one theme of this book. In the United States today it is no longer possible to remain narrowly within the study of primary literary texts and the commentaries on them. To remain at the frontier of research and teaching, the American student or teacher of literature is likely to feel the need to have expert knowledge of philosophy, social theory, psychoanalysis, anthropology, linguistics, or history. The present situation in the study of literature in the United States is, as I have elsewhere argued

(Miller, 1987b) characterized by the almost universal triumph of theory. This is true in spite of the continued active presence of what Paul de Man (1986) called "the resistance to theory." I suggest that, paradoxically, the most effective form of the resistance to theory these days (in fact at any time) is a certain form of the triumph of theory.

But, first, what do I mean by the "triumph of theory?" I mean what is evident on every side, not only in the development of a large number of powerful, competing theoretical discourses, each with its somewhat barbarous code name—hermeneutic, phenomenological, Lacanian, feminist, reader response, Marxist, Foucaultian, structuralist, semiotic, deconstructionist, new historicist, cultural critical, and so on—but the accompanying immense proliferation of courses, curricula, books, handbooks, dissertations, essays, lectures, new journals, symposia, study groups, centers, and institutes, all overtly concerned with theory or with what is called "cultural studies." Taken together these form a "hidden university" crossing departmental, disciplinary, and institutional boundaries. Much of the frontier work in literary studies is taking place today in this hidden university. This is not the place to try to characterize each of the kinds of literary theory I have named. It takes Vincent Leitch over four hundred pages to sketch out the main modes and their presuppositions (Leitch, 1988). What needs to be stressed here is the large number of competing theories and their incoherence. They cannot be synthesized into one grand all-inclusive theory of literature. The victory of theory has transformed the field of literary study from what it was when I entered it forty years ago. In those happy days, as I have said above, we mostly studied primary works in the context of literary history, paying some overt attention in our teaching to the basic presuppositions of the so-called New Criticism: the primacy of metaphor, the universality of the principle of organic unity and so on. Now it is necessary to be acquainted with a large number of incompatible theories, each usually based in disciplines outside literature, and each claiming our allegiance.

The present-day triumph of theory is no doubt overdetermined. It has many and incompatible "causes," or, to try to avoid begging the question by slipping in the word "causes," it would be better to say, "concomitant factors." The conflict of diverse assumptions among the different theories is itself one such factor, because their obvious incoherence forces theoretical reflection. If everyone shares the same assumptions, they can be taken for granted. Explicit theory does not then appear to be necessary. Among other factors are the demographic changes that are making the United States more and more of a multilingual country. It makes less and less sense to base literary study exclusively on canonical works in English literature. Another factor reducing the importance of literature written in England is the rise of the United States as a major world power accompanied by a decline in the importance of England. Another force for change is the women's movement, which has had and is having enormous effects on American culture. Technological changes like the jet airplane, which can bring scholars and critics from all over the world together for a conference, computers, tape recorders, and copying machines have enormously speeded up the dissemination of new work from place to place within the United States, from Europe and other continents to the United States, and from the United States to the rest of the world.

One of the important factors associated with the turn to theory is its function as a response to a need generated by a widespread loss of confidence in the unequivocal value of studying primarily works in the traditional male-dominated canon of English literature plus Homer, Virgil, Dante, Cervantes, and so on in English translation. The traditional justification for the study of the canon—that such study transmits from the old to the young the fundamental values of our culture, that Arnoldian "best that has been known and thought in the world"—also has been put in doubt. It is not that defenses of study of the traditional canon on these grounds are not currently being made, far from it, but they are likely to be made in a way that makes their ideological motivation evident. Such defenses no longer go without saying. Our consciousness has been raised, in large part by the works of theory itself. We are likely to feel that no choice of books for a syllabus, for example, or no choice of ways to read those books, is politically innocent. Such choices are no longer easily justified by appeal to a universal consensus or to universal standards valid for any time, place, institution, or particular classroom.

At the same time it is important to remember that, as recent empirical studies by the Modern Language Association of America have discovered (Franklin 1988), the traditional canon still forms the backbone of English curricula in most American colleges and universities. Study of the traditional canon has by no means been weakened as much as some critics of the teaching of literature in our colleges and universities have claimed. Nevertheless, discussion of the justification of the canon *is* taking place. At the practical curricular and pedagogical level, however, the result is more a matter of new works and new approaches to canonical works being added to more traditionally organized courses than anything like a radical overturning of the received canon. In a similar way, in spite of all the attention being paid the new forms of literary theory, as the studies by the Modern Language Association found, an immense number, perhaps the majority, of courses are still taught according to the methods and assumptions of the New Criticism.

The triumph of theory is to a considerable degree defined as a response to the new social, demographic, and technological developments and as an attempt to think one's way out of them. The teacher wants to be justified in what he or she does. Appealing to theory is one way of seeking that justification. To put it another way, one of the major functions of literary theory is as a critique of ideology, that is, a critique of the taking of a linguistic reality for a material one. The ideology in question in this case includes the hidden (but ideology is by definition hidden) assumptions of our procedures of teaching literature and of the general institutionalization of literary study. The result of this appeal to theory is that more and more in the United States literary theory has become a subject of study for its own sake. This is most conspicuous in the widespread development of courses devoted to the explicit study of theoretical texts as such, not as simply ancillary to the study of primary literary texts. It is also present in the inclusion of works of theory within courses that are not overtly "theoretical." Such courses, it would seem, are all to the good insofar as they recognize the importance of reading and using the works of theory. Courses of both sorts make the study of theory "academically respectable," as the saying goes. They institutionalize theory within the normal curriculum, but also marginalize it as one more field of study among others.

On the other hand, it is easy to see the danger to the effective functioning of theory inherent in such courses. They may be a subtle form of the resistance to theory. This may be so even when such courses are taught, as they usually are, by scholars who are deeply interested in theory and do not intend to do it any harm. Literary theory or critical theory, paradoxically, is, or ought to be, praxis. In this case at least, theory *is* praxis, thinking *is* action, rather than being its speculative opposite. To put it another way, the distinction between theory and praxis in this case breaks down into something that is self-divided in another way or in other ways. It is self-divided, for example, in the by no means symmetrical reciprocity between theory and reading, or between pedagogical theory and the results of pedagogy. Literary theory, that is to say, is of little or no use unless it is "applied," used. Theory must be active, productive, performative.

What theory performs or produces is, or ought to be, new readings in the broadest sense of the word. But these readings in their turn are performative rather than merely passive or cognitive. They make something happen. The readings in question would of course include new readings of the works of theory. They should be "readings" in a strong sense of the word, that is, active, critical, rhetorical, "interventionist" readings, as opposed to mere summaries of the manifest thematic context of the texts read. Theory itself is of no use unless it is read in this sense. Only then will it facilitate readings of other texts, readings that, as Jacques Derrida (1984) says in "Mochlos," are radically inaugural in the sense that they implicitly or explicitly propose a new "contract" with the university and with the society or the state that university serves. "For example," says Derrida, "when I read a sentence from a given text in a seminar (a statement of Socrates, a fragment of *Das Kapital* or *Finnegans Wake*, a paragraph of *The Conflict of Faculties*) I do not merely fulfill an already existing contract; I am also writing, or preparing for signature, a new contract with the institution, between the institution and dominant forces of society. Here, as in any negotiation—a pre-contractual negotiation always transforms a former contract—is the moment for every imaginable ruse and strategic ploy" (Derrida forthcoming).

This impressive proliferation of theoretical reflection about literature is without doubt the most "transferable" aspect of literary study in the United States today. I have named some of the technological advances, especially the immense development of telecommunications and ease of travel, that have made Western literary theory available in other countries around the world. I found colleagues in the People's Republic of China remarkably well informed about Western theory and very interested in further translation of Western literary theory. The same can be said for other countries around the world I have visited.

Literary theory is much more exportable than the local institutions of literary study in the United States. But there would not be so much interest in Western literary theory around the world, for example in the People's Republic of China, if it did not respond to some local social and cultural need in the countries that are translating it, writing about it, and making use of it in teaching and writing. I see this appropriation of literary theory as part of a rapid world-wide cultural change that results in part from technological changes like the personal computer and the fax machine but has other components as well, such as the proliferation of multinational corporations. In this new world of a multilingual copresence that crosses all national boundaries, literary study will more and more become a new form of comparative literature, no longer the separate study of national literatures. Comparative study demands explicit theoretical reflection. The "triumph of theory" is not an accident but a response to profound cultural, social, and technological innovations that are transforming our world. Such intercommunication among countries and cultures is by no means incompatible with maintaining local specificities in language and institutional forms. As Western theory is translated and assimilated throughout the world, it will be transformed in ways that cannot be anticipated, transformed to fit the new language and the local needs. As we learned, this is happening now in the People's Republic of China. It will be a matter of deep interest to watch the transformations that accompany the transfer of this particular aspect of Western academic study.

The most recent development in literary studies in the United States, a major change in focus currently going on, is the shift from language-based study to history-based study. This is most conspicuous in the work of the so-called "new historicists," for example Stephen Greenblatt and his colleagues at Berkeley and their associates at many other colleges and universities. It should be remembered that the theoretical presuppositions of the various scholars sometimes grouped as new historicists are diverse and to some degree contradictory, as in the case with any strongly innovative and influential movement. Moreover, the renewed interest in the historical contexts of literature is present in many other sorts of critics too, in Marxists, Foucaultians, and in more traditional scholars interested in the historical backgrounds of literature. It has been part of the work of the so-called deconstructionists all along. This new interest in the historical or cultural contexts of literature is rapidly producing a vigorous new discipline called "cultural critique" or "cultural studies." Sometimes this new enterprise is located within traditional departments of English, French, or German, sometimes in many new centers or institutes of cultural studies appearing in colleges and universities around the country.

This renewed attention to history is all to the good if it does not return to naive assumptions about the way literature is determined by history or merely reflects it. To put this another way, part of the strength of the new turn to history comes from insights, learned from structuralism and "deconstruction," into the complexities of the rhetorical or figurative dimensions of texts, both "literary" in the usual sense and "extra-literary" in the sense of being historical documents of one sort or another. The question of the actual relation between a given literary text, say a play by Shakespeare, and its historical context, say 16th-century treatises about hermaphroditism (see Greenblatt, 1988), must itself be a topic of sophisticated theoretical reflection. Simply placing the play in its context and asserting that the context explains or accounts for the text is not enough.

Identification of the actual ways in which literature and history are related is a major frontier of theory today as well as of critical practice (see Miller, 1988). Three acts of reading are necessary to this: a reading of the historical documents, a reading of the literary work in "the light" of those documents, and a reading of the relation between the two. The latter involves an especially difficult and controversial theoretical topic: the text-to-text relation. None of these acts of reading goes without saying. The insights of language-oriented theories, most especially so-called "deconstruction" as practiced by Jacques Derrida, Paul de Man, and a large number of younger literary scholars, are indispensable to any serious investigation of the relations of literature to history. One of the most important of deconstruction's insights is a recognition of the perlocutionary or performative aspect of the act of reading or teaching a work of literature. Reading makes something happen. It is, to borrow Austin's phrase, a way of doing things with words (Austin, 1975), not just a reflection or representation of some state of affairs imaginary or real. Works of literature (as well as criticism and the reading of literature) have a performative role in making history. It is a matter of great importance that the new investigations of the historical relations of literature recognize this dimension of the role of literature in society. It is in this region of literary study that attention to what I have called "the ethics of reading" has importance (Miller, 1987a, 1990).[2] The "ethics of reading" involves questions of an obligation or responsibility incurred by the act of reading or teaching a work of literature, an obligation to the text read, to the students to whom one teaches it, and to those who may read an essay one publishes on the work. The ethical and the political effects of reading and teaching literature are not necessarily the same. Both need to be recognized and interrogated as parts of the new theoretical work relating literature to history and seeing literature as performative, as making something happen.

The new historicism and rhetorical reading or "deconstruction" can therefore cooperate in the work of what at the beginning of this essay I called "critique of ideology." Since this claim is controversial, although essential to the argument I am making for a social function of the study of literature, let me make it clear what I mean by "ideology." Discussion of this paper at the 1988 Symposium at the Chinese Academy of Social Sciences focused sharply on my argument that literary study can and should be a critique of ideology. Our colleagues in the literature institutes of CASS, it seems, are accustomed to think of the social function of literature as the reinforcement of a consciously promulgated ideology, not its criticism. We in the United States would not ordinarily use the word "ideology" in a positive sense to name the primary values of our culture. The word, for us, generally has a negative connotation. It names either unconscious and prejudiced presuppositions or the conscious program of some group. Nevertheless, the word "ideology" in the West also is a focus of controversy. It has several contradictory meanings, both within Marxist thought and outside it. By "ideology" I do not mean the conscious values and concepts deliberately promulgated and enforced by what the French Marxist, Louis Althusser, calls "state apparatuses" (Althusser 1971, p. 127), but rather, as Althusser defines ideology in the essay just quoted and elsewhere, a largely unconscious or taken-for-granted, but therefore all the more powerful, system of valuation and judgment, an imaginary rewriting of the real material conditions under which men and women in a given society live their lives. "Ideology," says Althusser, "is a system (with its own logic and rigor) of representations (images, myths, ideas, or concepts, depending on the case) endowed with a historical existence and role within a given society" (Althusser, 1977, p. 231). Or, to cite another definition, I mean by "ideology" what Paul de Man means when he says, "What we call ideology is precisely the confusion of linguistic with natural reality, of reference with phenomenalism" (de Man, p. 11).

To put what I mean by "critique of ideology" in another way, whatever the case in other countries, the study of literature in the United States should now and in the coming decades have as its primary goal the teaching of good reading. What social or ethical good, it may be asked, is that? Courses in rhetorical reading have an essential role in a democratic society, I answer, in teaching citizens the skills necessary to read all the signs with which they are surrounded and to resist being repressed or oppressed by imaginary formulations of their real relations to the material, social, gender, and class conditions of their existence. Ideological formulations, defined as I have defined them, are false, illusory. They bamboozle us. Although it may be true that there is no society without its ideology, the errors caused by mistaking a linguistic reality for a natural reality are always potentially dangerous. Such errors cause much remedial social and personal suffering. It is better to know the truth. Unlike Friedrich Nietzsche, who thought there were some truths mankind could not stand knowing, I hold, on the contrary, that the truth will make you free. The teaching and study of literature, seen as training in good reading and thereby as critique of ideology, make an indispensable contribution to that liberation.

Notes

1. Gerald Graff's brilliant *Professing Literature: An Institutional History* (1987) is the most recent and best account of the development of teaching and scholarship in literature in the United States. But it is a feature of the profession of literature in the United States today that there has been an increasing reflection on the historical and institutional aspects of that profession. Graff's book is only one among an increasing number of books and articles on the topic. For salient examples, see Oleson and Voss (1979), Webster (1979), Weber (1982), Culler (1987), and Leitch (1988). Graff has been kind enough to read a draft of the present essay and to make many suggestions here and there for additions or changes. I have adopted most of his suggestions and express herewith my gratitude to him.

2. My remarks about the "triumph of theory" here are expanded from three paragraphs in Miller (1990, pp. 82-84).

References

Althusser, L. (1971). Ideology and ideological state apparatuses. *Lenin and philosophy* (B. Brewster, Trans., pp. 127-186). London: New Left Books.

Althusser, L. (1977). Marxism and humanism. *For Marx* (B. Brewster, Trans., pp. 219-248). London: New Left Books.

Austin, J. L. (1975). *How to do things with words* (2nd ed.). Cambridge, MA: Harvard University Press. (Originally published 1962)

Brooks, C. (1947). *Well wrought urn.* New York: Harcourt Brace.

Brooks, C., and Warren, R. P. (1938). *Understanding Poetry.* New York: Holt, Rinehart and Winston.

Culler, J. (1987). Criticism and institutions: The American university. *Poststructuralism and the question of history.* Cambridge: Cambridge University Press.

de Man, P. (1986). *The resistance to theory.* Minneapolis: University of Minnesota Press.

Derrida, J. (1983). The principle of reason: The university in the eyes of its pupils. *Diacritics, 13,* 3-20.

Derrida, J. (1984). Mochlos ou le conflit des facultés. *Philosophie, 2,* 21-53.

Derrida, J. (forthcoming). The conflict of faculties: A mochlos. In M. Riffaterre (Ed.), *Languages of knowledge and inquiry.* New York: Columbia University Press.

Franklin, P. (1988, February 13). Literary scholarship: New titles, old canon. *MLA Newsletter.*

Frantzen, A. J., & Venegoni, C. L. (1986). The desire for origins: An archaeological analysis of Anglo-Saxon studies. *Style, 20,* 142-156.

Frye, N. (1957). *Anatomy of criticism.* Princeton, NJ: Princeton University Press.

Graff, G. (1987). *Professing literature: An institutional history.* Chicago: University of Chicago Press.

Greenblatt, S. (1988). *Shakespearean negotiations: The circulation of social energy in renaissance England.* Berkeley and Los Angeles: University of California Press.

Krieger, M. (1956). *The new apologists for poetry.* Minneapolis: University of Minnesota Press.

Leitch, V. B. (1988). *American literary criticism from the thirties to the eighties.* New York: Columbia University Press.

Macksey, R., & Donato, E. (1970). *The languages of criticism and the sciences of man.* Baltimore: Johns Hopkins University Press.

Miller, J. H. (1987a). *The ethics of reading.* New York: Columbia University Press.

Miller, J. H. (1987b). The triumph of theory, the resistance to reading, and the question of the material base. *PMLA, 102,* 281-291.

Miller, J. H. (1988). Literature and history: The example of Hawthorne's "The Minister's Black Veil." *Bulletin of the American Academy of Arts and Sciences, 41,* 15-31.

Miller, J. H. (1990). *Versions of Pygmalion.* Cambridge, MA: Harvard University Press.

Oleson, A., & Voss, J. (Eds.). (1979). *The organization of knowledge in modern America: 1860-1920.* Baltimore: The Johns Hopkins University Press.

Stevens, W. (1957). *Opus posthumous.* New York: Knopf.

Weber, S. (1982). The Limits of professionalism. *Oxford Literary Review, 5,* 59-74.

Webster, G. (1979). *The republic of letters.* Baltimore: The Johns Hopkins University Press.

6

Contemporary Philosophy in the United States

JOHN R. SEARLE

Philosophy as an academic discipline in America has considerably fewer practitioners than do several other subjects in the humanities and the social sciences, such as sociology, history, English, or economics; but it still shows enormous diversity. This variety of points of view is made manifest by the fact that most professional philosophers in the United States are expected to publish original research, and their differing points of view are expressed in the large number of books published each year as well as in the many professional philosophy journals. Nearly all professional philosophers in the United States are professors at institutions of higher education, and as there are over two thousand colleges and universities and nearly all of these have philosophy departments, the number of professional philosophers is correspondingly large.

Because of this diversity, generalizations about the discipline as a whole, as I am about to make, are bound to be misleading. The subject is too vast and complex to be describable in a single article. Furthermore anyone who is an active participant in the current controversies, as I am, necessarily has a perspective conditioned by his or her own interests, commitments, and convictions. It would be impossible for me to give an "objective" account. In what follows I am not therefore trying to give a neutral or disinterested account of the contemporary philosophical scene, but rather trying to say what in the current developments seem to me important.

In spite of its enormous variety, there are certain central themes in contemporary American philosophy. The dominant mode of philosophizing in the United States is called "analytic philosophy." Without exception, the best philosophy departments in the United States are dominated by analytic philosophy, and among the leading philosophers in the United States, all but a tiny handful would be classified as analytic philosophers. Practitioners of all types of philosophizing that are not in the analytic tradition—such as phenomenology, pragmatism, existentialism, or Marxism—feel it necessary to define their positions in relation to analytic philosophy. Indeed, analytic philosophy is the dominant mode of philosophizing, not only in the United States, but throughout the entire English-speaking world, including Great Britain, Canada, Australia, and New Zealand. It is also the dominant mode of philosophizing in Scandinavia, and it is becoming more widespread in Germany, France, Italy, and throughout Latin America. I have found that I can go to all of these parts of the world and lecture on subjects in contemporary analytic philosophy before audiences that are both knowledgeable and well trained in the techniques of the discipline.

Analytic Philosophy

What, then, is analytic philosophy? The simplest way to describe it is to say that it is primarily concerned with the analysis of meaning. In order to explain this enterprise and its significance, we first need to say a little bit about its history. Although the United States now leads the world in analytic philosophy, the origins of this mode of philosophizing lie in Europe. Specifically, analytic philosophy is based on the work of Gottlob Frege, Ludwig Wittgenstein, Bertrand Russell, and G. E. Moore, as well as the work done by the logical positivists of the Vienna Circle in the 1920s and 1930s. Going further back into history, one can also see analytic philosophy as a natural descendant of the empiricism of the great British philosophers, Locke, Berkeley, and Hume, as well as the transcendental philosophy of Kant. Going back even further, one can see many of the themes and presuppositions of the methods of analytic philosophy as far back as the work of Plato and Aristotle. We can best summarize the origins of modern analytic philosophy by saying that the empiricist tradition in epistemology together with the foundationalist enterprise of Kant were tied to the methods of logical analysis and the philosophical theories invented by Gottlob Frege in the late 19th century. In the course of his work on the foundations of mathematics, Frege invented symbolic logic in its modern form and developed a comprehensive and profound philosophy of language. Although many of the details of his views on language and mathematics have been superceded, Frege's work is crucial for at least two reasons: first, by inventing modern logic, specifically the predicate calculus, he gave us a primary tool of philosophical analysis; and second, he made the philosophy of language central to the entire philosophical enterprise. From the point of view of analytic philosophy, Frege's work is the greatest single philosophical achievement of the 19th century. Fregean techniques of logical analysis were later expanded to include the ordinary language analysis of the work of Moore, Wittgenstein, and the school of linguistic philosophy that flourished in Oxford in the 1950s. In short, analytic philosophy attempts to combine certain traditional philosophical themes with modern techniques.

Analytic philosophy has never been fixed or stable, because it is intrinsically self-critical and its practitioners are always challenging their own presuppositions and conclusions. However, it is possible to locate a central period in analytic philosophy—the period comprising, roughly speaking, the logical positivist phase immediately prior to World War II and the post-war linguistic analysis phase. We can see both the pre-history and the subsequent history of analytic philosophy as defined by the central doctrines of that historical period.

In the central period, analytic philosophy was defined by a belief in two linguistic distinctions, combined with a research program. The two distinctions are, first, that between analytic and synthetic propositions, and second, that between descriptive and evaluative utterances. The research program is a traditional philosophical research program of attempting to find foundations for such philosophically problematic phenomena as language, knowledge, meaning, truth, mathematics, and so forth. One way to see the development of analytic philosophy over the past 30 years is to see it as the gradual rejection of these two distinctions, and a corresponding rejection of foundationalism as the crucial enterprise of philosophy. However, in the central period, these two distinctions served not only to identify the main beliefs of analytic philosophy, but for those who accepted them, they along with the research program, defined the nature of philosophy itself.

Analytic Versus Synthetic

The distinction between analytic and synthetic propositions was supposed to be the distinction between propositions that are true or false as a matter of definition or of the meanings of the terms contained in them (the analytic propositions) and propositions that are true or false as a matter of fact in the world and not solely in virtue of the meanings of the words (the synthetic propositions). Examples of analytic truths would be such things as "Triangles are three sided plane figures," "All bachelors are unmarried," "Women are female," "2 + 2 = 4," and so forth. In each statement, the truth of the proposition is entirely determined by its meaning. These propositions are true by the definitions of the words they contain. Such propositions can be known to be true or false a priori, and in each case they express necessary truths. Indeed, it was a characteristic feature of the analytic philosophy of this central period that terms such as "analytic," "necessary," "a priori," and "tautological" were taken to be coextensive. Contrasted with these were synthetic propositions that, if they were true, were true as a matter of empirical fact and not as a matter of definition alone. Thus propositions such as "There are more women than men in the United States," "Bachelors tend to die earlier than married men," and "Bodies attract each other according to the inverse square law" are all said to be "synthetic propositions;" and if they are true, they express a posteriori empirical truths about the real world that are independent of language. Such empirical truths are, according to this view, never necessary, but rather, contingent. And thus, for philosophers holding these views, the terms "a posteriori," "synthetic," "contingent," and "empirical" were taken to be more or less coextensive.

It was a basic assumption behind the logical positivist movement that all meaningful propositions were either analytic or empirical, as defined by the conceptions I have just stated. The positivists wished to build a sharp boundary between the meaningful propositions of science and everyday life on the one hand, and nonsensical propositions of metaphysics and theology on the other. They claimed that all meaningful propositions are either analytic or synthetic: disciplines such as logic and mathematics fall within the analytic camp; the empirical sciences and much of common sense fall within the synthetic camp. Propositions that were neither analytic nor empirical propositions, and which were therefore in principle not verifiable, were said to be nonsensical or meaningless. The slogan of the positivists was called the "verification principle," and in a simple form it can be stated as follows: All meaningful propositions are either analytic or synthetic, and those that are synthetic are empirically verifiable. This slogan was sometimes shortened to an even simpler battle cry: The meaning of a proposition is just its method of verification.

The Distinction Between Evaluative and Descriptive Utterances

Another distinction, equally important in the positivist scheme of things, is the distinction between utterances that express propositions which can be literally either true or false and utterances that are not used to express truths or falsehoods, but rather, to give vent to our feelings and emotions. An example of a descriptive statement would be, "The incidence of crimes of theft has increased in the past ten years." An instance of the evaluative class would be, "Theft is wrong." The positivists claimed that many utterances which had the form of meaningful propositions were not in fact used to state propositions that were verifiable as either analytic or synthetic, but rather were used to express emotions and feelings. Propositions of ethics look as if they are cognitively meaningful, but they are not; they have only "emotive" or "evaluative" meaning. The propositions of science, mathematics, logic, and much of common sense fall in the descriptive class; the utterances of aesthetics, ethics, and much of religion fall in the evaluative class. It is important to note that in this conception evaluative propositions are not, strictly speaking, either true or false, because they are not verifiable as either analytic or empirical.

The two distinctions are crucially related in that all of the members of the analytic-synthetic distinction fall within the descriptive class of the descriptive-evaluative distinction. The importance that these two distinctions had for defining both the character of the philosophical enterprise and the relationships between language and reality is hard to exaggerate. As a consequence of the distinction between descriptive and evaluative propositions certain traditional areas of philosophy, such as ethics, aesthetics, and political philosophy, were essentially abolished as realms of cognitive meaningfulness. Propositions in these areas were, for the most part, regarded as nonsensical expressions of feelings and emotions, not as utterances that can be, strictly speaking, either true or false. Since the aim of the philosopher is to state the truth, and since evaluative utterances cannot be either true or false, it cannot be one of the aims of philosophy to make any evaluative utterances. The philosopher might analyze the meaning of evaluative terms, and he might examine the logical relationships among these terms, but the philosopher, qua philosopher, can make no first-order evaluations in aesthetics, ethics, or politics, as these first-order evaluations are not, strictly speaking, meaningful. They may have a sort of secondary, derivative meaning, called "emotive meaning," but they lack scientifically acceptable cognitive meaning.

If the task of philosophy is to state the truth and not to provide evaluations, what then is the subject matter of philosophy? Since the methods of the philosopher are not those of the empirical sciences, since his or her methods are a priori rather than a posteriori, it cannot be his or her aim to state empirical truths about the world. Such propositions are the propositions of the special sciences. The aim of the philosopher, therefore, is to state analytic truths concerning logical relations among the concepts of our language. In this period of philosophy, the task of philosophy was taken to be the task of conceptual analysis. Indeed, for most philosophers who accepted this view, philosophy and conceptual analysis were the same. Where traditional philosophers had taken their task to be to discuss the nature of the good, the true, the beautiful, and the just, the positivist and post-positivist analytic philosophers took their task to be to analyze the meaning of the concepts, "good," "true," "beautiful," and "just." Ideally the analysis of these and other philosophically interesting concepts, such as "knowledge," "certainty," and "cause," should give necessary and sufficient conditions for the application of these concepts. They saw this task as the legitimate heir of the traditional philosophical enterprise, but an heir purged of the metaphysical nonsense and confusion that had discredited the traditional enterprise.

If we combine the assumption that philosophy is essentially a conceptual, analytic enterprise with the assumption that its task is foundational—that is, its task is to provide secure foundations for knowledge—then the consequence for the positivists is that philosophical analysis tends in large part to be reductive. That is, the aim of the analysis is to show, for example, how empirical knowledge is based on, and ultimately reducible to, the data of our experience, to so-called sense data. (This view is called "phenomenalism.") Similarly, statements about the mind are based on, and therefore ultimately reducible to, statements about external behavior (behaviorism). Necessary truth is similarly based on conventions of language as expressed in definitions (conventionalism); and mathematics is based on logic, especially set theory (logicism). In each case, the more philosophically puzzling phenomenon is shown to have a secure foundation in some less puzzling phenomena, and indeed, the ideal of such analysis was to show that the puzzling phenomena could be entirely reduced to less puzzling phenomena. Phenomenalism supposedly gave science a secure foundation because science could be shown to be founded on the data of our senses. Since the form of the reduction was analytic or definitional, statements about empirical reality could be translated into statements about sense data. Similarly, according to behaviorism, statements about mental phenomena could be translated into statements about behavior.

Within the camp of analytic philosophers who thought the aim of philosophy was conceptual analysis, there were two broad streams. One camp thought ordinary language was in general quite adequate, both as a tool and as a subject matter of philosophical analysis. The other camp thought of ordinary language as hopelessly inadequate for philosophical purposes, and irretrievably confused. These philosophers thought that we should use the tools of modern mathematical logic, both for analyzing traditional philosophical problems and, more importantly, for creating a logically perfect language for scientific and philosophical purposes in which certain traditional confusions could not even arise. There was never a rigid distinction between these two camps, but there were certainly two broad trends, one that emphasized ordinary language philosophy and one that emphasized symbolic logic. Both camps, however, accepted the central view that the aim of philosophy was conceptual analysis, and that in consequence philosophy was fundamentally different from any other discipline; they thought that it was a second-order discipline analyzing the logical structure of language in general, but not dealing with first-order truths about the world. Philosophy was universal in subject matter precisely because it had no special subject matter other than the discourse of all other disciplines and the discourse of common sense.

It is a further consequence of this conception of philosophy that philosophy is essentially a linguistic or conceptual enterprise. For that reason, the philosophy of language is absolutely central to the philosophical task. Indeed, in a sense, the philosophy of language is not only "first philosophy," but all philosophy is really a form of philosophy of language. Philosophy is simply the logical investigation of the structure of language, as language is used in the various sciences and in common life.

The Rejection of These Two Distinctions
and the Rejection of Foundationalism

Work done in the 1950s and 1960s led to the overcoming of these two distinctions (between analytic and synthetic propositions and between evaluative and descriptive utterances); and with the rejection of these two distinctions came a new conception of analytic philosophy—a conception that began to be worked out in the 1970s and 1980s and is still being developed. The rejection of these two distinctions and of the foundationalist research program led to an enormous upheaval in the conception of the philosophical enterprise and in the practice of analytic philosophers. The most obvious problem with traditional analytic philosophy was that the reductionist enterprise failed. In every case, the attempts to provide reductionist analyses of the sort proposed by the phenomenalists and behaviorists were unsuccessful, and by 1960 the lack of success was obvious. In addition, there were a series of important theoretical developments. For the sake of simplicity, I will concentrate on five major developments of the period: Quine's rejection of the analytic-synthetic distinction, Austin's theory of speech acts, Wittgenstein's criticism of foundationalism, Rawls's work in political philosophy, and the changes in the philosophy of science due to Kuhn and others.

Quine's Attack on the Analytic-Synthetic Distinction

Perhaps the most important criticism of the analytic-synthetic distinction was made by W. V. O. Quine in a famous article entitled, "Two Dogmas of Empiricism" (Quine, 1953). In this article, Quine claimed that no adequate, noncircular definition of analyticity had ever been given. Any attempt to define analyticity had always been made using notions that were in the same family as analyticity, such as synonomy and definition; consequently, the attempts to define analyticity were invariably circular. However, an even more important objection that emerged in Quine's article was this: the notion of an analytic proposition is supposed to be a notion of a proposition that was immune to revision, that was irrefutable. Quine claimed that there were no propositions that were immune to revision, that any proposition could be revised in the face of recalcitrant evidence, and that any proposition could be held in the face of recalcitrant evidence provided that one was willing to make adjustments in one's other propositions. Quine argued that we should think of the language of science as like a complex network that impinges on empirical verification only at the edges. Recalcitrant experiences at the edges of science can produce changes anywhere along the line, but the changes are not forced on us by purely logical considerations; rather we make various pragmatic or practical adjustments in the network of our sentences or beliefs to accommodate the ongoing character of our experiences. Language, in this view, is not atomistic. It does not consist of a set of sentences that can be assessed in isolation. Rather, it consists of a holistic network, and in this network sentences as groups confront experience; sentences individually are not simply assessed as true or false. (This holism of scientific discourse was influenced by the French philosopher of science, Duhem, and the view is frequently referred to as "the Duhem-Quine hypothesis.")

Most philosophers today accept some version of Quine's rejection of the analytic-synthetic distinction. Not everybody agrees with his actual argument (I, for one, do not), but now there is a general skepticism about our ability to make a strict distinction between those propositions that are true by definition and those that are true as a matter of fact. The rejection of the analytic-synthetic distinction has profound consequences for analytic philosophy, as we shall see in more detail later. At this point it is important to point out that if there is no well-defined class of analytic propositions, then the philosopher's propositions cannot themselves be clearly identified as analytic. The results of philosophical analysis cannot be sharply distinguished from the results of scientific investigation. In the positivist picture, philosophy was not one among the other sciences, but rather, stood outside the frame of scientific discourse and analyzed the logical relations between that discourse, its vocabulary, experience, and reality. Philosophers, so to speak, analyzed the relation between language and reality from the side. But if we accept Quine's rejection of the analytic-synthetic distinction, then philosophy is not something that can be clearly demarcated from the special sciences. Rather it is adjacent to and overlaps with other disciplines. It differs from other disciplines in its generality, but its propositions do not have any special logical status or special logical priority with regard to the other disciplines.

Austin's Theory of Speech Acts

The British philosopher J. L. Austin was suspicious of both the distinction between analytic and synthetic propositions and the distinction between evaluative and descriptive utterances. During the 1950s, he developed an alternative conception of language (Austin, 1962). His first observation was that there is a class of utterances which are obviously perfectly meaningful, but which do not even set out to be either true or false. A man who says, for example, "I promise to come and see you" or a qualified authority who says to a couple, "I now pronounce you man and wife" is neither reporting on nor describing a promise or a marriage, respectively. Such utterances should be thought of not as cases of *describing* or *stating*, but rather as *doing*, as *acting*. Austin baptized these utterances "performatives" and contrasted them with "constatives." The distinction between constatives and performatives was supposed to contain three features: constatives, but not performatives, could be true or false; performatives, on the other hand, although they could not be true or false, could be felicitous or infelicitous, depending on whether or not they were correctly, completely, and successfully performed; and finally, performatives were supposed to be actions, doings, performances, as opposed to mere sayings or statings. But as Austin himself saw, the distinctions so drawn did not work. Many so-called performatives turned out to be capable of being true or false, for example, warnings could be either true or false. And statements, as well as performatives, could be infelicitous. For example, if one made a statement for which one had insufficient evidence, one would have made an infelicitous statement. And finally, stating is as much performing an action as promising or ordering or apologizing. The abandonment of the performative-constative distinction led Austin to a general theory of speech acts. Communicative utterances in general are actions of a type he called "illocutionary acts."

One great merit of Austin's theory of speech acts is that it enabled subsequent philosophers to construe the philosophy of language as a branch of the philosophy of action. Since speech acts are as much actions as any other actions, the philosophical analysis of language is part of the general analysis of human behavior. And since intentional human behavior is an expression of mental phenomena, the philosophy of language and the philosophy of action are really just different aspects of one larger area, the philosophy of mind. In this view, the philosophy of language is not "first philosophy," it is a branch of the philosophy of mind. Although Austin did not live to carry out the research program implicit in his initial discoveries, subsequent work, including work by the present author, has carried this research further.

By treating speaking as a species of intentional action we can give a new sense to a lot of questions. For example, the old question, "How many kinds of utterances are there?" is too vague to answer. But if we ask "How many kinds of illocutionary acts are there?" we can give a precise answer since the question asks, "How many possible ways are there for speakers to relate propositional contents to reality in the performance of actions that express illocutionary intentions?" An analysis of the structure of those intentions reveals five basic types of illocutionary act: We tell people how things are (Assertives), we try to get them to do things (Directives), we commit ourselves to doing things (Commissives), we express our feelings and attitudes (Expressives), and we bring about changes in the world through our utterances, so that the world is changed to match the propositional content of the utterance (Declarations). (For details see Searle, 1979, 1983.)

Wittgenstein's Rejection of Foundationalism

The single most influential analytic philosopher of the 20th century, and, indeed, the philosopher whom most analytic philosophers would regard as the greatest philosopher of the century, is Ludwig Wittgenstein.

Wittgenstein (1958) published only one short book during his lifetime, which represents his early work, but with the posthumous publication of his *Philosophical Investigations* in 1953, a series of later writings began to become available. Now, we have a sizable corpus of the work he did in the last 20 years of his life. Through painstaking analysis of the use of language, particularly through analysis of psychological concepts, Wittgenstein attempts to undermine the idea that philosophy is a foundational enterprise. He asserts, on the contrary, that philosophy is a purely descriptive enterprise, that the task of philosophy is not to reform language, nor to try to place the various uses of language on a secure foundation. Rather, philosophical problems are removed by having a correct understanding of how language actually functions.

A key notion in Wittgenstein's conception of language is the notion of a language game. We should think of the words in language as like the pieces in a game. They are not to be understood by looking for some associated idea in the mind, nor some procedure of verification, nor even by looking at the object for which they stand. Rather, we should think of words in terms of their use, and referring to objects in the world is only one of many uses that words have. The meaning of a word is given by its use, and the family of uses that a group of words has constitutes a language game such as the language game we play in describing our own sensations or the language game we play in identifying the causes of events. This conception of language leads Wittgenstein to the rejection of the conception that the task of philosophical analysis is reductionist or foundationalist. That is, Wittgenstein rejects the idea that language games either have or need a foundation in something else, and he rejects the idea that certain language games can be reduced to certain other kinds of language games. The effect, Wittgenstein says, of philosophical analysis is not to alter our existing linguistic practices nor to challenge their validity, it is rather simply to describe them. Language neither has nor needs a foundation in the traditional sense.

I said that Wittgenstein was the single most influential philosopher in the analytic tradition, but there is a sense in which it seems to me he has still not been properly understood, nor have his lessons been fully assimilated by analytic philosophers. I will have more to say about his influence later.

Rawls's Theory of Justice

The conception of moral philosophy in the positivist and post-positivist phase of analytic philosophy was extremely narrow. Since, strictly speaking, according to the positivists, moral utterances could not be either true or false, there was nothing that the philosopher could say, qua philosopher, by way of making moral judgments. The task for the moral philosopher was to analyze moral discourse, to analyze the meaning and use of moral terms, such as "good," "ought," "right," "obligation," and so on. It is important to see that this conception of moral philosophy was a strict logical consequence of the acceptance of the distinction between evaluative and descriptive utterances. For if evaluative utterances cannot be either true or false, and if first-order moral discourse consists in evaluative utterances, and if the task of the philosopher is to state the truth, it follows that the philosopher, qua philosopher, cannot make any first-order moral judgments. As a philosopher, all he can do is the second-order task of analyzing moral concepts.

Some philosophers of the positivist and post-positivist period rejected this narrow conception of moral philosophy, and a series of attacks were mounted on the distinction between evaluative and descriptive utterances, including some attacks by the present author in the mid-1960s (Searle, 1964). It remained, however, for John Rawls in 1971 to reopen the traditional conception of political and moral philosophy with the publication of his book, *A Theory of Justice*. For the purposes of the present discussion, the important thing about Rawls's work was not that he refuted the traditional dichotomy of descriptive and evaluative utterances, but rather that he simply ignored it and proceeded to develop a theory of political institutions of a sort that has a long philosophical tradition which the positivists thought they had overcome. Rawls, in effect, revived the social contract theory, which had long been assumed to be completely defunct, but he did it by an ingenious device. He did not attempt, as some traditional theorists had done, to show either that there might have been an original social contract or that the participation of individuals in society involved a tacit contract. Rather, he used the following thought experiment as an analytic tool: Think of the sort of society that rational beings would agree to if they did not know what sort of position they themselves would occupy in that society. If we imagine rational beings, hidden behind a veil of ignorance, who are asked to select and agree on forms of social institutions that would be fair for all, then we can develop criteria for appraising social institutions on purely rational grounds.

The importance of Rawls for our present discussion is not whether or not he succeeded in developing new foundations for political theory, but rather the fact that his work gave rise to a renewed interest in political philosophy, and this was soon accompanied by a renewed interest in the traditional questions of moral philosophy. Moral and political philosophy had been confined to a very small realm by the positivist philosophers, and for that reason seemed sterile and uninteresting. Very little work was done in that area, but since the 1970s it has grown enormously, and is now a flourishing branch of analytic philosophy.

Post-Positivist Philosophy of Science

Throughout the positivist period the model of empirical knowledge was provided by the physical sciences, and the general conception was that the empirical sciences proceeded by the gradual but cumulative growth of empirical knowledge through the systematic application of scientific method. There were different versions of scientific method, according to the philosophers of that period, but they all shared the idea that scientific empirical propositions are essentially "testable." The most influential version of this idea is that empirical propositions are testable in the sense that they are falsifiable in principle. That is, in order for a proposition to tell us how the world is, as opposed to how it might be or might have been, there must be some conceivable state of affairs that would render that proposition false. Propositions of science are, strictly speaking, never verifiable but rather simply survive repeated attempts at falsification. Science in this sense is fallible, but at the same time it is rational and cumulative.

This picture of the history of science was very dramatically challenged in Thomas Kuhn's book *The Structure of Scientific Revolutions* (Kuhn, 1962). According to Kuhn, the history of science shows not a gradual and steady accumulation of knowledge but rather periodic revolutionary overthrows of previous conceptions of reality.

The shift from Aristotelian physics to Newtonian physics and the shift from Newtonian physics to relativistic physics are both illustrations of how one "paradigm" is replaced by another. When the burden of puzzling cases within one paradigm becomes unbearable, a new paradigm emerges and the new paradigm provides not just a new set of truths but rather a whole new way of looking at the subject matter. "Normal science" always proceeds by puzzle solving within a paradigm. Revolutionary breakthroughs, however, are not a matter of puzzle-solving within a paradigm; they are a matter of overthrowing one paradigm and replacing it with another.

Just as Kuhn challenged the picture of science as essentially a matter of a steady accumulation of knowledge, so Paul Feyerabend challenged the conception of there being a unitary rational "scientific method" (Feyerabend, 1975). Feyerabend tried to show that the history of science reveals not a single rational method but a series of opportunistic, chaotic, desperate (and sometimes even dishonest) attempts to cope with immediate problems. The lesson that Feyerabend draws from this is that we should abandon the constraining idea that there is such a thing as a single rational method that applies everywhere in science and adopt an "anarchist" view, a view according to which "anything goes." Reactions to Kuhn and Feyerabend, not surprisingly, differ enormously among analytic philosophers. Kuhn sometimes seems to be arguing that there is no such thing as the real world existing independently of our scientific theories, which it is the aim of our scientific theories to represent. Kuhn, in short, seems to be denying realism. Most philosophers do not take this denial of realism at all seriously. Even if Kuhn is right about the structure of scientific revolutions, this in no way shows that there is no independent reality that science is investigating. Again, most philosophers would accept Feyerabend's recognition of a variety of methods used in the history of science, but very few people take seriously the idea that there are no rational constraints whatever on investigation. Nonetheless, the effect of these authors has been important in at least the following respect. The positivists' conception of science as a steady accumulation of factual knowledge and of the task of the philosopher as the conceptual analysis of scientific method have given way to an attitude to science that is at once more skeptical and more activist. It is more skeptical in the sense that few philosophers are looking for the one single method that pervades every enterprise called "science." It is more activist in the sense that philosophy of science interacts more directly with scientific results. For example, recent philosophical discussions of quantum mechanics, or of the significance of Bell's theorem within quantum mechanics, reveal that it is now impossible to say exactly where the problem in physics ends and the problem in philosophy begins. There is steady interaction and collaboration between philosophy and science on such philosophically puzzling questions.

Some Recent Developments

The results of the changes I have just outlined are to make analytic philosophy on the one hand a more interesting discipline, but on the other hand a much less well-defined research project. In the way that the verification principle formed the core ideology of the logical positivists and in the way that conceptual analysis formed the core research project of the post-positivistic analytic philosopher, there is now no commonly agreed on ideological point of reference nor is there a universally accepted research program. For example, 30 years ago conceptual analysis was taken to be the heart of analytic philosophy, but many philosophers now would deny that it is the central element in the philosophical enterprise. Some philosophers, indeed, would say that the traditional enterprise of attempting to find logically necessary and sufficient conditions for the applicability of a concept is misconceived in principle. They think the possibility of such an enterprise has been refuted by Quine's refutation of the analytic-synthetic distinction, as well as by Wittgenstein's observation that many philosophically puzzling concepts do not have a central core or essence of meaning, but rather have a variety of different uses united only by a "family resemblance." Many other philosophers would say that conceptual analysis is still an essential part of the philosophical enterprise, as indeed it has been since the time of Plato's dialogues, but it is no longer seen to be the whole of the enterprise. Philosophy is now, I believe, a much more interesting subject than it was a generation ago because it is no longer seen as something separate from, and sealed off from, other disciplines. In particular, philosophy is now seen by most analytic philosophers as adjacent to and overlapping with the sciences. My own view, and I feel it is fairly widely shared, is that words like "philosophy" and "science" are in many respects misleading, if they are taken to imply the existence of mutually exclusive forms of knowledge. Rather it seems to me that there is just knowledge and truth and that in intellectual enterprises we are primarily aiming at knowledge and truth. These may come in a variety of forms, whether in history, mathematics, physics, psychology, literary criticism, or philosophy. Philosophy tends to be more general than other subjects, more synoptic in its vision, more conceptually or logically oriented than other disciplines, but it is not a discipline that is hermetically sealed from other subjects. The result is that many areas of investigation that were largely ignored by analytic philosophers of a generation ago have now become thriving branches of philosophy, such as cognitive science, the philosophy of biology, and the philosophy of economics. In what follows, I will confine my discussion to five major areas of philosophical research: cognitive science, the causal theory of reference, intentionalistic theories of meaning, truth-conditional theories of meaning, and Wittgenstein's conception of language and mind.

Philosophy and Cognitive Science

Nowhere is the new period of collaboration between philosophy and other disciplines more evident than in the new subject of cognitive science. Cognitive science from its very beginnings has been interdisciplinary in character and is in effect a joint property of psychology, linguistics, philosophy, computer science, and anthropology. There is, therefore, a great variety of research projects within cognitive science, but the central area of cognitive science, the hardcore ideology of cognitive science, rests on the assumption that the mind is best viewed on the analogy with a digital computer. The basic idea behind cognitive science is that recent developments in computer science and artificial intelligence have enormous importance for our conception of human beings. The basic inspiration for cognitive science went something like this: Human beings do information processing. Computers are designed precisely to do information processing. Therefore one way to study human cognition, and indeed perhaps the best way to study human cognition, is to study it as a matter of computational information processing. Some cognitive scientists think that the computer is just a metaphor for the human mind; others think that the human mind is literally a computer program. It is fair to say that without the computational model there would not have been a cognitive science as we now understand it.

Historically, this conception of human cognition was ideally suited to the 20th-century analytic tradition in philosophy of mind because the analytic tradition was always resolutely materialistic. It was anti-mentalistic and anti-dualistic. The failure of logical behavioralism did not lead to a revival of dualism, but to more sophisticated versions of materialism. I will now briefly summarize some of the recent developments in materialistic philosophies of mind that led to the computational theory of the mind.

The logical behaviorists' thesis was subject to many objections, most importantly the objection that it leaves out the internal mental phenomena. In science and common sense it seems more natural to think of human behavior as *caused by* internal mental states rather than the mental states as simply *consisting in* the behavior. This weakness in behaviorism was corrected by the materialist *identity thesis,* sometimes called "physicalism." According to the physicalist identity theory, mental states are just identical with states of the brain. We do not know in detail what these identities are, but the progress of the neurosciences makes it seem overwhelmingly probable that every mental state will be discovered to be identical with some brain state. In the early version of the identity thesis it was supposed that every type of mental state would be discovered to be identical with some type of physical state, but after some debate this began to seem more and more unplausible. There is no reason to suppose that only systems with neurons like ours can have mental states and indeed no reason to suppose that two human beings who have the same belief must therefore be in the same neurophysiological state. So, "type-type identity theory" naturally gave way to "token-token identity theory." The token identity theorists claimed that every particular mental state was identical with some particular neurophysiological state, even if there was no type correlation between types of mental states and types of physical states. But that only leaves open the question, "What is it that two different neurophysiological states have in common if they are both the same mental state?" To many analytic philosophers it seemed obvious that the answer to our question must be that two neurophysiological states are the same type of mental state if they serve the same *function* in the overall ecology of the organism. Mental states in this view can be defined in terms of their causal relations to input stimuli, to other mental states, and to external behavior. This view is called "functionalism." And it is a natural development from token-token identity theory.

But now the functionalist has to answer a further obvious question: "What is it about the states that gives them the causal relations that they do have?" If mental states are defined in terms of their causal relations, then what is it about the structure of different neurophysiological configurations that can give them the same causal relations? It is at precisely this point that the tradition of materialism in analytic philosophy converges with the tradition of artificial intelligence. The computer provides an obvious answer to the question I have just posed. The distinction between the software and the hardware, the program and the physical system that implements the program, provides an ideal model for how functionally equivalent elements at a higher level can be realized in or implemented by different physical systems at a lower level. Just as one and the same program can be implemented by quite different physical hardware systems, so one and the same set of mental processes can be implemented in different neurophysiological or other forms of hardware implementations. Indeed, in the most extreme version of this view, *the mind is to the brain as the program is to the hardware.* This sort of functionalism came to be called "computer functionalism," or "Turing machine functionalism," and it coincides with the strong version of "artificial intelligence" (strong AI), the version that says having a mind is just having a certain sort of program.

I have refuted strong AI in a series of articles (Searle, 1980a, 1980b). The basic idea of that refutation can be stated quite simply. Minds can't be equivalent to programs because programs are defined purely formally or syntactically and minds have mental contents. The easiest way to see the force of the refutation is to see that a system, say oneself, could learn to manipulate the formal symbols for understanding a natural language without actually understanding that language. I might have a program that enables me to answer questions in Chinese simply by matching incoming symbols with the appropriate processing and output symbols, but nonetheless I still would not thereby understand Chinese. However, although the project of computer functionalism is almost certainly a failure, the results of the enterprise are in many respects quite useful. Important things can be learned about the mind by pursuing the computer metaphor and the research effort has not necessarily been wasted. The most exciting recent development has been to think of mental processes not on the model of the conventional-serial digital computer, but rather to think of brain processes on the model of parallel-distributed processing computers. And indeed, the most exciting recent development, in my view, in cognitive science has been the development of such "neural net models" for human cognition.

In concluding this section, I want to point out that in my view the chief weakness of analytical philosophy of mind, a weakness it shares with the past three hundred years in the philosophy of mind, has been its assumption that there is somehow an inconsistency between mentalism and materialism. Analytic philosophers, along with the rest of the Cartesian tradition, have characteristically assumed that "mental" implies "nonmaterial" or "immaterial" and that "material" or "physical" implies "nonmental." But if one reflects on how the brain works, it seems that both of these assumptions are obviously false. What that shows is that our whole vocabulary, our whole terminology of mental, physical, and so forth, needs wholesale revision.

The Causal Theory of Reference

A central question in analytic philosophy of language, since Frege (and indeed in philosophy since the time of Plato), has been: How does language relate to the world? How do words hook onto things? In answering these questions, the analytic tradition characteristically had found a connection between the notion of reference and the notion of truth. An expression, such as a proper name, refers to or stands for or designates an object because associated with that name is some descriptive content, some concept of the object in question, and the object in question satisfies or fits that descriptive content. The expression refers to the object only because description is *true of* the object. This is the standard reading of Frege's famous distinction between sense and reference, between *Sinn und Bedeutung*. Expressions refer to objects in virtue of their sense and the sense provides a description, a "mode of presentation," of the object in question. Analogously with general terms, general terms are true of an object because each general term has associated with it a cluster of features and the term will be true of the object if the object in question has those features.

In the 1970s, this conception of the relation between language and reality was attacked by a number of philosophers, most prominently Donnellan (1970), Kripke (1972), and Putnam (1975). A variety of arguments were mounted against the traditional conception of meaning and reference, and the common thread running through these arguments was that the descriptive content associated with a word provided neither necessary nor sufficient conditions for its application. A speaker might refer to an object even though the associated description that he had was not true of that object; a speaker might have a description that was satisfied by an object even though that was not the object he was referring to. The most famous version of this argument was Putnam's "twin earth" example. Imagine a planet in a distant galaxy exactly like ours in every respect except that on this planet what they call "water" has a different chemical composition. It is not composed of H_2O but has an extremely complicated formula that we will abbreviate as XYZ. Prior to 1750, prior to the time when anyone knew the chemical composition of water, the people on twin earth had in their minds exactly the same concept of water as the people on earth. Nonetheless our word "water" does not refer to the stuff on twin earth. Our word "water," whether or not we knew it in 1750, refers to H_2O; and this is a matter of objective causal relations in the world that are independent of the ideas that people have in their heads. Meanings in this view are not concepts in people's heads, but objective relations in the world.

Well, if associated ideas are not sufficient for meaning, then what is? The answer given by the three authors I have mentioned is that there must be some sort of causal connection between the use of the word and the object or type of entity in the world that it applies to. Thus if I use the word "Socrates," it refers to a certain Greek philosopher only because there is a causal chain connecting that philosopher and my current use of the word. The word "water" is not defined by any checklist of features, rather "water" refers to whatever stuff in the world was causally related to certain original uses of the word "water," and these uses subsequently came to be accepted in the community and were then passed down historically through a causal chain of communication.

There is a very natural way of connecting the computer-functionalist conception of the mind with the causal theory of reference. If the mind is a computer program, and if meaning is a matter of causal connections to the world, then the way the mind acquires meanings is for the system that implements the computer program to be involved in causal interactions with the world.

Intentionalistic Theories of Meaning

Much of the best work in speech-act theory done after the publication of Austin's *How to Do Things with Words* in 1962, and the present author's *Speech Acts* in 1969, attempted to combine the insights of Paul Grice's account of meaning with the framework provided by the theory of speech acts. In a series of articles beginning in the late 1950s, Grice (1957, 1968) had argued that there is a close connection between the speaker's intentions in the performance of an utterance and the meaning of that utterance. In his original formulation of this view, Grice analyzed the speaker's meaning in terms of the intention to produce an effect on the hearer by means of getting the hearer to recognize the intention to produce that very effect. Thus for example, according to Grice, if a speaker intends to tell a hearer it's raining, then in the speaker's utterance of the sentence, "It's raining," the speaker's meaning will consist in his intention to produce in the hearer the belief that it's raining by means of getting the hearer to recognize his intention to produce that very belief. Subsequent work by Grice altered the details of this account, but the general principle remained the same: meaning is a matter of a self-referential intention to produce an effect on a hearer by getting the hearer to recognize the intention to produce that effect. Grice combined this analysis of meaning with an analysis of certain principles of conversational cooperation. In conversation, people accept certain tacit principles, which Grice calls "maxims of conversation"—they accept the principles that the speaker's remarks will be truthful and sincere (the maxim of quality), that they will be relevant to the conversational purposes at hand (the maxim of relation), that the speaker will be clear (the maxim of manner), and that the speaker will say neither more nor less than is necessary for the purposes of the conversation (the maxim of quantity).

There has been a great deal of controversy about the details of Grice's analysis of meaning, but the basic idea that there is a close connection between meaning and intention has been accepted and has proved immensely useful in analyzing the structure of certain typical speech-act phenomena. My own view is that Grice confuses the part of meaning that has to do with representing certain states of affairs in certain illocutionary modes and the part of meaning that has to do with communicating those representations to a hearer. Grice, in short, confuses communication with representation. However, the combination of an intentionalistic account of meaning, together with rational principles of cooperation, is immensely fruitful in analyzing such problems as those of "indirect speech acts" and figurative uses of language such as metaphors. So, for example, in an indirect speech act a speaker characteristically will mean something more than what he actually says. To take a simple example, in a dinner table situation a speaker who says, "Can you pass the salt?" would usually not just be asking a question about the salt-passing abilities of the hearer, he would be requesting the hearer to pass the salt. Now the puzzle is: How is it that speakers and hearers communicate so effortlessly when there is a big gulf between what the speaker means and what he actually says? In the case of a metaphor, a similar question arises: How does the speaker communicate his metaphorical meaning so effortlessly when the literal meaning of the sentence he utters does not encode that metaphorical meaning? A great deal of progress has been made on these and other problems using the apparatus that Grice contributed to the theory of speech acts.

One of the marks of progress in philosophy is that the results of philosophical analysis tend to be appropriated by other disciplines, and this has certainly happened with speech-act theory. Speech-act theory is now a thriving branch of the discipline of linguistics and the works of Austin and Grice, as well as my own, are as well known among linguists as they are among philosophers.

Truth-Conditional Theories of Meaning

Philosophers such as Quine and his former student, Donald Davidson, have always felt that intentionalistic theories of meaning, of the sort proposed by Grice (1957, 1968), Searle (1984) and others, were philosophically inadequate, because the intentionalistic notions seemed as puzzling as the notion of meaning itself and perhaps would necessarily involve linguistic meaning in their ultimate analyses. So Quine (1960) and Davidson (1984) attempted to give accounts of meaning that did not employ the usual apparatus of intentionality. The most influential version of this attempt is

Davidson's (1984) project of analyzing meaning in terms of truth conditions. The basic idea is that one knows the meaning of a sentence if one knows under what conditions it is true or false. Thus one knows the meaning of the German sentence *Schnee ist weiss*, if one knows that it is true if and only if snow is white. Now since a theory of meaning for a language should be able to state the meaning of each of the sentences of the language, and since the meanings of the sentences of the language are given by truth conditions, and since truth conditions can be specified independently of the intentionalistic apparatus, it seems to Davidson that a theory of truth (i.e., a theory of the truth conditions of the sentences) of a language would provide a theory of meaning for that language.

In order to carry out the project of explaining meaning in terms of truth, Davidson employs the apparatus of Tarski's semantic definition of truth, a definition that Tarski had worked out in the 1930s (Tarski, 1935). Tarski points out that it is a condition of adequacy on any account of truth that for any sentence s and any language L, the account must have the consequence that:

s is true in L if and only if p,

where for s can be substituted the structural description of any sentence whatever, for L, the name of the language of which s is a part, and for p, the sentence itself or a translation of it. Thus for example, in English, the sentence "Snow is white" is true if and only if snow is white. This condition is usually called "convention T" and the corresponding sentences are called "T-sentences."

Now Davidson notes that convention T employs the fact that the sentence named by s has the same meaning as the sentence expressed by p, and thus, Tarski is using the notion of meaning in order to define the notion of truth. Davidson proposes to turn this procedure around by taking the notion of truth for granted, by taking it as a primitive, and using it to explain meaning.

Here is how it works. Davidson hopes to get a theory of meaning for a speaker of a language which would be sufficient to interpret any of the speaker's utterances by getting a theory that would provide a set of axioms that would entail all true T-sentences for that speaker's language. Thus if the speaker speaks German, and we use English as a metalanguage in which to state the theory of the speaker's language, Davidson claims we would have an adequate theory of the speaker's language if we could get a set of axioms which would entail a true T-sentence stated in English for any sentence that the speaker uttered in German. Thus, for example, our theory of meaning should contain axioms which entail that the speaker's utterance *Schnee ist weiss* is true in the speaker's language if and only if snow is white. Davidson further claims that we could make this into an empirical theory of the speaker's language by proceeding to associate the speaker's utterances with the circumstances in which we had empirical evidence for supposing that the speaker held those utterances to be true. Thus, if we hear the speaker utter the sentence *"Es regnet,"* we might look around and note that it was raining in the vicinity, and we might then form the hypothesis that the speaker holds true the sentence *"Es regnet"* when it is raining in his immediate vicinity. This would provide the sort of empirical data on which we would begin to construct a theory of truth for the speaker's language.

It is important to note that we are to think of this as a thought experiment and not as an actual procedure that we have to employ when, for example, we try to learn German. The idea is to cash out the notion of meaning in terms of truth conditions, and then cash out the notion of truth conditions in terms of a truth theory for a language, a theory that would entail all the true T-sentences of the language. The empirical basis on which the whole system rests is the evidence we could get concerning the conditions under which a speaker holds a sentence to be true. If the project could in principle be carried out, then we would have given an account of meaning which employed only one intentionalistic notion, the notion of "holding true" a sentence.

Over the past 20 years, there has been quite an extensive literature on the nature of this project and how it might be applied to several difficult and puzzling sorts of sentences—indexical sentences, sentences about mental states, modal sentences, and so on. Enthusiasm for this project seems to have waned somewhat in recent years.

In my view, the central weakness of Davidson's enterprise is as follows: Any theory of meaning must explain not only what a speaker represents by his or her utterances, but also how he or she represents them, under what mental aspects the speaker represents the truth conditions. For this reason, a theory of meaning can not just correlate the speaker's utterances with states of affairs in the world, but must explain what is going on in the speaker's head that enables the speaker to represent those states of affairs under certain aspects with the utterances that the speaker makes. Thus, for example, suppose that snow is composed of H_2O molecules in crystalline form, and suppose the color white consists of light wave emissions of all wave lengths, then

> The sentence *Schnee ist weiss* is true if and only if H_2O molecules in crystalline form emit light of all wave lengths.

Now this second T-sentence is just as empirically substantiated as the earlier example,

> *Schnee ist weiss* is true if and only if snow is white.

Indeed, it is a matter of scientific necessity that the state of affairs described by the former is identical with the state of affairs described by the latter. But the former example simply does not give the speaker's meaning. The speaker might hold true the sentence *Schnee ist weiss* under these and only these conditions and not know the slightest thing about H_2O molecules and wave lengths of light. The T-sentence gives the truth conditions, but the specification of the truth conditions does not necessarily give the meaning of the sentence, because the specification does not yet tell us how the speaker represents those truth conditions. Does he represent them under the aspect of snow being white, or does he represent the truth conditions of what is the same fact in the world, under the aspect of frozen H_2O crystals emitting light of all wave lengths? Any theory that cannot give that information is not a theory of meaning.

There are various attempts to meet these sorts of objections, but, in my view, they are not successful. In the end all truth definitional accounts of meaning, like the behaviorist accounts that preceded them, end up with a certain "indeterminacy" of meaning. They cannot account in objective terms for all of the subjective details of meaning, and both Davidson and Quine have acknowledged that their views result in an indeterminacy.

Wittgenstein's Legacy

Wittgenstein's work covers such a vast range of topics, from aesthetics to mathematics, and covers these topics with so much depth and insight that it continues to be a source of ideas and inspiration for analytic philosophers and is likely to continue to be so for many years to come. I will mention only three areas.

Philosophical Psychology

One of Wittgenstein's main areas of research was psychological concepts such as belief, hope, fear, desire, want, and expect, as well as sensation concepts such as pain and seeing. Perhaps his single most controversial claim in this area concerned a private language. He claims that it would be logically impossible for there to be a language that was private in the sense that its words could only be understood by the speaker because they referred to the speaker's private inner sensations and had no external definition. Such a language would be absurd he said, because, for the application of such words, there would be no distinction between what seemed right to the speaker and what really was right. But unless we can make a distinction between what seems right and what really is right, we cannot speak of right or wrong at all, and hence we cannot speak of using a language at all. "An inner process," says Wittgenstein (Wittgenstein, 1958), "stands in need of outward criteria." Wittgenstein is here attacking the entire Cartesian tradition, according to which there is a realm of inner private objects, our inner mental phenomena, and the meanings of the words that stand for these entities are entirely defined by private ostensive definitions. No other single claim of Wittgenstein's has aroused as much controversy as the "private language argument." It continues to be a source of fascination to contemporary philosophers, and many volumes have been written about Wittgenstein's analysis of psychological concepts.

Following a Rule

Wittgenstein is part of a long tradition that emphasizes the distinction between the modes of explanation of the natural sciences and the modes of explanation of human behavior and human cultural and psychological phenomena generally. His analysis of this problem chiefly deals with the phenomenon of human behavior that is influenced or determined by mental contents and, most important, by the phenomena of human beings following a rule. What is it for a human being to follow a rule? Wittgenstein's analysis of this stresses the difference between the way that rules guide human behavior and the way that natural phenomena are results of causes. Wittgenstein throughout emphasizes the difference between causes and reasons, and he also emphasizes the role of interpretation and rule following. On the most extreme interpretation of Wittgenstein's remarks about following a rule, he is the proponent of a certain type of skepticism. According to one interpretation of Wittgenstein, he is arguing that rules do not determine their own application, that anything can be made out to accord with a rule, and consequently anything can be made out to conflict with a rule. If taken to its extreme, this would have the consequence that, logically speaking, rules do not constrain human behavior at all. And if that is right, then mental contents, such as knowledge of meanings of words or principles of actions or even beliefs and desires, do not constrain human behavior, because they are everywhere subject to an indefinite range of different interpretations. Wittgenstein's solution to this skepticism is to propose that in fact interpretation comes to an end when we simply accept the cultural practices of the community in which we are embedded. Interpretation comes to an end, and we just act on a rule. Acting on a rule is a practice, and it is one that in our culture we are brought up to perform. The skeptical implications of Wittgenstein's account of rule following are resolved by an appeal to a naturalistic solution: We are simply the sort of beings who follow culturally and biologically conditioned principles.

This interpretation of Wittgenstein is largely due to Saul Kripke (1982) and it has aroused considerable controversy. My own view is that Kripke has misinterpreted Wittgenstein in certain crucial respects, but whether or not his interpretation is correct, it has been a source of continuing discussion in contemporary philosophy.

Philosophical Skepticism

Important work on philosophical skepticism has been continued by philosophers who operate in the Wittgensteinian tradition, notably, Thomson Clarke and Barry Stroud. These philosophers point out that a really serious analysis of our use of epistemic discourse shows that the problem of skepticism cannot be overcome simply by the usual analytic philosopher's methods of pointing out that the skeptic raises the demand for justification beyond that which is logically appropriate. Clarke and Stroud (1984) claim that the problem of skepticism goes deeper than this solution will allow. Following Wittgentstein in investigating the *depth* grammar of language, they find that any solution to the skeptic's predicament, that is, any justification for our claims to have knowledge about the world, rests on a much deeper understanding of the difference between ordinary or plain discourse and philosophical discourse. Work in this line of research is continuing.

Overall Assessment

I have not attempted to survey all of the main areas of activity in contemporary analytic philosophy. Most important, I have left out contemporary work in ethics. Perhaps of comparable importance, I have had nothing to say about purely technical work done in logic. There is furthermore a thriving branch of analytic philosophy called "action theory," which should be mentioned, at least in passing. The general aim of analytic action theory is to analyze the structure of human actions in terms of the causal relations between such mental states as beliefs, desires, and intentions, and the bodily movements that are in some sense constitutive of the actions. Finally, it is worth calling attention to the fact that among analytic philosophers there has been a great revival of interest in the history of philosophy. Traditional analytic philosophers thought of the history of philosophy as mostly the history of mistakes. Some of the history of the subject could be useful for doing real philosophy; but the overall conception was that the history of philosophy had no more special relevance to philosophy than the history of mathematics to mathematics or the history of chemistry to chemistry. This attitude has changed recently, and there is now a feeling of the historical continuity of analytic philosophy with traditional philosophy in a way that contrasts sharply with the original view of analytic philosophers that they marked a radical, or indeed revolutionary break with the philosophical tradition.

It is too early to provide an assessment of the contribution that will be made by work done in philosophy at the present time, or even in the past few decades. My own view is that the philosophy of mind and social philosophy will become ever more central to the entire philosophical enterprise. The idea that the study of language could replace the study of mind is itself being transformed into the idea that the study of language is really a branch of the philosophy of mind. Within the philosophy of mind, perhaps the key notion requiring analysis is that of intentionality, that property of the mind by which it is directed at or about or of objects and states of affairs in the world independent of itself. Most of the work done by analytic philosophers in the philosophy of mind has tended to cluster around the traditional mind-body problem. My own view is that we need to overthrow this problem. In its traditional version, it was based on the assumption that mental and physical properties were somehow different from each other, and therefore, there was some special problem, not like other problems in biology, as to how both could be characteristics of the human person. Once we see that so-called mental properties really are just higher level physical properties of certain biological systems, I believe this problem can be dissolved. Once it is dissolved, however, we are still left with analyzing what is the central problem in the philosophy of language and in cognitive science, as well as the philosophy of mind, namely, the way that human representational capacities relate the human organism to the world. What is called "language," "mind," "thinking," "speaking," and "depicting" are just different aspects of this mode of relating to reality.

I believe the causal theory of reference will be seen to be a failure once it is recognized that all representation must occur under some aspect or other, and that the extensionality of causal relations is inadequate to capture the aspectual character of reference. The only kind of causation that could be adequate to the task of reference is intentional causation or mental causation, but the causal theory of reference cannot concede that, ultimately, reference is achieved by some mental device, because the whole approach behind the causal theory was to try to eliminate the traditional mentalism of theories of reference and meaning in favor of objective causal relations in the world. My prediction is that for these reasons, the causal theory of reference, although it is at present by far the most influential theory of reference, will prove to be a failure.

Perhaps the single most disquieting feature of analytic philosophy in the 50-year period that I have been discussing is that it has passed from being a revolutionary minority point of view held in the face of traditionalist objections to becoming itself the conventional establishment point of view. Analytic philosophy has become not only dominant, but intellectually respectable, and like all successful revolutionary movements, it has lost some of its vitality by virtue of its success. Given its constant demand for rationality, intelligence, clarity, rigor, and self-criticism, it is unlikely that it can succeed indefinitely, simply because these demands are too great a cost for many people to pay. The urge to treat philosophy as a discipline that satisfies emotional rather than intellectual needs is always a threat to the insistence on rationality and intelligence. However, in the history of philosophy, I do not believe we have seen anything to equal the history of analytic philosophy for its rigor, clarity, intelligence, and, above all, its intellectual content. There is a sense in which it seems to me that we have been living through one of the great eras in philosophy.

References

Austin, J. L. (1962). *How to do things with words.* Oxford: Clarendon Press.

Ayer, A. J. (1936). *Language, truth and logic.* Oxford: Oxford University Press.

Ayer, A. J. (Ed.). (1959). *Logical positivism.* New York: Free Press.

Block, N. (Ed.) (1980). *Readings in philosophical psychology* (Vols. 1 & 2). Cambridge, MA: Harvard University Press.

Davidson, D. (1980). *Essays on actions and events.* Oxford: Clarendon Press.

Davidson, D. (1984). *Inquiries into truth and interpretation.* Oxford: Clarendon Press.

Donnellan, K. (1970). Proper names and identifying description. *Synthese, 21,* 335-358.

Feigl, H., & Sellars, W. (Eds.). (1949). *Readings in philosophical analysis.* New York: Appleton-Century-Crofts.

Feyerabend, P. (1975). *Against method.* London: Humanities Press.

Grice, H. P. (1957). Meaning. *Philosophical Review.* Ithaca, NY: Cornell University Press.

Grice, H. P. (1968). Utterer's meaning, sentence-meaning, and word-meaning. *Foundations of Language, 4,* 1-18.

Haugeland, J. (Ed.). (1981). *Mind design: Philosophy, psychology, artificial intelligence.* Cambridge: The MIT Press.

Kripke, S. (1972). Naming and necessity. In G. Harman & D. Davidson (Eds.), *Semantics of natural language.* Dordrecht: D. Reidel.

Kripke, S. (1982). *Wittgenstein on rules and private language.* Cambridge, MA: Harvard University Press.

Kuhn, T. (1962). *The structure of scientific revolutions* (Foundations of the Unity of Science Series, Vol. 2, No. 2). Chicago: University of Chicago Press.

Putnam, H. (1975). The meaning of meaning. *Philosophical papers, Vol. 2: Mind, language and reality* (pp. 215-271). Cambridge: Cambridge University Press.

Quine, W. V. O. (1953). *From a logical point of view.* Cambridge, MA: Harvard University Press.

Quine, W. V. O. (1960). *Word and object.* Cambridge: The Technology Press of MIT and New York; John Wiley.

Rawls, J. (1971). *A theory of justice.* Cambridge, MA: Harvard University Press.

Russell, B. (1956). *Logic and knowledge: Essays 1901-1950*. (R. C. Marsh, Ed.) London: Allen & Unwin.

Searle, J. R. (1964, January). How to derive "ought" from "is." *Philosophical Review,* Vol. 73.

Searle, J. R. (1969). *Speech acts: An essay in the philosophy of language*. Cambridge: Cambridge University Press.

Searle, J. R. (1979). *Expression and meaning*. Cambridge: Cambridge University Press.

Searle, J. R. (1980a). Minds, brains, and programs. *Behavioral and Brain Sciences*, pp. 417-124.

Searle, J. R. (1980b). Intrinsic intentionality. *Behavioral and Brain Sciences*, pp. 450-456.

Searle, J. R. (1983). *Intentionality: An essay in the philosophy of mind*. Cambridge: Cambridge University Press.

Searle, J. R. (1984). *Minds, brains and science*. London: BBC Publications and Cambridge, MA: Harvard University Press.

Stroud, B. (1984). *The significance of philosophical skepticism*. Oxford: Clarendon Press.

Tarski, A. (1935). Der Wahrheitsbegriff in den formalisierten Sprachen. *Studia Philosophica, Vol. I*, pp. 261-405.

Wittgenstein, L. (1922). *Tractatus logico-philosophicus*. New York: Harcourt, Brace.

Wittgenstein, L. (1958). *Philosophical investigations* (G. E. M. Anscombe, Trans.). London: Basil Blackwell & Mott, Ltd. (Originally published in 1953).

7

Blurring the Disciplinary Boundaries

Area Studies in the United States

RICHARD D. LAMBERT

For this review, I define an area specialist as someone who devotes all or a substantial portion of his or her professional career to the study of another country or region of the world. Area studies is what area specialists do. For historical reasons, most Americans do not include the study of western European countries nor that of their own country in that term. If they included study of the United States, most disciplinary scholars would be area specialists. The term area specialist normally refers to a person whose work is focused on one or another country in Latin America, eastern Europe, the Middle East, Africa, South and Southeast Asia, and East Asia. As we will note, while identification of specialists tends to be with a broad region of the world, the long-term trend among area specialists in the United States is for narrower and narrower geographic specialization, moving from world region to country to section of the country.

I want to note at the outset that I will be describing area studies as the field is currently organized in the United States, where laissez-faire growth has produced almost a pure market profile of this intellectual enterprise. While I have no systematic information on area studies in other countries, it seems clear that they have not, nor should they, follow this laissez-faire model. Indeed, many of the issues central to the academic debate about area studies in the United States—the relative value of an area versus a disciplinary focus, research technology versus content, and applied versus pure research—are peculiarly American. They do not seem to trouble scholars in other countries quite so much. Moreover, in many other countries the topical and disciplinary focus of area studies is determined by the interests of public policy, in particular, a government's need to devise an effective political or economic strategy with reference to a country or region. Indeed, in many countries, much of area studies is carried out within government agencies or in separate academies that are responsible and responsive to government needs. In the United States, while there are individuals within government agencies who have a responsibility for providing policy-relevant information, the bulk of the basic research and writing on other countries is carried out in a university setting by scholars who set their independent agendas and who, in some cases, see themselves as not only independent of government policy but opposed to it. The fact that area studies in the United States is so firmly rooted in the university setting also gives it a teaching function often not found in other countries where area specialists confine their professional work to research and writing.

In the discussion that follows, there is no assumption that the American pattern is the one that other countries should adopt. In several respects, the way in which area studies is institutionalized in other countries has much to recommend it. There are, however, some trade-offs which the choice of one or another model introduces and I shall try to identify some of these. In addition, there are some intellectual issues that occur everywhere in the concentrated study of other countries, and I shall try to highlight those.

Recognizing the National Need for Specialists

As most countries discover, the development of a substantial cadre of people who are expert on other parts of the world tends not to happen without a deliberate governmental decision to create such a cadre and the investment of the resources necessary to bring it about. Without special effort, some disciplinary scholars may, over time, become a little more cosmopolitanized in their perspective, but the creation and maintenance of a corps of area specialists, particularly specialists on countries outside of their own cultural tradition, is unlikely to occur. The position in the United States preceding the 1940s is typical of the early stages of development of area studies more generally. Before World War II, only a handful of American scholars dedicated their professional lives to the study of countries outside of western Europe. It was the missionary, the ex-foreign service officer, and, to a lesser extent, the itinerant businessperson or immigrant national of the country who provided the bulk of American expertise on many countries of the world. Looking back, it was an odd view of the world that they provided for us, one which we are even now trying to supplant in the same way that many European countries must try to dislodge their colonial perspective.

In the days before World War II, the few area specialists on the faculty of universities tended to be historians, students of classical literatures, or an occasional linguist. It was American participation in World War II, and our need to deal successfully with many countries whose names most Americans had barely heard of, that created a need for a larger cadre of area specialists with a greater knowledge of the contemporary societies of the world. To meet this need, during World War II the few existing academic area specialists on each world area were brought together on a few university campuses to train students to be specialists on other countries. After the war, the military need for these programs disappeared, and many programs were dismantled. However, with help from several major private foundations, 14 organized campus-based area studies programs remained, many of them expanded versions of the small nuclei that had survived from the prewar days.

A Basic Organizational Decision

The basic decision that was made during the war, a decision whose consequences were not even debated at the time, was to place these programs on campuses and to staff them with civilian professors, even though the people being trained in these centers at that time were all military personnel. They were, in fact, enclaved and had little to do with the rest of the campus. It might have made as much sense at the time to make the area centers free-standing, governmentally supported units outside the university system. Had this decision been taken, these army specialized training units might have been the prototypes of the "academy" style of organization of area studies that is so typical in other countries.

This almost accidental decision—to fit area studies into the university context—produces structural and intellectual benefits:

- It allows the intellectual strength of the academic disciplines to constantly feed into area studies without having to cross an institutional boundary.
- It makes the recruitment of very good students and faculty more likely because they do not have to leave their academic institution to become area specialists.
- It makes a wide range of disciplines available to students to broaden their training.
- It brings into area studies a wide range of academic disciplines, particularly in the humanities, that would not be so likely to be represented in separate academies or government organizations.
- It insulates basic research from the pressure by government to make it serve exclusively government-defined national interests, or worse, to provide rationalizations for the policies of particular regimes.
- It combines area research with teaching, to the benefit of both.

Drawbacks of locating area studies on campuses, as against establishing them as free-standing entities, are equally apparent:

- It is difficult to guarantee that issues of great importance to national interest will be adequately researched.
- It is difficult to ensure that universities will provide staff positions for specialists on marginal societies or topics—for instance, central Asian languages or the Sri Lankan economy—even though the national need may be great.
- It is difficult to ensure that campus-based specialists will be able to devote their time fully to their area specialty.
- It is difficult to provide the special resources necessary to the production and maintenance of specialists when they are widely dispersed.
- It is difficult to assure that the orientation of research will be from the perspective of the home-country national interest. In general, the focus and style of university research tends to be overly scholarly and not directed to the needs of policymakers.

In different national settings, the balance of benefits and drawbacks of the university versus the academy model of area studies may be different. In any event, in the United States, the decision to sustain area specialists on university campuses was made at the very beginning.

Rapid Growth

The rapid expansion in the number of area specialists was one of the remarkable features of post-World War II academic development in the United States. In particular, the successful launching of *Sputnik* by the Soviet Union led to the creation of a major U.S. government funding program to support the training of area specialists. All of a sudden, there was another reason why American ignorance of other countries was costly. Competitors in science and technology, and more recently in business, had crept up on us unawares. Skilled other-country watchers were needed. There are now about 600 self-declared area studies programs on American campuses which range in size from only a few to hundreds of faculty and students. At the top of the range in numbers and quality, 80 or so programs annually receive support from the government. Between 1959 and 1981, these government-supported programs produced 88,000 students receiving academic degrees in language and area studies (Lambert, Barber, Jorden, Twarog, & Merrill, 1984). Over the past 5 years, the period of rapid expansion in area studies, with the possible exception of Japanese studies, has come to an end. There is now a stable corps of about 7,000 academic area specialists (Lambert, et al., 1984), scattered throughout higher education, both within and outside organized centers.

Area Studies as a Highly Differentiated Enterprise

As with most scholarly developments in the United States, the current pattern of area studies is the result of an essentially laissez-faire process of growth. To be sure, the national government has occasionally tried to reshape it, mainly through special financial support for underrepresented disciplines and unstudied countries and by attempting to raise the level of language competency. By and large, however, the growth of area studies has been the result of many separate institutional and individual decisions unrelated to government support. As a result, the very general term "area studies" hides vital differences among area studies that make generalizations extremely difficult. Accordingly, the first thing that must be done in any discussion of area studies in the United States is to unreify; it is not a single phenomenon. There are some features of area studies that are shared very generally by those who dedicate all or a large part of their scholarly careers to area studies. I will discuss the intellectual and organizational implications of some of them. However, there are many more that may apply to scholars in one set of disciplines studying one country or region and be totally inappropriate for others. As I shall show, we are dealing with a highly variegated, fragmented phenomenon, not a relatively homogeneous intellectual tradition like those in the various social science disciplines.

Elements Within Area Studies

In considering area studies and area specialists in the American context, one must look at several elements, including degree of specialization, factual knowledge, language competency, country or region of focus, and discipline. Indeed, area studies is best seen as a general rubric that covers many very different intellectual enterprises. The following classificatory variables are minimal criteria for specifying which aspect of area studies we are talking about.

Degree of Specialization

The American laissez-faire pattern has led to the diffusion of studies of other countries of the world throughout the academic world. Except for the least studied countries—for instance, Burma and Rwanda—research and writing on other areas of the world is by no means limited to a small, highly specialized, highly trained set of area specialists. As it does in its education system more generally, the United States democratizes area studies. This is not the case in many countries, as noted earlier, where a small cadre of area specialists located in special institutes outside teaching universities conduct almost all of their research on other countries. The American system raises real questions as to who an area specialist is.

In the American context, the degree of area specialization is a continuum ranging from the person who conducts a single piece of research on another country and then moves on to another topic, to the scholar whose entire professional life is devoted to research and teaching on a particular area. The latter group comprises a minority of those who are publishing scholarly work on other parts of the world. Even within organized area studies programs— the American equivalents to the academies—a substantial portion of the faculty does not spend the bulk of its professional time in an areal specialization. A recent survey (Lambert et al., 1984) indicated that even among those listed on the faculty of the federally funded language and area studies centers that train most of our future area specialists, organizationally the inner core of area studies, only 77% spent 25% or more of their professional time studying or teaching about an area.

This pattern of relatively open scholarly entry into the study of other countries has costs and benefits. On the positive side:

- It allows for the continual infusion of fresh ideas and perspectives.
- It protects against the enclaving of area studies away from main currents within academic disciplines.
- It lessens the danger of dependence on a very few people for information on other societies.
- It reduces the likelihood of a descent into very narrowly defined, country- specific esoterica.

The pattern has drawbacks as well:

- It may swamp serious scholarly work on other countries in a sea of uninformed dilettantism.
- It squanders scholarly resources that might be better spent on in-depth studies.
- It intrudes issues of the advancement of the discipline per se or of the technology of research analysis into the selection of topic and the conduct of research; the importance of the research to the understanding of a country or region becomes a secondary consideration.

- It dilutes the training of specialists so that attaining genuine expertise on a country or region is displaced by non-area-related disciplinary training.

In an attempt to minimize the negative effects of the American system of open access to scholarship on other countries, the natural tendency of those with a life-long commitment to scholarship on another area is to develop ever more rigorous criteria for defining who is truly an expert. To give some idea of the proportion of the inner core of specialists to all scholars writing on a region, we recently supplied a list of names of all scholars who had written a scholarly article on one of the countries of South Asia in the past 5 years (Lambert et al., 1981). We asked respondents to indicate those whom they considered to be experts. Of a list of 2,046 academics who had recently published scholarly work on South Asia, 762 or 37% were judged to be truly expert. South Asia, with its English-speaking tradition, may make the proportion of experts to total scholars a little lower than would be true of China or Japan, but even for those countries, the experts would probably make up a minority of those publishing scholarly work on the region.

Broad Factual Knowledge

The criteria normally used to distinguish the serious area specialist are that he or she has mastered a substantial amount of factual information on the area, has extensive and recent experience of direct contact with the area, and has a high level of competency in a language of an area. These criteria show up most clearly in the training of specialists. The attainment of the "old hand" status of someone who has accumulated a substantial amount of knowledge on a wide variety of topics relating to a country or region—somewhat akin to what an educated native would have—is built into the curriculum by enrolling the student in coursework relating to the area in a wide variety of disciplines. In practice, this is difficult to accomplish. Given the heavy disciplinary focus of much of American graduate education, it is not surprising to find that few students actually distribute the courses in their training very far from their major discipline. Nonetheless, the goal of the formal training and a great deal of the informal reading and experience that follows it is meant to provide specialists with a large base of factual knowledge about the country or region of specialization.

Indeed, it is this quality of knowing many things about another society that makes it possible for them to relate effectively to nationals of that society. Intellectually, the general knowledge base anchors their research in the reality of the local society, minimizing to the greatest extent possible the distortions arising from the superimposition of American cultural and academic perspectives on societies where they are not relevant. Some groups of area scholars—most notably South Asianists and Southeast Asianists—have gone so far as to deliberately try to import analytic concepts indigenous to the societies they study into their own analyses. A similar phenomenon occurred with the importation of the Latin American notion of *dependencia* into American scholarship on Latin America. This insistence on a locally rooted, factual base and a leaning toward indigenous conceptual constructs tends to separate these area specialists from others in their field who see their work as universal and not bound to any particular society. As area specialists point out, however, many aspects of the discipline are not universal but in reality represent hidden area studies of the United States. Out of just such symbolic battles are major academic wars spawned.

In-Country Experience

In the early years of area studies, it was possible for specialists to write and teach about other countries without ever having visited them. In the case of some closed societies to which American scholars are not admitted, this may still be the case. It is a rare area specialist now who does not make periodic visits to the country he or she is studying, and students are not permitted to complete their training without collecting data for a dissertation or enrolling in advanced language training in the country of specialization. The rhythm of academic life in the United States may limit student visits to an academic year or less (probably somewhat less than is needed to get an adequate exposure to the country), but almost every area studies student makes that visit. And becoming an "old hand" requires repeated visits over the course of a career.

The need for in-country experience, however, raises major structural and intellectual issues. In the early days of area studies in the

United States, except for a few societies from which Americans were entirely excluded, American students and professors had reasonably free access to most societies to conduct their research. Gradually, however, more and more restrictions on the topic, sponsorship, and location of research have been introduced by one government after another. From the perspective of the host country, American research became viewed increasingly as an extractive industry in which data were gathered by Americans on short trips to the country, often by hiring local academics to carry out the data collection, and then taken home to be analyzed and published in the United States. Moreover, Americans have a taste for problems, and, particularly in studies of politics and economics, their views often ran counter to those held by policymakers in the countries they studied. In addition, the American intellectual style, especially in the social sciences, was increasingly viewed as ethnocentric and irrelevant by indigenous scholars. Add to this the vagaries of official relations between particular countries and the United States, of which the student or faculty member may be the victim. Accordingly, governmental and academic screening of topics are now routinely grafted on the visa clearance process so that, today, acquiring in-country experience for a student or scholar is a complex and risky venture. Denial of access for research makes it extremely difficult for a student or a professor to continue as an area specialist.

The intellectual costs of this process are less clear but nonetheless important. Because the "safe" topics tend to lie in the humanities, there is a distinct shadow effect, which means the willingness of social sciences students and faculty to spend a career in the study of particular countries is sharply curtailed. As other countries develop their own cadres of area specialists and seek to give them in-country research experience, issues of dyadic relationships of each country with the others will require a host of complex bilateral negotiations unless a collective international solution to this problem is found.

Language Competency

An even more tangible definer of the area expert is the command of a language of the area. The need for language competency differs from one topic or discipline to another. The econometrician or the demographer who can work with published aggregate data may have less need for language competency than does the anthropologist engaged in village studies, or the student of literature. And someone studying a region where the use of English is widespread may still work effectively as an area specialist without a competency in a language of the area. However, a command of a regional language and its use in research is becoming increasingly important in area studies scholarship.

In large part as a result of the needs of area specialists, the United States has developed a very substantial capacity to teach foreign languages. In 1982, the organized area studies programs on American campuses taught 76 different languages, from Amharic to Quechua and Zulu. Since the purpose of learning most of these languages is for use by area specialists in active research within a country, there is a very heavy emphasis on attaining a high level of competency in the modern spoken version of the language, although, as we will indicate, there are still substantial residues of classical and literary languages. To emphasize the importance of the spoken vernacular, a major national effort has been made to develop a common measure of language competency independent of the number of months or years that a student has spent learning a language. This measure, referred to as the ACTFL/ILR standard, is tested in a face-to-face oral interview. It uses the educated native speaker as a reference point, and it specifies particular linguistic tasks that a student must perform to mark levels of competency. Currently, there is major debate within the United States about the relative utility of this standard for the less commonly taught languages, but in the end, some form of a common metric across all, or almost all, languages is likely to emerge.

For countries initiating or expanding area studies, the demands of the introduction of language instruction are substantial. For one thing, the number of languages to be covered is immense. For instance, to fully staff a South Asia program, all 14 official languages of India should be taught. In Africa, there are 2,000 different languages, many of which have distinctive dialects. Even to cover Latin America, in addition to Spanish and Portuguese, some of the indigenous Indian languages, such as Quechua, must be covered. American area programs, in practice, concentrate on one or two major languages spoken within their region, but all add one or two other languages of the area. Thus, from a national perspective, a large number of the major languages of the world are covered.

The time demands for learning a language vary considerably. Languages are roughly divided into four categories of difficulty for American learners. In the first category, which comprises the western European languages, such as French, Spanish, and Italian, it is estimated that 840 classroom hours are required to allow an American student to achieve a minimal ability to satisfy routine social demands and limited work requirements. In the fourth category, which includes Arabic, Chinese, Japanese, and Korean, 2,400 hours are required. Obviously, for native speakers of other languages, the levels of difficulty would be different. The basic point, however, is that in all countries the successful development of area studies requires heavy investment both by the country and by the individual in language learning, particularly for those languages most difficult to learn. More than any other feature, this commitment of language-learning time tends to distinguish area specialists.

"Ologizing" Area Studies: Country or Region

The tendency of any intellectual tradition to create guild-like definitions of qualification for membership is, of course, universal. I mention it here because it highlights one of the long-term intellectual trends in area studies in the United States. The combination of a high degree of specialization and of the need for substantial amounts of factual knowledge about a country or region, repeated visits to that country or region, and high levels of language competency results in what I would call "ologizing" area studies. That is, the study of Japan becomes the property of Japanologists; of China, Sinologists; of the Soviet Union, Sovietologists. The growth of the "ologist" tradition is most notable among specialists on areas where mastery of the regional languages is most time-consuming: East Asia, the Middle East, central Asia, and, to a lesser extent, the Soviet Union and eastern Europe.

The "ologizing" movement in area studies in the United States is a natural consequence of the need to draw a boundary separating the real experts from dilettantes, because of the fully laissez-faire recruitment system. In many other countries where the open scholarship tradition in area studies is less evident, "ologizing" may be built into institutional structures. In the United States, it is more informal; it represents a constant tension. In either case, its impact on the intellectual direction of the field can be substantial. "Ologizing" means that recruitment to area studies is constrained by high entrance requirements, both on the part of established scholars and of students. This makes the interface between area studies and its various disciplinary components more troublesome. In general, it tends to push the disciplinary balance of area specialists away from the social sciences and toward the humanities, where language competency and substantive knowledge of other countries are more likely to be found and where the fungibility of interest from one topic to another is greatest. "Ologizing" particularly tends to exclude the "hard" end of the social sciences (e.g., econometrics, demography, and political modeling), where the supremacy of analytic technique over substantive content finds its greatest adherents. On the other hand, it does make for research that is more fully informed and more reflective of the country or region being studied, which is no mean accomplishment in itself.

I have spent so much time on the "ologist" tradition because it has major policy implications for a country seeking to inaugurate or expand area studies. It must decide whether to diffuse research on other countries widely throughout the academic community in each of the relevant disciplines or to concentrate resources on producing fewer specialists with a deep, all engrossing, concentration on an area and its languages. I have no data on the situation in other countries. My impression is that, in the main, they have chosen the "ologist" model. The American experience indicates that there are advantages and costs to each approach.

Area Studies Tribes

There are, in fact, totally distinct tribes of scholars focusing on each of the major world areas, tribes that are just as distinct as the regions they study. In fact, it has been remarked that American specialists on particular countries or regions take on some of the characteristics of the societies they study. As with tribes, most of the interaction is within the tribe and not with people outside the tribe. For instance, individuals specializing on Japan and China will have relatively little to do with each other professionally, and for either to share an intellectual endeavor with a specialist on, say, Latin America or Egypt, is quite unlikely. There are some bridges. It is interesting that the metaphor of the Pacific Rim has brought together the Latin Americanists and the East Asianists in a curious coalition. Recently, a bridging scholarly group was formed to investigate the Muslim world stretching from the Middle East all the way across Asia to the east coast of China. Its research domain runs across the turfs of some of the area studies tribes. It will be interesting to see how durable the Pacific Rim coalition is. But, by and large, the world area studies tribes inhabit relatively watertight intellectual domains.

The regions represented in area studies reflect the broad cultural subdivisions of the world. The boundaries follow old colonial empires, especially the old British foreign office partitioning of the world. Afghanistan goes with India and Pakistan, but Burma goes with Southeast Asia. Africa breaks at the Sahara. East Europe follows the cold war. Central Asia is a no-man's-land. Within each of these regions, one or a few countries get the lion's share of attention: China and Japan in East Asia, Thailand and Indonesia in Southeast Asia, India in South Asia, Egypt in the Middle East, Mexico and Brazil in Latin America, the Soviet Union in East Europe, and Kenya and Nigeria in Africa. But "tribal" identification is, by and large, with the region, not the country.

One peculiarity of the American area studies tribal identifications is that western Europe is not a tribe. Most American scholars studying western European countries see themselves strictly as disciplinarians and not as area specialists. This lack of tribal identification derives in part from historical reasons. The development of area studies in the United States was principally a reaction to scarcity: Until World War II, there were very few scholars who had any knowledge of most of the non-Western world. Hence area studies grew as a deliberate attempt to increase their numbers. At the time, there was no shortage of scholars studying Europe. However, the reluctance of European specialists to identify themselves as an area studies tribe was and is, above all, an intellectual preference. They tend to see themselves as members of a discipline who happen to be studying a phenomenon in a European country. In an important sense, expatriates became the true Europeanists. It is interesting to note that now that there are more doctoral dissertations on Chinese history than on all of European history written each year in the United States, some West European scholars are developing an area studies "tribe" of their own.

There are many examples of the differences in intellectual style among the various world-area scholarly tribes. A few examples will suffice. For instance, they differ on the extent to which they reflect the tradition of the oriental classicists, the scholars rooted in the great civilizations of the past. Orientalism is not an issue at all in Latin American or African studies. While most historians in Soviet and East European studies concentrate on the pre-Bolshevik period, there are few equivalents to the classicists there. But for a scholar studying China or India, the classical civilization is part of everyday life. Serious scholars, even social scientists, must master it to make any sense of the contemporary society. Indeed, the appreciation of the relevance of history more generally to contemporary studies varies immensely from one world-area group to another.

In addition, the world-area studies groups differ considerably in terms of their penetrability, the degree to which "ologizing" has taken over. South Asian and African studies are porous. They are subject to a considerable amount of movement of scholars in and out of the fields. The heavy investment required for entry into Chinese and Japanese studies makes for tighter boundaries. Latin American studies is somewhere in between. And more generally, the distribution of academic disciplines differs from one world-area studies group to another. Latin American, African and South Asian studies belong to the social scientists, although in the latter, the humanists are beginning to shift the balance. Chinese and East European studies belong to the humanists.

The implications of the tribalization of area studies are twofold. First, each world-area studies group has its own tradition, definitions of scholarship, and set of relationships with the countries being studied and the scholars in that country. Countries seeking to expand area studies will need to tailor their effort to the special needs of the particular area they are studying.

The second implication is that the territory lying between the tribes tends to be plowed by others. It takes special effort to make the separate groups interact since their natural tendency is to reflect the more disparate features of the countries they study. Comparative studies is one route to such interaction but it has weak roots in area studies. And broader considerations of multinational affairs outside of the dyadic relationships of a particular country and the United States tend to be left to an entirely different set of academic specialists, the international relations experts. Indeed, even political science area specialists tend to focus not on the external relations of the countries they study but on their internal political systems.

Discipline

I refer to the specialists on particular world areas as distinct "tribes" because each has its own culture and social organization, and each tribe has relatively little to do with the others. This, in part, reflects differences in the regions they study, but it is also a by-product of the fact that campus-based area centers and the external funds that support them are area-specific. However, disciplinary differences in area studies are not so tribal. In part because of the structure of the field—both the organized centers and the professional organizations that bind individual specialists are defined by area, not by discipline—there is much greater contact by area specialists with other specialists across disciplinary boundaries. And students training to be specialists are usually required to take courses on their area in other disciplines than their major discipline.

Nonetheless, the basic reference point for most area specialists is the discipline in which he or she resides, and the long-term tendency is for more and more disciplinary specialization. This clear disciplinary emphasis carries over into the training of future specialists. While there is some attempt to expose area studies students to a variety of disciplines as they relate to their area of specialization, the overwhelming proportion of their training remains within a single discipline, and in the social sciences about 80% of the courses that students take are not area-specific, but are confined to their discipline.

Given the heavy disciplinary specificity of most students' training and specialists' research interests, it follows that the most useful way to think of area studies is not as an interdisciplinary tradition of scholarship but as a set of subdisciplines, each of which lies inside the larger tradition of the discipline. Looking at area studies as a set of subdisciplines, how are area specialists distributed across the academic disciplines? Table 1 provides the most recent information on the disciplinary spread of area specialists in the United States, shown separately for each world area. The data in this table present the percentage of the faculty from different disciplines in each world area studies group in all of the governmentally supported area studies programs. Only those who reported that they spent 25% or more of their professional time working on the area are included. The number at the bottom of each column is the

Table 7.1: Percentage of Area Specialists[a] by Discipline and by World Area

Discipline	Africa	East Asia	East Europe	Inner Asia	Latin America	Middle East	South Asia	Southeast Asia
History	5.0	21.9	16.7	20.0	10.0	17.6	8.0	5.2
Language-related	20.0	22.0	29.5	39.7	40.0	25.0	31.3	39.0
Arts	8.0	9.7	3.9	0.0	4.5	4.7	8.0	11.5
Religion and philosophy	3.2	0.0	5.1	2.0	0.0	0.0	5.3	8.7
Area studies	0.0	2.0	0.4	4.9	40.0	0.9	10.5	0.0
Economics	13.6	8.0	5.9	3.4	0.0	9.1	2.9	5.9
Anthropology	19.9	15.0	5.5	1.9	0.0	17.0	6.5	8.0
Sociology	5.2	3.0	3.8	2.0	0.0	8.0	2.4	2.3
Psychology	0.0	0.0	0.4	0.0	0.0	0.5	0.0	0.7
Archaeology	0.0	0.0	0.0	0.0	0.0	0.0	3.5	0.7
Geography	5.2	5.0	1.3	3.9	0.0	2.7	4.1	2.4
Political science	8.9	8.0	8.9	10.8	0.0	8.2	7.1	10.3
Applied and professional	4.0	7.6	10.8	0.0	14.1	4.1	6.0	7.3
N	100	237	204	15	219	170	122	47

[a]Faculty of government-supported, organized area programs who spend 25% or more of their professional time on the area.

total number of faculty included and gives a fair idea of the core of specialists training most of the next generation of area studies students. There are a number of more complete enumerations of specialists, including those not affiliated with centers, but the disciplinary distribution is similar (Lambert et al., 1984).

It will be noted that while area specialists are found in a large number of disciplines, in general, it can be said that the more a discipline is focused on what are presumed to be universal principles rather than substantive particularities, the less hospitable that discipline will be to area studies. Psychology, which is rapidly becoming a biology-based science, economics, with its center of gravity in econometrics and macroeconomic theory, and, to a lesser extent, sociology are less well represented than anthropology and political science, where elegant description-oriented analyses are still admired. It can be seen from Table 1 that the heart of area studies lies in just four disciplines: language and literature, history, political science, and anthropology. In all world area groups, except Southeast Asian studies, about two thirds of the specialists are in these disciplines. More than half of the Southeast Asian specialists are in these four disciplines.

It can also be seen from Table 1 that the distribution varies by world region. Inner Asian studies is so small and so recent that specialists on that area concentrate on history, language studies and a nondisciplinary concentration on the area itself. History is well represented in East Asian and East European studies. Language and literature is well represented in most world area groups. Economics is relatively strong in African, Latin American, and Southeast Asian studies, but never reaches more than 15% in any of them. Anthropology is strong in the developing societies, but sociology is underrepresented everywhere. This distribution of scholars by degree of specialization, world area, and discipline is the result of a laissez-faire system of recruitment and growth in the American university setting. Other countries may well produce very different patterns.

Area Studies as a Transdisciplinary Enterprise

It is a mistake to think of area studies as predominantly an interdisciplinary enterprise. It is not inherently interdisciplinary if that term implies individuals from different disciplines joining in a common intellectual endeavor. On most occasions, it would be better described as transdisciplinary. If one looks at the set of scholars who have a long-term professional concern with a particular part of the world, it spans many disciplines. But that does not mean that scholars from these disciplines are engaged in intellectual collaboration across disciplinary lines. They happen to be working on the same geographic area, but each scholar's perspective is usually bound by his or her discipline. Area studies programs are predominantly nondisciplinary; the topics of research are usually chosen because of their importance for an understanding of a society. The conceptual and methodological superstructure of Western- oriented disciplines is often not very helpful in this endeavor. Furthermore, area studies may be considered subdisciplinary in that research by individual area specialists, particularly in the social sciences, tends to concentrate on particular subsections, rather than the full range of specialties, within each discipline.

The organized area studies programs on American campuses, which gather together scholars from different disciplines who share the same area focus, vary in size from a dozen or so faculty members to almost one hundred. The complement of faculty members usually includes teachers of the languages of the area, as well as scholars in a substantial number of academic disciplines. Similarly, the professional organizations that serve the scholarly interests of the field are transdisciplinary, that is, they will draw members from a large number of disciplines, but members' scholarly work lies within their own disciplines.

The same picture of transdisciplinarity is evident in the training of students who will be the specialists of the future. While the area studies program in which the student is training to become a specialist will normally offer courses in many disciplines, to a student it resembles a cafeteria in which each course is anchored in its own discipline. It is often left to the student to blend them together. Indeed, most students training to be specialists take the overwhelming proportion of their courses within their major discipline, and those courses are, by and large, not related to their area. A recent survey (Lambert et al., 1984) of the transcripts of students receiving fellowships to become area specialists showed that only 6.4% of the courses that these students took were on the area in a discipline other than their own major. In fact, 75% of all the courses they took were in their major discipline, and only 25% of their courses were related to the area, no matter what discipline they were offered in. It is clear that the training of specialists still comprises a gentle graft of a little bit of area and language training on top of a largely discipline-focused graduate education. In the United States, there is no equivalent to what one finds in other countries where students are being trained almost exclusively in language and other courses related to a particular country. The American tradition of area studies as a nonenclaved endeavor with a very loose definition of expertise is reflected in the education of area specialists.

Area Studies as an Interdisciplinary Enterprise

The true blending of disciplinary perspectives in area studies is most frequent in two types of activity. The first of these is in conferences, symposia, and thematic sessions at professional association meetings. A sample of the topics of representative conferences and professional meeting sessions dealing with China, or on other world areas, which have been held in the United States within the past few years would reveal a pattern of broadly defined themes on which scholars from a number of disciplines present separate papers; taken together they make up a multidisciplinary perspective. It is the topic of the conference, symposium, or session that drives the disciplinary mix.

The second type of blurring of disciplinary boundaries occurs in the research of individual area specialists. Once again, it is the topic that blurs the disciplinary boundaries. As individual scholars work on a particular topic relating to a country or world area, their research will inevitably draw on relevant parts of other disciplines. Since topics of scholarship in area studies are often selected because they are substantively important to understanding a particular country, they frequently do not respect disciplinary boundaries. Accordingly, the work of an individual researcher becomes transdisciplinary with respect to a particular research topic.

Individual area specialists, in the course of their scholarly careers, will often take up topics that naturally belong in a variety of disciplines. If I may be permitted to cite my own career as an example, I have published separate scholarly articles and books on patterns of collective violence, the history of a political party, the economic implications of cultural values, patterns of urban morphology, industrial labor markets, social stratification, ethnic relations, religion, educational development, linguistic aspects of language skill attrition, and language policy. The style of analysis in these publications ranges from descriptive prose to highly abstract statistical modeling. Similar eclecticism can be found in the writings of many other area specialists. Intellectual interest follows the topic, and is informed, but not bound, by a particular discipline. However, in only two of these studies did I actually collaborate with a scholar in another discipline: one with an economist, not in the analysis of labor markets where it might have been expected, but in a book jointly authored on the history of economic philosophy in Asia; and the other with a linguist on language skill attrition. In the other studies, if there was some relevant intellectual apparatus that had to be borrowed from another discipline, I acquired it. My own experience is not unrepresentative of that of other area specialists.

Area Studies as a Nondisciplinary Enterprise

Such intellectual eclecticism has its costs, however. For one thing, it guides the choice of topics of research into domains where the methodological and conceptual superstructure of disciplines is less intrusive. It will be noted that the two formal collaborations in which I engaged were in disciplines with a high methodological and conceptual orientation—economics and linguistics. Moreover, both in the case of these collaborations and in other research domains I explored, the topics selected for research either fell well within my own discipline of sociology or lay in aspects of other disciplines that a generalist might have some hope of mastering.

In one sense, such research might be called interdisciplinary, since it crosses disciplinary boundaries. However, the better term is nondisciplinary, since the topics often fall in domains where the conceptual and methodological apparatus of particular disciplines is least relevant. Indeed, for area specialists working on many topics, the normal disciplinary apparatus is often seen to be narrowly culture-bound and largely irrelevant to the phenomenon being studied. Dissertation students engaged in field work often go through a sort of intellectual crisis as they discover that the conceptual baggage with which their home university faculty sent them into the field seems unsuited to the analysis of the situation in which they find

themselves. The tension is legendary between U.S.-based dissertation supervisors rooted in their disciplines and home cultures and
students working abroad, whose research must reflect the society
they are studying. It can be no less a problem for the established
scholar who often must face two ways, one toward a disciplinary
audience back home and the other toward a substantively oriented
set of colleagues sharing his or her interest in a particular country
or area. In fact, it is often this tension that makes it difficult for area
studies scholarship to feed back into the disciplines. There are
exceptions, of course. For instance, specialists on socialist economies are often as econometric in orientation as specialists on capitalist economies, and their research is increasingly changing the
nature of macroeconomic theory. However, the core of area studies in the social sciences lies in the nontechnical, frequently nondisciplinary end of the discipline.

The tendency to nondisciplinarity shows up in scholarly activities
usually thought of as interdisciplinary. This is true not only in the
topics that span disciplines but in the disciplines most often engaged in interdisciplinary ventures. I mentioned earlier that there
are four core disciplines which provide the bulk of the specialists in
area studies: anthropology, history, literature, and political science.
Not only do these disciplines predominate in area studies, but it is
precisely at their juncture point—a kind of historically informed
political anthropology, using materials in the local languages—that
much of the genuinely interdisciplinary work in area studies occurs.
History operates as a swing discipline, facing both the humanities
and the social sciences, and the principal thrust of a particular
research theme determines where in the spectrum it will lie. A large
portion of the interdisciplinary conferences, symposia, book collaborations, and jointly taught courses fall within this range of disciplines.

Most of the social science used in area studies tends to be at the
"soft" end of the spectrum because of the heavy representation of
the humanities within several of the area studies "tribes." The
research is closely tied to topics that normally fall within the humanities. Area specialists who are in the social sciences are likely to have
a great deal more contact and shared intellectual activity with
humanists than do most of their nonarea-oriented disciplinary colleagues. This tie to the humanities presents an unusual opportunity
for intellectual cross-fertilization through dialogue with scholars in

disciplines with which they normally have little contact. For instance, few nonarea- oriented social scientists engage in much intellectual interchange with classicists or philologists, who comprise an important part of area studies. Indeed, the early founders of area studies in the United States, in East Asian, South Asian, and Middle Eastern studies, tended to be scholars whose interests lay in the great classical civilizations and languages of those areas. Almost as a side activity, they occasionally wrote and taught on other aspects of China, Japan, the Middle East, and South Asia. This anchoring of area studies in the classical period with its mix of philology, textual exegesis, archaeology, religious studies, and philosophy gives it a special antiquarian patina.

The pervasive humanities aspect of much of area studies is immensely enriching. However, for many social scientists not engaged in area studies, particularly those at the "hard" end of the spectrum, the close ties of area studies with the humanities reinforces their perception that area studies is not a scientific activity. From the perspective of the "hard" social scientist, the humanities are nondisciplinary. The fact that humanistic disciplines have their own distinctive conceptual and methodological framework does not alter their judgment since these disciplines do not follow the social science paradigm. To the extent that social science research in area studies leans toward the humanities, it is likewise considered nondisciplinary.

Area Studies as a Subdisciplinary Endeavor

So far, we have talked of entire disciplines or groups of disciplines. However, area studies is not typically a blend of all aspects of its constituent disciplines. Rather, within each discipline there are particular subdisciplinary domains within which area specialists in the United States tend to work. We mentioned earlier that there are, indeed, economists who are area specialists. However, the majority (59%; Lambert et al., 1984) of them work in just three subfields: agricultural, development, and planning economics. For a discipline in a capitalist society, it is surprising that so little of the work of area specialists is in the subfields of economics which one might expect to be of interest to business leaders: Only 8.8% had to do with markets and only 6.4% with industry.

Policy Application

In fact, one of the most striking features of American area studies research is that it is only loosely related to public or private policymaking. Of 5,928 publications by area specialists between 1976 and 1981, only 16% had any policy relevance, using a very loose definition of that term. The bulk of those (55%) dealt with economic or social development within the country being studied and not with external affairs. Publications on foreign policy, broadly defined, comprised only 13.5% of all articles and books during this period, and less than 6% had any possible relevance to military or strategic planning. Whatever else it may be, American area studies is not an applied enterprise. Contrary to the view of many foreign governments and scholars, only in the most indirect sense does area studies serve the needs of the American government or American business. In many other countries, area studies is tied much more directly to the practical needs of policymakers. One of the advantages of bringing specialists together in extrauniversity centers and institutes is that collective agendas can be set to serve specific national objectives.

Under the American laissez-faire system, centralized narrowing and directing of the focus of research is not possible. Moreover, as I have indicated, the feeling of area-specific expertise tends to preserve the tribal orientation of area studies and keeps the field immensely fragmented. It can truly be said that area studies in the United States marches to a thousand different drummers.

References

Lambert, R. D., with Barber, E., Jorden, E., Twarog, L., & Merrill, M. (1984). *Beyond growth: The next stage in language and area studies*. Washington, DC: Association of American Universities.

Lambert, R. D., Baxter, C., Dimock, E., Embree, A., Ilchman, W., Talbot, P., Veit, L., Weiner, M., & Moore, S. J. (1981). *National targets for South Asian specialists*. New York: National Council on Foreign Languages and International Studies.

8

The Shaping of Business Management Thought

EARL F. CHEIT

The work of business managers is an attractive subject for research in the social sciences. The issues are interesting and important; they lend themselves well to the analytical techniques of most social science disciplines; and scholarship concerned with business management has practical consequences. Whatever its shortcomings, the field of management has not suffered from lack of scholarly attention or influence. Academics have profoundly shaped what managers do and how they do it.

Yet the essential nature of management remains elusive. More than a century of thoughtful attention to this field has not produced consensus on a definition of management, what must be taught in management education, or even on what to call the major institutions in which the subject is taught. Of the 25 American graduate institutions usually ranked among the leaders in the field, eight use

AUTHOR'S NOTE: The author is pleased to acknowledge the research assistance of Brian Shaffer, doctoral student, Graduate School of Business, University of California, Berkeley, and the helpful comments of his colleagues Robert Harris, Baruch Lev, Raymond Miles, Charles O'Reilly, and David Vogel on an earlier version of this manuscript.

"Management" in their title, 15 use "Business" or "Business Administration," and two use neither. In this chapter, "Business School"
will refer to the institution, and "Management Education" to the
curriculum.

What is generally agreed upon is that the work of managing is in
significant part an art; that its practitioners are gradually gaining
some professional status; and that although the search for a science
of management began at the turn of the century, the scientific basis
for the field is still new and fragile. It was just 12 years ago that the
Swedish Academy of Science awarded its first Nobel prize in the
field to Professor Herbert A. Simon for his work on decision making by business managers. Although his influence remains strong,
Simon's hope for "a bridge" between management theory and descriptive and empirical studies so that "theory could provide a
guide to the design of 'critical' experiments and studies" has not
been realized.

Managing is an applied activity, a doing occupation, and management thought is, of course, shaped in part by the dominant management problems. One of the earliest management problems was
identified by Chandler (1962, 1977), who demonstrated that the
need for management grew rapidly in the latter half of the 19th
century as the organizational form of American business evolved
from small family-run firms to large complex enterprises. These
large enterprises relied increasingly on the division of labor and on
geographically dispersed operating units, and depended for their
success on how well they were administered. For this new role,
owners needed a new type of employee, the salaried manager.
Business management education was designed to train this new
type of practitioner.

The current state of the field of business management education
is the product of two stages of development which started at the
turn of the century, and a third more recent one, the influence of
which is just beginning.

The Old Consensus, 1900-1940

During the first half of the 20th century, the concept of management, as well as the curriculum in business schools, represented a
consensus of the views of both practitioners and professors. Practice

played an important role in instruction, most of which was at the undergraduate level and was frequently offered by instructors from the world of business. Because the entry-level employment needs of business firms were most influential in shaping the concept of the manager and of management education, the emphasis in the curriculum was on how to perform the functions of business. And there was agreement among practitioners and professors about the importance of the principles of management, a body of thought that later became known as the classical theory.

The Classical Theory

In a careful analysis of the many principles of management formulated in this period, Massie (1965) showed that six of them are common to the work of all classical theorists. He lists:

1. *Unity of Command.* No member of an organization should receive orders from more than one superior.
2. *The Scalar Principle.* Authority and responsibility should flow in a clear unbroken line from the highest executive to the lowest operative (thus the organization chart).
3. *The Exception Principle.* Routine decisions should be delegated to subordinates, and only important and non-recurring issues should be referred to superiors.
4. *Span of Control.* The number of subordinates reporting to a superior should be limited, usually to five or six.
5. *Organizational Specialization.* Work should be divided into units with specialized activities.
6. *The Profit Center Concept.* Large organizations should be divided into integrated, self-contained units, each with its own facilities and staff support; each should operate on a competitive basis in an effort to maximize profits.

By 1940, the importance of the classical theory was firmly established. It had evolved from a workplace perspective into a management view of the firm. Based on experience and insight, the classical theory examined management in a functional framework; it identified as uniquely managerial the task of organizing; it energized managers to generalize from their experience and to contribute to a large body of work on the principles of management; it attracted, and still does, many followers among practitioners; and, in a variety of forms, became part of the university curriculum, despite the fact that it has many academic critics who feel it lacks scientific foundations.

Empirical Studies

Although the classical theory dominated management thought before World War II, two empirical studies that would later command more interest were being conducted during those years.

The first was the Hawthorne Studies, an analysis of production workers in a telephone equipment factory, by Elton Mayo (1933), a Harvard industrial psychologist and pioneer in field experiments. Mayo found that the needs and limitations of workers—rest periods, social interaction on the job, relationship to superiors—were critical elements in their productivity. His findings became the basis of the human relations approach to management. Mayo's studies imply a strong, positive relationship between worker satisfaction and productivity, an assumed relationship that has increasingly and profoundly influenced management thought and practice.

The other empirical study of great significance was the work of Berle and Means (1932), who documented the changing role of managers in business corporations. Through an analysis of corporate ownership, Berle and Means argued that in cases where stock ownership is widely distributed it becomes passive and separated from control—that control of these large corporations has effectively passed to management. As I note later, the implication of this finding of separation of ownership and control remains an important issue today. For now, we may simply observe the irony of the Berle and Means argument, namely, that managers—the new type of employee identified by Chandler—had within a half-century gained control of the firms and indeed of the owners who had hired them.

Management as Tools, Functions, Policy, and Environment

Following World War II the field of business management began to change in ways that soon destroyed the old consensus about management and management education. Before World War II, the most influential body of work about management, the classical theory and its related assumptions, was produced by practitione: s. But by the end of the 1950s, the main influence on management thought was coming from the universities where, because of the growth of business schools and their new emphasis on scholarship, the classical theory came under challenge by social scientists.

In response to critical studies by Gordon and Howell (1959) and Pierson (1959), business schools began to support research in management issues and increasingly to require that their faculty members become productive scholars. The approach to the well-established functional fields of business, such as finance and accounting, began to change, transformed by new research approaches and by the demand by business firms for graduates with specialized knowledge, the MBA. Faculty members began learning about the new fields of management science and organizational behavior and formulating new concepts of the nature of business enterprise and of the managerial process. One of the first consequences of these changes was a new challenge to the classical theory.

Challenges to the Classical Theory

The earliest challenge to the classical theory and its prescriptive reliance on principles came from the Harvard Business School, which over several decades before World War II had developed the highly influential case method of instruction, an approach that sought to simulate management problem situations and asked students to recommend solutions based on the facts of the situation.

But the most direct challenge to the classical theory came from Simon (1945). Acknowledging that practitioners' principles could be useful as general observations about managing, Simon contended that they do not withstand rigorous analysis. Using several of the most commonly accepted principles designed to increase efficiency—specialization, unity of command, and span of control—Simon demonstrated that upon careful analysis, when put into practice these principles are revealed to be mutually incompatible. For example, unity of command holds that members of an organization should be arranged in a determinate hierarchy. Simon contended that this principle is incompatible with the principle of specialization, which holds that decisions should be made at that point in the organization where they can be made most expertly. For any given situation, these two criteria need to be weighted.

Simon did not advocate discarding classical principles, but he argued that it is inappropriate to approach management by assuming the validity of any single principle. All principles should be seen rather as "criteria for describing and diagnosing administrative situations." Whether administration could aspire to be a science could only be determined by study and experience. Simon (1945) observed that at their present stage, management principles were more like proverbs, and concluded that: "Even an 'art' cannot be founded on proverbs."

In another work of enduring significance, McGregor (1960) challenged the implicit assumptions of the classical theory about the attitudes and capabilities of workers. These assumptions, which he called Theory X, are that people have an inherent dislike of work and will avoid it if they can, that they will put forth effort only if they are coerced or controlled, and that the average person wants to avoid responsibility.

McGregor said that findings from research in the behavioral sciences warranted radically different assumptions, which he called Theory Y: that expenditure of effort at work is as natural as play or rest; that people will use self-direction and self-control in working for objectives to which they are committed; that under proper conditions, people will not only accept, but will seek responsibility; that the potentialities of people are not fully used and that workers could contribute much more than they were now doing to help solve organizational problems.

This surge of academic analysis radically transformed the status of management thought. Not only was the classical theory being challenged, but new disciplines (and old ones that were being transformed) were producing new analytical approaches to management and new conceptions of the functions themselves. What had once seemed like an orderly structure of principles built from a practitioner's understanding of the actual management process now became a jumble of contending schools of thought (Koontz, 1961). A key role in this transition was played by the development of two new fields, Management Science and Organizational Behavior.

Management Science

The modern origins of Management Science were the air defense operations of Great Britain in the early stages of World War II in which groups of scientists worked to incorporate radar into the tactics and strategy of air defense operations. For this reason their work was originally called "Operations Research" (or operations analysis or systems analysis). The approach was soon applied to non-military applications. By 1960, the field, now generally known as Management Science, was firmly established in management education. It raised high expectations. Its cautious enthusiasts saw it as "the scientific arm of the executive function." Its less restrained enthusiasts saw it as the science of management. Its critics saw it as little more than pretentiousness.

The reasons for these assessments become clearer when we put them in perspective. Whereas the classical theory emphasized practice, the early advocates of management science saw in their new field the scientific basis for key top management functions. And they stimulated expectations that this scientific basis would extend generally to issues of strategy for the firm.

The logic of management science was (and is) straightforward (Simon, 1960). The performance of a system is a function of two sets of variables, those that can be controlled and those that cannot. For those that can be controlled, it is possible mathematically to find rules for the optimum values; for the variables that cannot be controlled, the researcher tries to find procedures through which to check their values. The method is to model the system and manipulate its values.

Just as it succeeded in solving complex problems in military operations, management science was successful in bringing solutions to a series of important management problems, particularly those production and operations issues of a recurring nature that are capable of definition. Aided by the computer, management science has identified the best rules for problems such as replacement (when to do maintenance), inventory (how much to have), queueing (how to schedule arrival of service), routing (selecting the best path between given points), and many others, such as production planning, quality assurance, and raw material acquisition.

The computer itself has become a subject of systems study. Management information systems (MIS) (sometimes called decision support systems) are critically important in the support of the functions of a firm. Management science has been successful in identifying the computer's best uses and its limits in performing the firm's functions.

As management science research extended into issues of decision analysis (how to make the best decision under uncertainty and/or when the result depends on decisions by others) and management strategy (how to match the firm's capabilities to a changing environment), it fostered the expectation that a true science of management was within sight. This may explain both the harsh criticism of the classical theory and the irritated responses of its defenders.

The reality is that management science has not produced a science of management. It has, however, greatly influenced management thought and practice. The distinctive contributions of management science have been made in operations issues. Its techniques have become an essential part of everyday operations in activities as varied as banking, transportation, and manufacturing. Indeed it strongly affects the operations of most large organizations. It offers growing promise in manufacturing, in simulating and monitoring automatic handling equipment. Although management science is moving into the broader field of strategy, larger systems issues have been more effectively analyzed by the other new discipline, Organizational Behavior.

Organizational Behavior

The earliest university work in Organizational Behavior appeared after World War II and gained recognition as a discipline about the same time as Management Science. The origins of the field of Organizational Behavior are usually traced to the work of Mayo (1933) and Barnard (1938), and to the writings of Weber (1947) that stimulated research on complex organizations. More than any other management discipline, Organizational Behavior represents continuity with the classical theory as it became the subject of study and critical analysis.

The model used by the discipline is that the organization is a natural social system and instrument for carrying out objectives. The field of Organizational Behavior is structured in two parts: macro and micro. Improved performance of organizations is the goal of the applied work in the field, especially in the micro-organizational behavior area. Here the research objective has been to understand and predict how individuals will behave in an organizational context. Perhaps the most significant work has been that directed to worker satisfaction and its relationship to productivity.

Although it has never been conclusively demonstrated that high worker satisfaction leads to improved productivity, the human relations approach that grew out of Mayo's work assumed that it did. Today it is accepted that the relationship is much more complex. But as in other areas of micro-organizational analysis, research is making the nature of that complex relationship increasingly clear and showing how it is related to contextual variables such as the nature of rewards and supervisory style. Organizational theorists have demonstrated that conflict is not necessarily a sign of organizational weakness; that although collaboration is essential, the process of adaptation is facilitated by conflict in organizations that have methods for its resolution.

Work in this discipline has illuminated practice by, among other things, identifying the value of informal organization, and by showing that organizations do not have goals for all major decisions, but that decisions leading to goals are made by a coalition of managers whose preferences must be reconciled by the on-going process of learning and deciding (Cyert, 1968).

Managerial concepts and practices in dealing with personnel issues have in large part been shaped by the research in this productive field. Important personnel management issues such as recruitment, training, compensation, performance evaluation, and manpower planning, among others, are the subjects of strong, continuing interest in the field.

Using an approach from anthropology, researchers in organizational behavior have conceptualized organizational learning as organizational culture. They identify the premises that shape values and behavior. The concept of organizational culture is both highly informative and useful as a source of strategy.

Research in macro-organizational behavior focuses on questions such as: Why do organizations exist? Do organizations have universal properties? To what extent do they control their own destinies? From a managerial perspective, the most productive macro studies have been those linking organizational form and business strategy. Strategy is revealed by these studies to be an intelligent adaptation to complex environmental changes. Chandler's *Strategy and Structure* (1962) was the original work. Miles and Snow (1978, 1986) have extended this work in a modern context, useful for multinational enterprise. They show that in response to global competition new organizational forms—what they call unique combinations of strategy, structure and process—are emerging.

For scholars, the most interesting issues in macro-organizational behavior have centered on why certain types of organizations survive and multiply and others fail and go out of existence. Several models have been developed. One (the population ecology model) uses a biological—Darwinian—approach, emphasizing natural selection. In contrast, the resource dependency model emphasizes adaptation. Organizations, it holds, can act to strengthen the odds on their survival.

Transformation of Older Fields

At the same time that the new fields were developing, older, simpler conceptions of management—the well-established functional fields—were also undergoing an important transformation. Finance, an offshoot from the discipline of economics at the turn of the century, is one of the oldest of the functional fields of business management. For 50 years its main concern was how corporations raise funds—an important issue, to be sure, but one that was regarded as a staff specialty because its scope limited its concerns to the practices, institutions, and instruments in financial markets.

In the 1960s, the field was transformed from corporate finance to market finance and became an integral part of management. Its focus was enlarged from the issue of raising funds to the more general concern of the wise uses of funds. It now considers how the firm should decide to commit funds and what the optimal uses of funds are. These questions extend the field from the liability and equity side of the balance sheet to the asset side, thus getting to the question of the firm's goals, that is, how can the firm act in the best interest of its shareholders? In developing answers to these questions, scholarship has had a profound impact on practice, on the role of financial institutions, and on money managers. Indeed, in the last few years, as the field has moved to the study of the micro-structure of capital markets, the time lag from professional journals to professional practice is at most a few years.

Accounting is often called "the language of business." Although its foremost function has always been stewardship, which remains important both in public auditing and within the operation of firms, the field has come to emphasize information economics, expanding its role to include providing information for all types of decisions. Using information theory, accounting research has provided an analytic framework for identifying the costs and consequences of regulation. The combination of agency and information theory suggests a role for accounting in monitoring the activity of the agent, as well as in formulating contracts. Most recently, scholars have begun to study the behavioral aspects of accounting and control.

Economic theory has played a crucial role in the development of finance and accounting. The transition to the approach of the optimal uses of funds was made possible by research using economic theory, and in both fields it has continued to be central to later developments, such as agency theory and modern accounting research.

Marketing, another functional field that began as an offshoot from economics at the turn of the century, has undergone a similar, though less dramatic, transformation. Before 1960, it was heavily vocational and, like finance, focused on documenting existing practice and the structure of markets. Its main concerns were the distribution system and methods of selling and advertising. In the 1960s, marketing began to use advanced survey and statistical techniques in order to follow what has been called the first law of marketing: "Make what people want to buy." Research has focused on how buyers form preferences and make decisions.

Market research into issues of consumer motivation and consumer behavior has required sophisticated use of statistical and psychological concepts. Although its theoretical foundations are less firm than those of finance, the field also has become an integral part of management decision making because of the growing importance of marketing strategy.

The Management Curriculum

These and other new fields and changes in the functional fields have transformed the curriculum of business schools. An analysis of the relative importance of fields of study in the required portion of the MBA curriculum in 12 institutions shows that in the academic

year 1987-1988, Management Science and Organizational Behavior
accounted for 29% of the required portion of the two year program.[1]
These two new fields were given exactly as much importance in the
curriculum as the three oldest (although now transformed) functional fields, Accounting, Finance, and Marketing. Statistics, at 9%,
had the same relative importance as one traditional functional field.

Two newer fields of study, Business and Public Policy and Policy
and Strategy, together accounted for 12%. They represent a recent
and rapidly growing concern with strategies for dealing with the
external environment of business. One, the interdisciplinary field of
Business and Public Policy, emphasizes nonmarket environmental
forces (such as legislation, regulation, and the political process), the
social role of the corporation, and ethical issues in management.
Communication was given 4% of the required course time. Last in
relative order of importance, at 2%, was Management. Most institutions have no course with this name, and when it is used, it is often
another name for Organizational Behavior. In sum, the significance
of the classical theory has been sharply reduced. In some institutions, it is no longer part of the curriculum.

What Happened to the Old Consensus?

By the beginning of the 1980s, both management thought and the
forces that shape it had changed profoundly. Although practitioner
advocates of the classical theory continue to contribute to popular
management literature, the new analytical concepts of management
are largely shaped by work performed in business schools and
universities. Whether the subject is portfolio insurance or strategic
planning, environmental scanning or marketing models, it is business school faculty members who do most of the research as well as
most of the writing. These faculty members are no longer practitioners—they are Ph.D.s. Twenty years ago they came from disciplinary
departments. Today a growing number are Ph.D.s from Business
Schools. They edit major journals; they teach future managers and
current managers who return to campuses in management development programs. And, although many companies conduct their own
management development programs, the instruction is often performed by faculty members from business schools.

This rise of academic stature has produced specialization and
increased emphasis on analytical tools and theory. Operating func-

tions, applied economics, and the classical theory have been replaced by behavioral science, applied mathematics, and financial theory. Uncertainty and growing interdependence have made strategy a key concern and enlarged the concept of the role of the manager. The concept of the manager as someone who carries out plans has been replaced by the concept of the manager as someone who makes plans and oversees their execution.

The work of practitioners now plays a role primarily outside of the university. Books such as *In Search of Excellence* (Peters & Waterman, 1982), which sought to identify the key characteristics of the best-managed business organizations in the U.S., are highly regarded among practitioners, but have relatively little influence in the MBA curriculum.

Management consultants now play an important bridging role between the new analytic concepts and practitioners. Although management consulting is as old as the field of management, its growth and expanding influence are a post-World-War-II phenomenon. While functionally driven, management consultants seek to apply the best concepts. The installation of management information systems is a current example in which the consultant must know the work of management science as well as the practical problems of the client. Consultants are important conceptualizers. They tend to be industry specialists, and a few write for academic journals.

The courses in the required portion of the current MBA curriculum can be grouped into four categories: (a) analytical tools; (b) the functional fields of business; (c) policy (the decisions made at the firm level taking into account all the functional fields); and (d) the external environment (the relationship of the firm to its social, political and legal environment). Ranked by this approach, the current curriculum gives greatest importance to analytical tools. Production as a functional field has been dropped, although, in some institutions Management Science is beginning to include it. Functions, environment, and policy follow in that order. Policy issues are given high priority in executive education, but much less emphasis in MBA programs. Before World War II, the rank order would have been: functions, environment, tools, and policy.

Although undergraduate business schools continue to flourish, the MBA has become the most important degree in the preparation of managers. Moreover, those who have earned it rise in management ranks more rapidly than those who have not. Surveys find that currently about one-fourth of senior corporate officers now have the MBA. This growing acceptance of the MBA means that men and women are, in effect, "commissioned into managerial jobs" by "getting a degree from a business school." This observation by *The Economist* concluded that, in America, "business schools perform the initiation rites common to other professions."

Given these circumstances, the required portion of the MBA program would seem to be a reasonable proxy for the academic view of the essentials of management—a view that, at the beginning of the 1980s came under sharp criticism. Its critics say that this model of management is neither coherent nor responsive to the needs of contemporary society, that the needs of management practice have outstripped management thought.

Criticism and Calls For Coherence

In the late 1950s critics of business schools deplored the dominance of their narrowly vocational orientation. By the 1980s, critics were saying that business schools' conception of management had become too academic, too theoretical. These conflicting criticisms reflect two important characteristics of business schools: (a) their dual academic and professional roles in universities and (b) the effect on the curriculum of their limited role in the certification of managers.

Unlike academic departments, in which work is judged entirely by other professors using the standards of the discipline, business schools are subject to two sets of judgments, reflecting the views of their two constituencies—one in the university, the other in professional practice. Academics expect professional schools to meet the scholarly standards of the university, whereas practitioners put highest value on competence demonstrably related to practice. The inward orientation is to theory and scholarship; the outward orientation is to applied problems and operations.

As for their limited role in certification, business schools are unusual among professional schools. Unlike Law, Medicine, Engineering, Public Health, and Architecture, where one cannot enter practice without certification by a professional school, the field of management requires neither certification nor attendance at a business school. In the absence of a certification link to practice, Business School faculty members in research universities are freer than those in other professional schools to pursue purely theoretical interests.

Moreover, many—at least one-half—of the graduates business schools initially do not enter the work force as managers; they begin their careers as accountants, analysts, and agents. Eventually many will become managers, even if only managers of specialized functions. The curriculum, much of which is devoted to these primarily staff roles, is increasingly specialized and academic, and not primarily about managing.

The new criticism of this inward orientation of business schools was triggered by a provocative article entitled "Managing Our Way to Economic Decline," by Robert H. Hayes and William J. Abernathy (1980). They argued that what passes for a sophisticated business school curriculum is, in fact, a shallow concept representing a view of the manager that encourages analytic detachment. It fails to develop the insight that comes with "hands-on" experience, and, perversely, encourages short-term cost reduction rather than long-term technological competitiveness. Hayes and Abernathy expressed a point of view that was obviously of great concern—orders for reprints set an all-time record for the 58-year-old *Harvard Business Review*. Other writers began to examine the issue. Two persuasive papers, by Harris (1984) and Teece and Winter (1984), show how reliance in the curriculum on neoclassical economic theory may contribute to the problems cited by Hayes and Abernathy.

Underlying these criticisms is a growing concern about American competitiveness. One key element of this concern is the declining rate of productivity growth; another is an apparent decline in the rate of innovation and discovery. Both are puzzling, and in the absence of other explanations, attention has focused on management.

Within four years the criticism that the wrong educational model is in use in business schools had been amplified and repeated enough that the American Assembly of Collegiate Schools of Business (AACSB) produced a study (Porter & McKibbon, 1988) of the status of management education and development. It concluded that:

- Young faculty members are too narrowly trained in their specialties.
- Research is too heavily oriented to the academic community.

- There is insufficient contact with real managerial problems.
- Insufficient attention is given to managing people and to the development of leadership.
- Insufficient attention is given to the international component of the curriculum.
- The curriculum currently lacks meaningful integration across functional areas.

Thus as management thought became solidly established in the university as part of the social sciences, it encountered the same problems as other disciplines. Its knowledge has become highly specialized and fragmented. Predictably, the AACSB study calls for more coherence in the curriculum.

Current Questions and Controversies

Since management studies draw on almost all of the social science disciplines, an all-inclusive list of current questions and controversies would be unmanageably long. Here I will briefly address six issues that reflect current research or practitioner concerns, or both.

How Significant is the Management Function?

Since the 19th century, it has been generally accepted that management is essentially a fourth factor of production. But how much does this management factor contribute to the result? Is management the difference between success and failure of firms? Of nations? A sudden change in top management will be reflected in the price of a firm's shares. Often it declines. Sometimes it rises. By market measures, management does indeed matter.

Although some organizational theorists contend that the key factors in organizational survival and advancement may be external factors over which managers have little or no control, such as environment, resources, or economic trends, it has long been an article of faith that management makes a crucial difference. "Every industrial community . . . depends for its prosperity and ultimate survival upon the knowledge and imagination of its managers," says a popular English handbook on management (Hooper, 1948). This view was advanced by Servan-Schreiber (1967) in his best selling book, *Le Défi Américain*, in which he attributed the success of American multinational firms in Europe to superior American management. Two decades later the same conclusions are being drawn about the superiority of Japanese management in explaining the economic success of Japan. Unfortunately for those who maintain that management is the main cause of shifts in national economic performance, market forces provide another explanation. The cost of capital and shifts in exchange rates also can explain shifts in the patterns of investment and trade.

Comparative studies of successful and unsuccessful firms have sharpened the issue. In a prize-winning study, Tushman, Newman, and Romanelli (1986) showed that managerial effort in reorienting firms was indeed the difference between companies that effectively coped with recent sudden environmental shifts and those that did not, and that this finding not only holds for a variety of industries but also for various countries.

Do Managers Behave Like Owners?

When Berle and Means (1932) wrote their pioneering study of the modern corporation, they described the limited role of the manager before the widespread distribution of stock. They wrote that the corporation was

> A group of owners, necessarily delegating certain powers of management, protected in their property rights by a series of fixed rules under which the management had a relatively limited play. The management of the corporation indeed was thought of as a set of agents running a business for a set of owners . . . they were strictly accountable and were in a position to be governed in all matters of general policy by their owners.

From their data on the distribution of stock ownership, Berle and Means argued that, in contrast to this description of ownership control, large corporations were in fact controlled by their managers.

Initially, Berle and Mean's argument posed an empirical question about stock ownership. Was it, in fact, so widely distributed that control had shifted from owners to managers? As evidence began to mount that the answer was "yes," researchers raised the next issue. Do managers behave differently from owners?

Research into this question suggests that in certain circumstances the answer is also "yes." The development of the social role of corporations is sometimes attributed to the managerial quest for legitimacy, given their power of self-perpetuation in corporations where shares are widely distributed. Research has produced strong evidence that firms controlled by managers are more likely to follow certain courses of conduct. In an important study, Amihud and Lev (1981) demonstrated that these firms are much more likely to carry out conglomerate mergers than are firms under ownership control. They argue that these conglomerate mergers are motivated in part by the desire of managers to diversify their career risks.

In the merger movement of the 1980s, finance specialists argued that corporate takeovers are a means to efficiency. Thus the market for corporate control provided an answer to the concern about managerial control raised by Berle and Means (1932). According to this argument, if management-controlled corporations become inefficient (fail to behave like owner-controlled corporations) that fact will be reflected in their stock prices, and they will become vulnerable to takeover by another firm that will make better use of the firm's assets (Jensen, 1984).

Today, the issue raised by Berle and Means—separation of ownership and control—is considered the classical statement of the agency problem: how to monitor performance and structure incentives to assure that the interests of managers (the agents) are aligned with those of owners (the principals). One answer, defended by some agency theorists, is the "Golden Parachute," a contract providing severance payments to managers who lose their jobs when control of the firm is changed. The justification for this arrangement is that when protected by the Golden Parachute, managers will not resist takeovers that increase the value of the owners' shares. The issues raised by separation of ownership and control proved to be of greatest interest to economists in the Chinese Academy of Social Sciences, where this chapter was discussed in a series of workshops connected with the 1988 Symposium.

Has Global Economic Interdependence Created the Need
for New Management Knowledge and Skills?

Some of the recent criticism of management education is that it fails to emphasize the management knowledge and skills that are needed for global operations, that it has not taken into account management practices that are particularly effective in the new competitive international environment. This criticism spurred a faddish interest in comparative management—especially in management practices in Japan—but that interest seems to be waning. While it produced a renewed emphasis on quality and the rediscovery of quality-control crusader, W. Edwards Deming, and his standard for "total quality control," relatively few new ideas emerged. One exception (perhaps the most successful of these new practices) is the "just-in-time" inventory practice used in Japan and now widely adopted in the United States. Development of the new flexible approaches may have been hindered by the large assembly-line solutions produced by simplistic applications of management science.

In a study of Japanese business firms, Gerlach (1987) concludes that Japanese competitive successes owe more to the alliances produced by inter-firm cooperation than to their much studied management practices within firms. His work implies that it is more important to understand industrial structure than management practices.

Many markets that were once domestic have become global. Global competition means rapid product imitation and change. It puts emphasis on the ability to innovate rapidly and the ability to capture value from technical innovation. These issues have revived interest in production, the management of technology, and international business. As I noted earlier, International Business was not a required MBA core course in the 12 institutions studied. International issues now are part of the functional fields. This reflects the widely held faculty view that, country-specific information aside, international operations demand no new management skills beyond those needed for successful competitive domestic operations.

How and When Should Management Be Taught?

One area of research that seems to have had little effect on teaching is research about what managers actually do. A growing number of studies shows that managers spend a great deal of time talking and acting. Because they work through people, interpersonal skills are extremely important to their success. These studies indicate that managing tends to be a doing, not a knowing, occupation.

Mintzberg (1975) is frequently cited. He contends that the classical theory is not supported by the facts of what managers actually do, and concludes that managerial work consists of the performance of defined series of roles.

The current MBA curriculum does not reflect these research findings. In contrast with the executive education, instruction is not tailored to the manager's task. Instead, in their MBA programs the leading business schools tend to do what they do best—train specialists in the foundations of the functions. It is left for the job and later education in management development programs to provide graduates with general management training. Since the essence of managing is making decisions, the business school view is that the best education helps future managers learn how to think, how to develop the analytical capacity to deal with problems not even known today. This argument dominates the thinking that shapes most university-based MBA programs and leads toward a more academic than professional model of instruction. While its critics complain, justifiably, that the current curriculum lacks coherence and fails to teach management (Samuelson, 1990), it is accepted by managers who place a high value on the MBA degree. Although opinion polls consistently show that business leaders believe MBA programs to be academic (perhaps too academic), their hiring practices reveal that they like the graduates and that they use the selection mechanism of educational credentials in deciding whether applicants meet job requirements.

What Are the Notable Advances and Limitations of Management Thought?

It is fair to say that in the three decades since Simon pointed out the need for empirical foundations for the classical theory, the field has made scientific progress. The strategy/structure issues, which pose the classical managerial problem, today can be analyzed in ways that warrant predictions about the ability of organizations with a given design to pursue a stated strategy. Indeed, most of the functional fields have developed a theoretical base or, at a minimum, analytical approaches to problems. The result is a high level of sophistication in research methods and significant progress in the analysis of particular problems in the functional fields.

In the area of task performance rules and routine decision making, as I noted in the discussion of Management Science, management clearly has become more scientific. Yet management studies have shown that simple decision rules are not adequate to explain the behavior of the firm, that the classical theory is in reality a set of broad guidelines whose value depends on the context.

Another notable advance is the strong interdisciplinary base of management studies. Most faculty members are trained in the social science disciplines, and the work of the functional fields draws on them, perhaps more than in any other professional field. Each of the functional fields relies on at least two of the social science disciplines.

Organizational Behavior combines the work of psychology, sociology, and more recently, in its work in organizational culture, anthropology. Psychology, statistics, and economics provide the disciplinary base for Marketing; Management Science draws on statistics, economics, and engineering.

In developing a theoretical base, Finance and Accounting have drawn heavily on economics and mathematics. Most of the functional fields now include an international element and rely on work in area studies. Business and Public Policy draws on history, law, political science, economics, sociology, and area studies.

Although the record of progress is impressive, the limitations of management thought are all too evident. First among them is the inability to answer the big questions. Thus, although Finance has made the most progress in its analysis of risk, finance theory cannot tell us how important financial decisions are made in individual firms. And although efficient market theory has enabled impressive empirical explanations of market behavior, it provides no explanation of major phenomena—for example, the drop of almost one-fourth of the value in the U.S. stock market on October 19, 1987. For the major movements of mergers and acquisitions, plausible explanations abound, but not scientific ones.

Management remains a blend of art and science. Its methods are increasingly complex, its language rational and technical. But management is still best perceived as a cluster of skills. Some are associated with science, others with daring. Fundamentally, managers succeed when they make things happen. But management thought cannot say exactly how or why.

Even so, management thought is far stronger about means than about ends. It can tell us much about how to reach an objective, but much less about the worth of the objective. A particularly vexing issue is the apparent short-term outlook of American managers and its effect on a variety of important business decisions. The decline in interest in production remains a puzzle. Key ethical issues, the fundamental justification for business and its social role, are not adequately understood.

Criticism of management and business schools reflects this two-culture problem: managers are seen as technicians, but are seen to lack the social vision and commitment to longer-term values that can command public support.

A New Consensus about Management?

Critics of current management practice generally agree that American economic problems—particularly those of productivity, the rate of technological innovation, and competitiveness—are due in part to management and the influence of business schools. The Graduate Management Admissions Council created a commission to address these issues. Its report (1990) emphasized the need for more managerial relevance in the MBA curriculum.

In a much-quoted observation on business education, Derek C. Bok (1988), President of Harvard University, endorsed a familiar theme: He blamed business schools for placing too much emphasis on analytic skills and finance, and not enough emphasis on manufacturing, production, international business, motivation of workers, and business-government relationships.

The effects of this criticism on management education are promising but still limited. There have been changes: signs of a revived interest in the functional field of production, efforts to strengthen the international dimension of the curriculum, and increased work on issues of strategy from a variety of perspectives.

These changes have potential importance, but in the leading business schools, writing and teaching are dominated by sophisticated analyses of the foundations of the functional fields. When the process of managing is addressed, the focus is still mainly on the management of the functions. Thus courses are offered in financial management or marketing management or human resources management, and now, in a few institutions, production, but rarely is there significant integration across functional fields. The AACSB study (Porter & McKibbon, 1988) calls this lack of integration "one of the most critical issues for business/management schools." Hence the calls for coherence.

At the beginning of the 1990s, business schools have reached a new peak of popularity—as measured by student interest. At the same time, however, management education is coming under increasing criticism on the ground that it has become inwardly absorbed and inadequately linked to the longer term needs of enterprise made necessary by changes in the world economy. Today, the dominant business problems are caused by external influences on the firm and by slow productivity growth. For managers, the challenge is how to deal with consequences of these new circumstances.

Under the names of policy and strategy, these broader issues have become a central concern of executive education, where the curriculum is almost wholly market driven. This approach enlarges the conception of the role of the manager from implementer and specialist to formulator of strategy for the organization. There is a growing interest in the direction of managing. As management thought is increasingly shaped by the new management problems, the prospects for coherence—a higher synthesis of art and science, an integration of the discipline—improve.

Notes

1. The 12 institutions whose curricula were analyzed by the author are: Berkeley, Carnegie-Mellon, Chicago, Columbia, Cornell, Dartmouth, Harvard, MIT, Northwestern, Stanford, UCLA, and Wharton.

References

Amihud, Y., & Lev, B. (1981, Autumn). Risk reduction as a motive for conglomerate mergers. *Bell Journal of Economics, 12*, 605-617.

Barnard, C. (1938). *Functions of the executive.* Cambridge, MA: Harvard University Press.

Berle, A., & Means, G. (1932). *The modern corporation and private property.* New York: Macmillan.

Bok, D. (1988, April). Proposals to keep the U.S. on top. *New York Times*, p. 28.

Chandler, A. (1962). *Strategy and structure: Chapters in the history of American industrial enterprise. Cambridge, MA: MIT Press.*

Chandler, A. (1977). *The visible hand: The managerial revolution in American business.* Cambridge, MA: Harvard University Press.

Cyert, R. M. (1968). Business management. In *International encyclopedia of the social sciences.* New York: Macmillan and Free Press.

Gerlach, M. (1987). Business alliances and the strategy of the Japanese firm. *California Management Review, 30*(3), 126-142.

Gordon, R. A., and Howell, J. (1959). *Higher education for business.* New York: Columbia University Press.

Graduate Management Admissions Council. (1990). *Leadership for a changing world: The future role of graduate management education.* Los Angeles: Author.

Harris, R. (1984). The values of economic theory in management education. *American Economic Review, 74*(5), 117-126.

Hayes, R., & Abernathy, W. (1980). Managing our way to economic decline. *Harvard Business Review, 58*(4), 67-77.

Hooper, F. (1948). *Management survey.* London: Pittman.

Jensen, M. (1984). Takeovers: Folklore and science, *Harvard Business Review, 62*(6), 109-121.

Koontz, H. (1961). The management theory jungle. *Academy of Management Journal, 4,* 174-188.

Massie, J. (1965). Management theory. In J. March (Ed.), *Handbook of organizations.* Chicago: Rand McNally.

Mayo, E. (1933). *The human problems of an industrial civilization.* Cambridge, MA: Harvard University Press.

McGregor, D. (1960). *The human side of enterprise.* New York: McGraw-Hill.

Miles, R., & Snow, C. (1978). *Organizational strategy, structure and process.* New York: McGraw-Hill.

Miles, R., & Snow, C. (1986). Network organizations: New concepts for new forms. *California Management Review, 28*(2), 62-74.

Mintzberg, H. (1975). The manager's job: Folklore and fact. *Harvard Business Review, 53*(4), 49-61.

Peters, T., & Waterman, R. (1982). *In search of excellence.* New York: Harper & Row.

Pierson, F. (1959). *The education of American businessmen.* New York: McGraw-Hill.

Porter, L., & McKibbon, L. (1988). *Management education and development: Drift or thrust into the 21st century.* New York: McGraw-Hill.

Samuelson, R. (1990, May 14). What good are B-schools? *Newsweek,* p. 49.

Servan-Schreiber, J. (1967). *Le Défi Américain* (The American Challenge, Ronald Steel, Trans.). New York: Atheneum.

Simon, H. (1945). *Administrative behavior.* New York: Macmillan.

Simon, H. (1960). *The new science of management decision.* New York: Harper & Row.

Teece, D., & Winter, S. (1984). The limits of neoclassical theory in management education. *American Economic Review, 74*(5), 117-126.

Tushman, M., Newman, W., & Romanelli, E. (1986). Convergence and upheaval: Managing the unsteady pace of organizational evolution. *California Management Review, 29*(3), 29-44.

Weber, M. *The theory of social and economic organization.* Glencoe, IL: The Free Press. (Original work published 1924).

9

A New Framework for Integration

Policy Analysis and Public Management

JOEL L. FLEISHMAN

Neither is it to be passed over in silence that this dedicating of colleges and societies only to the use of professory learning hath not only been an enemy to the growth of the sciences, but hath redounded likewise to the prejudice of states and governments; for hence it commonly falls out that princes, when they would make choice of ministers fit for the affairs of state, find about them such a marvellous solitude of able men; because there is not education collegiate designed to this end, when such as are framed and fitted by nature thereto, might give themselves chiefly to history, modern languages, books, and discourses of policy, that so they might come more able and better furnished to service of state.

—Francis Bacon, *Advancement of Learning, Book I*

Background

It is startling to realize that it was only 20 short years ago that what has now grown into the field of public policy analysis and management was first embodied in formal educational programs. Looking back over those two decades, one senses both amazement that the enterprise ever got under way and astonishment that so much has been accomplished in so short a span.

It all seemed to happen at once, apparently without any prearranged concert of effort. Although many of the individuals involved were known to one another, and indeed knew something of one another's general concerns about the inadequacy of training for public sector decision making, the kind of hand-wringing, morale-raising, resolve-inducing, course-setting conference that normally precedes an innovation of this character and extensiveness seems not to have taken place. Instead, within a span of 5 years starting in 1967, scholars at nine different institutions spontaneously designed a radically different kind of educational program for students wishing to prepare themselves for public sector decision-making careers. Programs of graduate study—at either the master's or doctoral level—were approved by the following institutions in the years indicated: Institute of Public Policy Studies, University of Michigan (1967); Kennedy School of Government, Harvard University (1968); Graduate School of Public Policy, University of California, Berkeley (1969); School of Urban and Public Affairs, Carnegie-Mellon University (1969); RAND Graduate Institute, now known as the RAND Graduate School (1969); the Fels Institute, University of Pennsylvania (1969), now known as the Department of Public Policy and Management; School of Public Affairs, University of Minnesota (1970); Lyndon B. Johnson School of Public Affairs, University of Texas (1970); and Institute of Policy Sciences and Public Affairs, Duke University (1971).

It is difficult to call to mind any analogous movement which managed to spring up simultaneously in nearly the same precise form in so many different institutional settings and with such uniform success. That it did so is powerful testimony to the obviousness and urgency of a need, but what that need was is not clear.

The nation was deeply divided over the Vietnam War, the civil rights movement was at its peak, and the war on poverty had begun in earnest. As a direct consequence of these and other demands for governmental action, the federal budget was badly strained by policies aimed at delivering guns and butter to the nation at the same time. As one means of both attempting to gain better control of federal expenditures and seeking the greatest possible effectiveness of such dollars as were to be spent, the Bureau of the Budget first fostered, and later mandated throughout the federal government, a system called Program Planning and Budgeting (PPBS), which was supposed to depend on careful, detailed analyses of the costs and benefits of proposed programs, with multiyear projections of costs. The analytic framework, along with the underlying economic, mathematical, and statistical techniques, had been brought into the Department of Defense by "the best and the brightest," recruited by Defense Secretary Robert McNamara during the Kennedy administration.

The application of that combination of analytic techniques to solve discrete problems of public policy had been pioneered at the RAND Corporation, principally in studies done under contract for the Department of the Air Force. The persuasiveness of those studies—especially the Strategic Basing Study—suggested to many in the governmental and scholarly communities alike that here was an entirely new way of framing public policy problems and of assessing a range of alternative solutions.

It seems to me, in retrospect, therefore, that it is not unreasonable to attribute, in a shorthand way, the origin of the public policy schools to a desire to produce a supply of "RAND-style" analysts. How else can one explain, in the absence of coordinated planning, not only the simultaneity of the programs but their substantial identity of curriculum—a curriculum that seemed to train students in precisely the analytic techniques first combined, so far as I know, by RAND researchers? It was surely the RAND paradigm which provided the framework for the analytic studies in the Department of Defense and became the basis of the growing PPBS/Policy Analyses/Planning/ Evaluation establishment in the Bureau of the Budget and the major federal departments. That establishment was instantly perceived by alert academics in key institutions as a potential market for universities to supply with graduates, a market likely to grow even larger. Moreover, it was a market for a fairly well-defined product—persons trained to do analyses like those done at RAND! Why, then, should it be a surprise to find that the RAND paradigm provided the overarching curricular framework in the new schools?

True, RAND did not furnish the complete skeleton—there was a so-called "missing chapter" in the RAND analyses which neglected to deal with the crucial political implementability issues and which academic curriculum designers took pains to remedy at the very start. But the bulk of the curriculum was indeed made up of RAND's unique framework of a combination of quantified costs and benefits, iterated and assessed alternatives, decisions sequenced into policies, and probability calculations as to likely outcomes.

To ascribe the initial idea to RAND should not and does not in any way diminish the credit due to the university-based scholars who instantly formulated an impressive curriculum grounded on that concept. Without the leadership of such scholars as Harvard's Richard Neustadt, Graham Allison, Frederick Mosteller, and Thomas Schelling, Michigan's J. Patrick Crecine, Berkeley's Aaron Wildavsky, and RAND's Charles Wolf, it seems almost certain that the RAND idea would not have spread so extensively and absolutely certain that it would not have spread so fast or be in so vigorous a state of intellectual health 20 years later.

It could not have been simply the discovery of a new way of thinking about public problems, however, that accounts for the speed and unanimity with which educational programs were created to refine and transmit that framework to new generations of students. Ideas of great promise are discovered and proclaimed virtually every day, but these usually take years to gain widespread acceptance. Aaron Wildavsky, founding Dean of Berkeley's Graduate School of Public Policy, has suggested that the proliferation of the Great Society domestic programs sparked a widespread conclusion that some reliable, generally acceptable methods and standards for evaluating their effectiveness were urgently required. This explanation is of significant consequence insofar as it provided a widely perceived reason for many universities, which normally move at a pace slower even than glacial, to feel justified in forging ahead at what must have seemed to many academic administrators as reckless speed. The Great Society had indeed spawned a legion of new agencies and programs, which triggered praise, criticism, and questions about their effectiveness. Moreover, it was also a time of widespread social protest—civil rights demonstrations by Blacks and their White supporters, urban rioting by ghetto dwellers, and persistent protests, principally by the young, about the Vietnam War and the bombing of Cambodia. Such circumstances created, I think, a sense of urgency about the need to train young people with the ideas and skills necessary to solve those and other social problems.

Even if the RAND paradigm did serve as both motivation and basis for curricular consensus, and even if the sociopolitical environment of the late 1960s and early 1970s did furnish an incentive for speedy implementation of the paradigm, there is another factor which helps to explain the speed with which the RAND paradigm was so widely adopted. It was the juxtaposition of a fresh, university-based approach, based on an intellectual framework that seemed to be working in practice, against the desultory background of existing programs in public administration. Those programs had held themselves out for about three decades as the centers of training for government service but, in fact, had not, for many years, played any significant role in the training of many of those who actually ended up in high policy-making positions in the federal government.

Public administration schools had, for the most part, been created in the wake of the "good government" movement, about 30 to 40 years earlier, with a goal of training neutrally competent personnel to serve as administrators in the government service. Very early in their history, they were led astray by their concern for neutrality. This view caused them to abjure any focus on policy, which they saw as value-laden and controversial as well as, in the then-conventional view, outside the domain of the civil service, which provided the model for what they were about. The curricular content of schools of public administration at that time was mainly applied political science, accounting, rudimentary public finance, and personnel administration. These schools were, for the most part, staffed with faculty who had come out of the underlying disciplines but had been cut off from the roots which nourished their intellectual vigor. Thus most of what they taught—that is, that which defined their courses as public administration—had become frozen as of the time the faculty separated themselves from their underlying fields, and had become merely a caricature of late-1960s political science, economics, or business administration. With courses short on sophistication, lacking in theory of any power, devoid of quantitative analysis or, indeed, rigorous analysis of any kind, generally unconcerned about costs and rarely weighing them against benefits, and always fearful of dealing with policy, public administration schools were not, by the 1960s, attracting students with any promise of attaining significant policymaking positions in government.

Even with respect to furnishing personnel for the lower levels of government, the public administration schools were swimming upstream. Most of those in government service who do, after many years in the civil service, end up in high policy-making positions in the federal, state, and local governments, were first employed by the government not as graduates of public administration schools but rather as practitioners of one or another of the established professions—about a quarter of them engineers, and other large fractions of lawyers, economists, and doctors.

Twenty years ago, the public administration schools were mainly preoccupied with the instruments of government—budgets, personnel practices, and organizational arrangements. Perhaps the most exciting idea which animated the new public policy schools was the opportunity to focus not on the means whereby government acts but on the ends to which government power may be put. That shift from means to ends freed students and faculty to consider entirely new ideas about policies and programs. Even as the new public policy analysis thereby shifted the focus from means to ends, it simultaneously raised the standing of these new creatures called policy analysts. By virtue of the prestige of quantitative analysis in the universities, the analysts were provided a much stronger and broader platform of methodological expertise from which to challenge the traditional substantive expertise of the career bureaucrats.

The consequence was to make policy analysis a powerful instrument with which to challenge the current enterprise and the prevailing conventional wisdom. In creating such potential for effective action at high levels, policy analysis brought to the governmental enterprise young people who, by temperament, background and training, were quite different from those who came from traditional public administration. These new policy analysts were, by definition, skeptical of received solutions and imaginative in generating alternatives. It must be acknowledged, therefore, that at least some of the energy which powered the creation of the public policy schools, and the growing attraction of students to them, came from the possibility for students to enter the professional world of government decision making with some heightened standing, with the standing, as it were, of intellectuals.

When one considers the combination of pressing social and governmental problems, the apparent lack of an adequate source of training in the skills to solve them, and the sudden arrival on the public landscape of a powerful-seeming package of skills and theory already being put to use in some parts of government, the sudden creation of nearly a dozen new schools of public policy seems not quite so inexplicable. Even that concatenation of circumstances, however, did not suffice to ensure the exact replication in those universities of the RAND paradigm, as we shall see from the ensuing discussion of the original public policy curriculum.

The Original Curriculum in Its Present Form

While the new schools went initially by a variety of names—"public policy," "public affairs," and "public policy analysis" were most common—the field quickly became known as "Public Policy." No one, so far as I know, has claimed authorship of that combination of words. Yet, irrespective of who coined the name, Public Policy very quickly acquired a specific meaning in the context of educational programs, a meaning that was frequently underscored to differentiate the new schools from the older public administration ones. That underscoring undoubtedly annoyed the faculties and graduates of the public administration schools, which is regrettable. But it was then thought necessary to establish a separate identity for the fledgling schools, a definition of the distinctiveness of the educational product they planned on producing.

The curriculum was, and is, markedly different from that of the public administration schools. What is first noticeable about the Public Policy curriculum is that all students must take the same combination of courses during the first year and a core of the same courses during the second year. It is, in short, a substantially required curriculum, with all students taking the same methods and theory courses, but leaving some choice among electives which, by and large, focus on the application of the theory and methods to particular areas of policy, such as international security policy, energy policy, or health financing. Also required is working as an intern or apprentice for a government official or a not-for-profit decision maker for a short period of time, usually during the summer.

A rigid list of prescribed courses is precisely what students have usually encountered in law schools and medical schools and increasingly find in business schools. It was, however, just the opposite of the cafeteria approach which prevailed in schools of public administration, and, indeed, in most graduate departments of political science. It is surely worth remembering, too, that at the very time the new Public Policy curriculum was adopting an inflexible set of requirements, many of the same universities were going through the agony of relaxing, in response to student demonstrations and protests in the name of "relevance," the course requirements theretofore imposed on undergraduates. Is that an irony, or was it, as I believe to have been the case, intended as a statement of what the founding fathers of Public Policy believe all education to be about—the commitment of an educational institution to a vision of particular skills, theory, and knowledge which students ought to know whether they realize it or not? That is why, perhaps, one of my Duke colleagues, Bruce Payne, calls "Public Policy" the only legitimate university response to the student demand for relevance. It provided relevance at the price of exacting standards.

The founders of Public Policy had such a vision and did not hesitate to embody it in required courses. The wisdom of their selection of subject matter has proved itself in the durability of the curriculum. It has not changed in any significant way from its first formulation 20 years ago, and, to the extent that there have been any changes, so far as I can tell, every one of them has grown organically out of, and continues to be substantially related to, subject matter that is found in the original course descriptions. As the primary interest of those reading this article centers on today's practices rather than yesterday's history, contemporary course descriptions seem more appropriate here.

Because the overarching intellectual framework of public policy is that of economics, with its concern for production functions of producers and consumers and its insistence on maximizing both resource efficiency—the biggest "bang for a buck"—and resource effectiveness—the highest and best use of a given resource—every program requires substantial coursework in microeconomics and some (Boston University, Carnegie-Mellon, George Washington, Maryland, Princeton, RAND, SUNY Albany, and Washington) also require lesser doses of macroeconomics (Friedman, 1987).

In their syllabus for Microeconomics I, the instructors at the RAND Graduate School explain the course objectives as follows:

> The course develops the methods of microeconomics which is the study of economic agents (buyers, producers, and sellers), how they act when facing constraints, and how they interact with one another. The underpinnings of demand and supply, the exceptions to this

model, and the analytical tools used to apply microeconomics to questions of public policy are developed. . . . The nature of benefits and costs and the tools of optimization and equilibrium analysis are emphasized in this development. An introduction to the effect of uncertainty on the traditional model is also included. Although this course emphasizes tools and methods, examples from national security economics, health economics, environmental policy, and other applied areas are used to illustrate the microeconomic paradigm and its exceptions. (Cave & Hildebrandt, 1986, p. 1)

All Public Policy schools do not teach precisely the same topics in microeconomics or the same number of courses as does the RAND Graduate School, but all require courses that substantially cover most of these concepts and tools.

As critical as the economic cast of mind is to the field of Public Policy, an even more salient characteristic is the insistence on training students to understand, interpret, use, and frequently actually carry out quantitative analysis at some reasonable level of sophistication. In the view of both critics and admirers alike, it is the quantitative stress that is the distinguishing hallmark of the Public Policy schools. The critics fault it for what such quantitative analysis leaves out—that which is *un*quantifiable—and the admirers praise it for giving policymakers a solid handle to grasp in thinking about the costs, benefits, and risks of proposed policies. Whether admired or criticized, quantitative analysis has been a central part of the curriculum from the beginning.

What students have encountered has been some combination, varying from school to school, of two basic kinds of quantitative methods. One group of methods deals with modeling and maximization, essentially providing the means and images to teach students how to maximize given objectives. The other basket of quantitative methods contains those used for making inferences from experience—experimental design, regression, and statistics.

An introductory note in the syllabus for the course taught at the Harvard University Kennedy School of Government in 1985 outlines a typical approach to the teaching of quantitative analysis:

The goal of Empirical Analysis is to equip Public Policy students with an intuitive understanding of the tools of data analysis and statistical inference as they are used in policy application. Our approach is to learn by doing. Many Public Policy students will directly use the

techniques we explore in other courses, independent work, and in
subsequent employment. In addition, virtually all of our students will
encounter policy arguments that rely on empirical analysis, and will
need to be able to evaluate their appropriateness. . . .

   We expect all students in the course to develop a basic facility for
conducting and especially interpreting statistical analyses. We rely on
some mathematical language and techniques, but attempt to develop
an intuition about appropriate application. (Bloom & Boersch-Supan,
1985, p. 1)

While efficiency and effectiveness may be the standards of judgment and the methods of analysis may be mathematical, the settings
out of which *public* policy arises, in which it usually is made, and to
which it always refers, are public institutions—a species of organizations greatly affected by politics, politicians, interest groups, and
bureaucracy. It is for that reason that the Public Policy curriculum
has, from the beginning, required what has usually been called
"political," "bureaucratic," or "organizational" analysis. The principal goal of such courses is to enable students to understand that
there are, almost always, political and bureaucratic factors which, if
not taken into account, may well make any policy chosen to maximize efficiency utterly impossible to implement, or, if implemented,
guaranteed to fail in achieving this objective.

   An excerpt from the syllabus used in teaching such a course at the
University of Minnesota focuses the content even more sharply:

   If one is to be an effective professional in planning and public affairs,
   one needs to be able to do more than simply analyze plans and policies.
   One needs to understand the actual concrete social and political context in which plans and policies will be deliberated and implemented.
   One further needs to know how to act and how to find one's way
   through the thicket. This course will help you understand how the
   thicket is organized and how the transactional and interactional games
   are played out at the state and/or local level. (Bolen & Einsweiler, 1987,
   pp. 1-2).

These, then, are the three strands of the core curriculum required
to some extent or other by all schools of Public Policy. In addition,
all programs have developed required workshop courses, essentially as laboratory sessions in which perspectives from all three
strands are woven together and applied to specific policy problems.

Workshops, or policy exercises as they are sometimes called, have the goal of enabling students to integrate economic, quantitative, and organizational analysis in solving specific problems.

Increasingly, too, one finds in the Public Policy schools a growing number of substantive policy courses with exactly the same goal as the workshops: training students to integrate all three components of the core by applying them to a single area of public policy. Only in that fashion, it is believed, can students come to understand fully both the uses and the limitations of particular methods of analysis.

In addition, from their inception, the Public Policy schools have offered courses or modules on ethical and moral aspects of public policymaking, although only at Duke University is such a course required of all graduate and undergraduate students. The substance of ethics courses varies widely from school to school. Some concentrate on issues involving unethical practices occasionally employed by politicians, administrators, and others, such as lying, willful deception, or making decisions on the basis of self- interest even when it runs contrary to the public interest. Other ethics courses are organized around a consideration of alternative values which, because they conflict with one another, force policymakers—and indeed the public—to choose one over the other or to compromise their conflict. Such problems of "hard choices," as Professors Dennis Thompson and Amy Gutmann describe them in their syllabus, include conflicts between liberty and paternalism, liberty and life, equity and efficiency, and equality and neutrality. In view of the inevitability with which ethical considerations enter into every personal and official decision, it would seem imperative that policy analysts be both sensitized to those considerations and adequately trained in the methods of careful thought about them.

The only other frequently found subject, currently offered at Harvard, Duke, and RAND, although required in no school, focuses on history and public policy. The pioneering Harvard course, created by Professors Ernest May and Richard Neustadt, is entitled "Uses of History for Analysis and Management." The 1986-1987 catalog description reads:

> Explores the uses (and misuses) of historical materials for policy analysis and advocacy: seeking analogies, tracing patterns, placing people, and orienting oneself to institutions and issues (each with its own history). Considers problems of interpretation and problems of

parochialism: time, space, race, and class. Draws examples from among important questions of this century in civil rights, welfare, defense, foreign affairs. Includes other examples from different centuries and countries. (p. 6c)

If government bureaus and legislative chambers are the arenas in which quantitative analysis of public policy must prove its mettle, history is the context in which the policies of high officials, such as presidents, cabinet secretaries, and senators, will ultimately be judged wise or foolish, right or wrong, beneficial or harmful. There is hardly any area of public policy in which alternative solutions are not somehow constrained by our previous attempts, successful or not, to deal with the same problems. Not only does a knowledge of the history clarify the nature of the problem and constrain the solutions that are possible, but it is also the case, to paraphrase Proust, that policy analysts who exert themselves to remember the mistakes of past policies can thereby free themselves from being condemned to repeat them.

Moreover, the simple act of defining the problem to be solved requires judgments which necessarily include choices of one event in history over another, as the point in time from which to begin the analysis. This in turn affects the reasonable range of possible solutions. To use an example from the Harvard course, how one defines a reasonable policy for resolving or ameliorating the hostilities between Israel, the Palestinians, and their neighboring Arab countries depends entirely on the date at which we begin the analysis. For it is that date, perhaps more than any other factor, which determines who is right and who is wrong today, as well as the fairness of the trade-offs which any policy designed to solve the problem will impose on all parties.

Finally from the very beginning, the Public Policy schools have manifested a keen and unwavering commitment to ensure that their students acquire practical analytic, managerial, or problem-solving experience in so-called real world settings. In some schools, the emphasis is on summer internships or apprenticeships, while in others, students do either individual or group analytical projects for clients, usually government officials but sometimes officers of private organizations, generally not-for-profit. Such experience is thought to be essential if students are to understand the forces which bear on the policy-making process and the influence that bureaucratic settings have on it.

Evolutionary Refinements in the Public Policy Curriculum

While the basic required courses in all Public Policy schools are essentially the same as those first offered 20 years ago, it goes without saying that their content has been continuously updated with refinements in analytical methods, the introduction of new theory as it evolves, and new research as it is conducted and reported in books and journals. In addition, one can also now see— quite beyond the expected proliferation of courses in substantive policy areas—some entirely new subjects. One of these has achieved sufficient importance to warrant clusters of courses at several schools.

It will come as no surprise that the most widespread new entrant into the Public Policy curriculum is the subject of management, usually called public or political management. Like so many other important parts of the nationwide Public Policy curriculum, public management first began to make noticeable headway at Harvard, where it is now part of the required curriculum, as it also is at Duke. As first taught at Harvard, it grew out of Professor Mark Moore's courses in political and organizational analysis and reflected, according to him, his frustration in teaching those courses in a descriptive manner. In other words, while other core courses in the Public Policy curriculum are explicitly prescriptive in their orientation— that is, they are designed to enable students to use particular theory and analytic methods to solve discrete problems—the political and organizational analysis courses tended to have a descriptive orientation that betrayed their largely political science background. Moore's goal, and that of his associates, in developing courses in public management was to refocus political and organizational analysis into prescriptive subject matter, with a point of view that is decidedly strategic. In their teaching, therefore, they always asked not only "What are the political forces or organizational tendencies which affect the kind of policy we can formulate?", but also "What do I, as analyst or manager, need to do, as I shape my policy prescriptions or implement the chosen policy, to ensure that the political forces and organizational tendencies do not succeed in frustrating or changing desirable policy in undesirable ways?"

It was not very long before Moore, at Harvard, and Robert Behn, at Duke, decided that it was, in fact, impossible to combine in a single course both the presentation and discussion of the descriptive material necessary to answer the first question and the prescriptive/strategic orientation required to answer the second. The result of Moore's frustration, and his vision, was the first of a series of new courses that focus on management. The catalog description of the introductory course at Harvard, entitled "Managing Organizational Production and Implementation," begins:

> This course introduces the subject of 'public management' and surveys the concepts and tools that managers use to shape the ongoing activities of organizations they direct or to implement specific policies. (Barzelay, Leone, & Moore, 1986-1987, p. 3c)

The second course in that same series, entitled "Political Management and Institutional Leadership," continues in exactly the same spirit:

> The objectives of this course are two: first, to enhance capacities for diagnosing and solving problems of political management, and second, to develop a concept of 'strategy' as an integrating concept for public managers. The focus of the first part of the course is on shaping mandates through negotiation with political and legislative overseers, and by managing relations with the press and interest groups. The focus of the second part of the course is on the concept of 'organizational strategies' and the design of strategic planning processes in public sector organizations. (Barzelay et al., 1986-1987, p. 6c)

The second of the two courses constitutes a particularly radical step. To use Moore's own metaphor, the usual management courses focus on "downward" management, that is, on the ways in which leaders at the top of a pyramid can accomplish the objectives they set for those below them. The great innovation of the second course is its focus on "upward and outward" management—teaching students how to negotiate with collateral and superior centers of power, whether above them in their own agencies or in other agencies, or in the legislative bodies which make the laws, or in politically powerful interest groups, or in the press.

Such an approach to management enables students to learn how to craft a policy that can gain support from the beginning outside their own immediate administrative environs. That is why Harvard calls the course "political" management—because policy choice is appropriately made in the political arena. It is in that arena of upward and outward management that public sector executives, it is estimated, spend more than half their working hours.

In "political management," perhaps more than in any other course, therefore, the spirit of the Public Policy schools, that which most dramatically differentiates it from public administration, comes through most strikingly. It is a contemporary spirit that denies any alleged division between policy and administration.

The content of these courses was, to some scholars and practitioners of policy analysis, uncomfortably similar to parts of the curriculum taught in the old public administration schools. Yet what prevents the Public Policy schools' courses in public management from having any similarity to the old public administration courses that covered similar topics—and emphatically I cannot speak to the current offerings of schools of public administration because I have not surveyed them recently—is the fact that the subject matter, as taught in Public Policy, is indissolubly wedded to the subject matter of the required courses dealing with sophisticated economics, analytics, and political and organizational analysis. Without that bond, it is possible that courses which deal with such matters as personnel management might, in time, conceivably degenerate into the simply descriptive exercises that generally characterized such courses in public administration. But the fact is that they *are* inextricably bound, by the required nature of the curriculum, to analytics and theory which are several orders of magnitude more sophisticated than virtually anything taught in schools of public administration at the time of the founding of the Public Policy schools.

Moreover, there is a second characteristic of such public management courses—and, in fact, of nearly all public policy courses—as they are taught in all Public Policy schools: their almost invariable decision-forcing character. Unlike the old public administration cases which simply recount an actual sequence of events about which the students are then asked questions, the public management courses in Public Policy schools present sets of facts which the students are obliged to use in formulating decisions about given problems. Sometimes the facts are hypothetical and sometimes they are historical, but virtually always they are presented in such a way as to force students to make a decision, rather than simply to comment on, praise, or criticize the decision that someone else has made. This is precisely the same step which schools of medicine took many years ago. Medical students are not simply taught the principles of anatomy and physiology; they are forced to diagnose an illness, chart a prognosis, and prescribe a treatment.

By teaching skills in the context of decision-forcing cases within courses characterized by a uniformly strategic orientation, premised on and utilizing sophisticated analytic techniques, the Public Policy schools seem to me to be in no danger of relapsing into the old public administration mold.

In the methodological vein, given the explosion in general and personal computing, one should not be surprised to find in Public Policy curricula a rapidly expanding body of instruction in the use of computers. Of all the Public Policy schools, Carnegie-Mellon offers the most courses—12 as of last count—and indeed offers not only a Master of Public Management (MPM) degree, with a management information systems concentration, but a totally separate degree program: Master of Science in Management Information Systems. The courses offered in the MPM concentration include "Information Systems for Public Managers," "Analysis and Design of Information Systems," "Management of Computer and Information Systems," and "Urban Information Systems." No other school of Public Policy offers so broad an array of such courses, although all of them require their students to use computers—both mainframe and personal—in analyzing data in the core courses. I suspect that, in 5 years' time, all schools of Public Policy will include many courses like those offered by Carnegie-Mellon.

Other curricular areas into which the Public Policy schools seem to be expanding include separate courses in budgeting and financial management, which are sometimes treated within public management courses. Duke, Harvard, Maryland, Michigan, Minnesota, and RAND now offer such courses.

In addition, in the past few years, some of the schools have begun to formulate courses in negotiation, both general and focused on labor relations. While negotiation and arbitration have always been key components in schools which train students whose careers will involve bargaining with labor unions, they have not always been dealt with in schools of Public Policy. That they are today is suggestive of a growing interest in so-called alternative decision-making techniques.

This term is used mainly to describe efforts to resolve disputes outside the traditional adversary avenues offered by the court system. In addition, negotiation is, as we have noted, one among several methods which public managers can use, quite aside from the narrow labor relations context, in formulating and implementing their organizational strategies. Such courses now appear in the Harvard and University of Maryland catalogs.

In the early days, the substantive policy courses, as well as most of the case examples used in the methodological courses, dealt almost always with domestic matters. It must be said, however, that most Public Policy curricula now include one or more elective courses dealing with some aspect of international relations policy. Harvard alone offers nine separate courses within its concentration area of international affairs and security and 10 different courses in the concentration on international development.

The Difference Between Public Policy and Other Fields of Study

Policy analysis is neither more nor less than a lens for viewing a subject, a frame designed to fit around a problem so as to help us come to grips with it. It is a useful framework for integrating knowledge about most problems which lend themselves to purposive individual or social action. Policy analysis is designed to force one to think ahead in order to identify and organize the information which both defines a given problem and appears to be necessary to fully explore solutions. A well-constructed policy analysis will also specify the analytic techniques which must be applied for understanding the underlying data, the decisions that need to be made to accomplish desired results, as well as their sequencing, and the statistical techniques for estimating the probability that particular outcomes will occur.

Policy analysis is not a discipline. Rather, it chooses the analytic methods, theories, and substantive knowledge generated by other fields that are useful to integrate into its own framework for application to particular problems at hand. Policy analysis differs from the disciplines on which it draws so heavily—principally political science and economics—in two major respects. First, while they are both predominantly descriptive, policy analysis is prescriptive, or "actionable," as Dean Charles Wolf of the RAND Graduate School describes it. Or, put another way, while they are both contemplative in nature, policy analysis is decisive in nature. And second, while each of the disciplines tends to a kind of orthodoxy in erecting boundaries around itself—defining what is and is not economics or political science—policy analysis is, by definition, heterodox, eclectic, integrative, and inclusive. In other words, the disciplines tend toward insularity, looking only at those parts of problems with which each regards itself competent to deal, while policy analysis aspires to be reasonably comprehensive, looking at the whole problem.

I stress the word "tend" because very often such generalizations are misleading. Political scientists frequently do engage in prescription, but I believe that it is accurate to describe their basic orientation as principally devoted to explaining political institutions and forces, with any prescription arising by way of inferences from the explanation. Prescription is entirely incidental to the principal role of the political scientist, as well as that of scholars in most other disciplines which describe themselves as "social science." While economic theory pays as much attention to normative as to descriptive issues, its normative framework is excessively narrow. As my Duke colleague, the economist Philip Cook, puts it, it is only a slight exaggeration to depict the roots of economics as growing principally from the notions "that each individual has clearly developed preferences, that those preferences are typically selfish, and that the aggregation of those preferences is the proper basis for a definition of the public interest." Moreover, in the jargon of empiricism, most social scientists study policy as what they call a "dependent"—that is, assumed—variable, while policy analysts regard policy as the "independent"—that is, manipulable—variable.

With policy analysis, the goal is not merely to describe problems but to solve them, to create and assess possible solutions. Policy analysis starts where economics and political science leave off, building on their descriptions and inferences to formulate alternative solutions and projecting the likely consequences. In so doing, policy analysis incorporates, at any one time, only a tiny fraction of the contents of the underlying disciplines, choosing those fragments which appear relevant to solving the problem at hand. To them, policy analysis then adds useful or pertinent elements from statistics, operations research, history, and ethics.

Because policy analysis is nourished, sustained, and continuously refined by the underlying basic disciplines, it is no surprise to discover that most of the faculty members in Public Policy schools, as well as a preponderance of those guiding policy analytic research in the government and private research institutes, are trained to the doctoral level in one of those disciplines. Usually they are economists or political scientists, but sometimes they are statisticians, engineers, or operations researchers. Most of the Public Policy faculty members think of themselves, therefore, as either economists or political scientists *and* policy analysts. When faculty vacancies occur, they are almost always described in terms of training in one of the underlying disciplines. That fact alone is a powerful metaphor for the way in which policy analysis stands on the shoulders of the underlying disciplines and takes account of their descriptive, analytic, and theoretic capacities in formulating policy prescriptions.

Policy analysis draws its intellectual paradigm from microeconomics, the source of which is Benthamite utilitarianism: rational calculation of causes and results, as well as costs and benefits. But policy analysis differs from economics by refusing to be bound, for the most part, by constraints on what it can take into account in calculation, constraints that economics not only accepts but postulates. For example, because it is a practical tool for solving problems in the real world, policy analysis routinely deals with messy data—the very opposite of the precise, neat, quantifiable information that is the heart of econometrics and economic models. The ideal of the economist is an elegant model premised on such quantified knowledge. The ideal of the policy analyst is to use the economist's framework but broaden it to accommodate political, value-laden, normative, historical, and other not-neatly-quantified factors.

Although it derives the mind-set from economics, policy analysis focuses on the realities of power, who exercises it, how, and to what ends. That is, of course, the very heart of the discipline of contemporary political science, which is why many have analogized policy analysis to what used to be called political economy. That phrase declares the reality that political—that is, value-laden—choices provide the energy and direction that drive economics' analytic framework.

Policy analysts are generalist problem solvers. Unlike those who specialize in such fields of applied knowledge as education, public health, and the old public administration, policy analysts, because of their role as generalists, do not become bounded by the substantive knowledge and perspectives of the problem areas to which they apply their analytic skills. The analytic framework, rather than the substantive problems, is their disciplinary substitute.

None of this is meant to suggest that policy analysts are somehow exemplary, some noble breed apart from everyone else. In fact, to describe them as different from other social scientists is only to underscore their prescriptive and integrative orientation. It must also be stressed that many other scholars, who study public problems and offer well thought-out solutions to them, choose to describe themselves not as policy analysts but as economists or members of some other basic social science discipline.

Moreover, the work done by policy analysts runs the same gamut of quality as that done by scholars and practitioners in any other social science. When it is good, it can be extremely helpful; when it is sloppy, fuzzy or careless, it can be worse than useless, indeed downright harmful, principally because it is designed specifically to be put into practice.

The Achievements of the Public Policy Schools

In the 20 years which have elapsed since the founding of the first schools of Public Policy, the movement of public policy analysis has established itself as a contributor to public policy discourse and policymaking of widely recognized importance. All of the original schools abound with students and are otherwise thriving. Their numbers have been augmented by subsequently established Public

Policy or public management degree programs, using some approximation of the same curricular mix, at over 20 other institutions.

The reason that other programs have been established and the enrollments of the original schools have continued to grow is that a growing market for their graduates has developed. That market has several components.

First, there are the public policy research organizations which support themselves by contract research for government or by foundation grants. In addition to RAND, there are the Urban Institute, founded, incidentally, in the same year as the original academic programs, and the American Enterprise Institute for Public Policy Research. There are also such research organizations as ABT Associates, Arthur D. Little, Battelle, the Research Triangle Institute, and the Southwest Research Institute.

In addition, one of the largest markets for Public Policy graduates has been for-profit consulting firms, which typically do analyses for both the private and the public sectors. All of the major national consulting firms, including McKinsey, Booz Allen, Cresap McCormick, and Bain, recruit Public Policy students. So do those of the major national accounting firms which have established public management divisions, such as Coopers and Lybrand. Almost one third of all Public Policy master's graduates are choosing to work for consulting firms.

Somewhere between one half and two thirds of the Public Policy graduates choose employment in the public sector, divided almost evenly between the federal government, on one hand, and state and local governments, on the other. In the federal establishment, they are, of course, legion in the Office of Management and Budget, as well as in the various policy analysis and program evaluation sections in the departments, commissions, and offices. Many of them, however, are in line positions in substantive program areas throughout the executive branch, and some are serving in important staff positions with individual members of Congress and congressional committees, as well as in the Congressional Budget Office. At the state and local levels, they are in budget offices, planning agencies, and in line positions in substantive agencies.

A small fraction of the graduates are working for private organizations, some in the public affairs divisions of for-profit corporations and others in not-for-profit agencies of one kind or other.

Various public interest organizations, such as those dealing with health, the environment, and consumer protection, have been attractive to graduates, as have foundations. In addition, some have found their way into trade associations—that is, lobbying organizations—representing particular groups of industries.

The annual increase in Public Policy graduates nationally is about 1,000, and, judging from the salaries reported by the schools, the demand for them seems to be continuing to grow. If the market were not absorbing the supply, the salaries would not be continuously rising. Perhaps that is a reflection of the reality noted by Aaron Wildavsky (1985): "When government is expanding, it needs more of everything so it might as well have analysts. When times are tough, agencies need people to tell them how to cut back" (p. 33).

The schools and their alumni, then, are indeed prospering. This has, of course, contributed to the sense of being part of a growing movement of individuals who approach public problems from the same vantage and with at least some of the same value orientations. That feeling has been fostered, too, by the creation of the Association for Public Policy Analysis and Management (APPAM), which is to the field of policy analysis what their respective disciplinary associations are to economics and political science. The membership of APPAM has been growing by about 10% a year, and now stands at about 1,500.

Like the analogous disciplinary organizations, APPAM annually sponsors national, indeed international, research conferences, which have grown better and larger with each passing year. The 1989 Research Conference, which took place in Arlington, Virginia, attracted 600 registered scholars and practitioners. The breadth and quality of the agenda were impressive.

Too exclusive a concentration on the institutional achievements of Public Policy poses the risk of neglecting the intellectual contributions of the field. It is indeed those contributions, both in their intrinsic merits and in their embodiment in schools, programs, research, and living human beings, which, in the end, are the justification for the energy and resources which went into the creation and sustenance of the new schools.

The roster of Public Policy's intellectual contributions is far too long to be listed exhaustively here, but a few examples will illustrate their significance. There is now far better understanding of the role of uncertainty in decisions and policies, traceable directly back to the fields of defense, international security policy, and arms control, which were, as pointed out earlier, the original sources of Public Policy education. Not only do we now better recognize the crucial role that uncertainty plays in all purposive action, but Public Policy has taken a lead in developing methodologies, such as those pioneered by Howard Raiffa, designed to enable decision makers to grapple with uncertainty effectively and responsibly. As Harvard's Richard Zeckhauser pointed out to me, if one compares any of today's economics journals on an applied subject with those of 20 years ago, one discovers that "the prevalence of uncertainty as a core topic has multiplied tenfold" (personal correspondence, February 2, 1988).

A related contribution of Public Policy is underscoring the importance of, as well as applying, game theory, interactive decision techniques, and bargaining to decision-making and policy-making processes. Largely, but not only, because of the influence of Public Policy scholars, we have come increasingly to understand the public policy arena as one that is highly dynamic, with not only the formal institutions of government frequently struggling with one another but with groups within groups, both inside and outside government, competing to shape outcomes to their preferred ends. While other social and behavioral sciences have also contributed to our understanding of this phenomenon, Public Policy has pioneered the application of methods which promise to be useful to students, scholars, and practitioners in coping constructively with those forces.

In perhaps its most significant contribution, Public Policy has led the way in helping the public rethink the whole range of issues surrounding the proper role of government. Almost certainly to a greater extent than other fields of study, Public Policy has highlighted the question of which social functions can best be served by government, which by nongovernmental institutions, and which by individual citizens. Scholars of Public Policy have probed many well-known cases of so-called market failure to discover whether and when public/private solutions would be more effective than private solutions alone, and, correspondingly, they have also probed many cases of government failure to ascertain when some greater involvement by the private sector, or some combination of sectors, would be more successful (Zeckhauser, 1986).

Of great importance in a democracy is yet another field of Public Policy scholarship, that which focuses on how best to organize government so as to maximize the likelihood that the interests of the citizenry are effectively served. This focus on principals and agents—on the citizens as principals and on government officials as their agents—is an area of Public Policy study that holds great promise for dealing with some of the public problems of greatest concern to the citizenry (Pratt & Zeckhauser, 1987).

The cumulation of so many persons using the same language, so to speak, has inevitably changed the character of public discourse on many issues. By creating a body of comparatively value-neutral, objective means of discussion of policy issues and policy-making, Public Policy has enabled partisans, decisionmakers, and observers to talk rationally and without excessive passion, at least sometimes, about controversial, value-laden problems. Moreover, by being more explicit about the costs and benefits, including who pays and who benefits and how much, as well as about the assumptions which underlie the selection of objectives to optimize and the criteria by which choices are made, it has made it easier for antagonists to detect with reasonable precision where they differ, thereby enabling them to find common ground. All essentially political decisions are compromises of one sort or another, and compromises are rarely achievable without clarification of the interests at stake between the parties to the controversy.

As important as any achievement of policy analysis is the difference it has made in democratizing discourse about public problems. As Aaron Wildavsky (1985) made clear, policy analysis is to public policy what the First Amendment's guarantee of a free press is to democracy as a whole:

> Traditionally, the main characteristics of bureaucracy are seen as security of tenure and a monopoly of expertise. The policy analytic movement in America has weakened tenure and destroyed monopoly. For every important area of policy in America, there are numerous rival centers of analysis. The bureaucracy has not only lost a monopoly of expertise in defense, but also in transportation and welfare and medical care. Civil servants can no longer claim they really know better than anybody else, a claim that our bureaucracy could make in most areas of policy through the 1950s. Consequently, information about public policy—how it works now, why it might work better, which

clienteles it might serve differently—while once a private preserve, has become public property; its provision has changed from monopoly to a competitive enterprise. (p. 33)

Moreover, by creating an objective framework of analysis based solidly on factual evidence that is quantified when possible, the very possibility of a better understanding of issues by all parties—decision makers as well as antagonists—has been substantially increased. By proliferating policy-analysis-based groups of individuals—who know and respect the rules and language of the same framework of reasoning and evidence—in the executive branch, in the Congress, among contending interest groups, within the academic and think-tank communities, as well as in the world of journalism, policy analysis has created a common ground for public discourse. What more beneficial contribution could any institution make to any society?

References

Barzelay, M., Leone, R., & Moore, M. (1986-1987). Course descriptions for "Managing Organizational Production and Implementation" and "Political Management and Institutional Leadership" at the John F. Kennedy School of Government, Harvard University. *Catalogue 1986-87*, 3c, 6c.

Bloom, H. S., & Boersch-Supan, A. (1985). Course syllabus for "Empirical Analysis I" at the John F. Kennedy School of Government, Harvard University, p. 1.

Bolen, R., & Einsweiler, R. (1987). Course syllabus for "PA5002: Policy Process II" at the Hubert Humphrey Institute of Public Affairs, University of Minnesota, pp. 1-2.

Cave, J., & Hildebrandt, G. (1986). Course syllabus for "Microeconomics I" at the RAND Graduate School, p. 1.

Friedman, L. S. (1987). Public policy economics: A survey of current pedagogical practice. *Journal of Policy Analysis and Management*, 6(3), 505.

May, E., & Neustadt, R. (1986-1987). Course description for "Uses of History for Analysis and Management," at the John F. Kennedy School of Government, Harvard University. *Catalogue 1986-87*, 6c.

Pratt, J. W., & Zeckhauser, R. (1987). *Principals and agents: The structure of business.* Boston, MA: Harvard Business School Press.

Wildavsky, A. (1985). The once and future school of public policy. *Public Interest*, 79, 33.

Zeckhauser, R. (1986). The muddled responsibilities of public and private America. In W. Knowlton & R. Zeckhauser (Eds.), *American society and private responsibility* (pp. 45-77). Boston, MA: Ballinger.

Index

About the Editors

David Easton is Distinguished Professor of Political Science at the University of California, Irvine, and Andrew MacLeish Distinguished Service Professor Emeritus at the University of Chicago. He was Co-Chair of the Western Center and Vice President of the American Academy of Arts and Sciences. He received his B.A. and M.A. from the University of Toronto and his Ph.D. from Harvard University, and has written numerous books and articles on political science. He has served on the boards of editors of several journals in political science. A former president of the American Political Science Association, he is a fellow of The Royal Society of Canada.

Corinne S. Schelling is Associate Executive Officer of the American Academy of Arts and Sciences. Trained as an economist, with a background in government service in international affairs, she has participated in a wide range of Academy studies on public policy and social science questions. Most recently she was co-editor of *Public-Private Partnership: New Opportunities for Meeting Social Needs* and assisted the editors of *The U.S. Business Corporation: An Institution in Transition*. She is now engaged in several joint projects between the American Academy and French scholars on immigration policy and urban problems.

About the Authors

Earl F. Cheit is Edgar F. Kaiser Professor of Business and Public Policy at the University of California, Berkeley. From 1976 to 1982, he was Dean of the School of Business Administration, and from 1981 to 1982, acting Vice-President, Financial and Business Management, at the University of California. Earlier he served in other administrative posts at the University. He holds several degrees, including a Ph.D in economics and a JD from the University of Minnesota. He has written extensively on higher education, as well as on various aspects of business management and industrial relations. He is Senior Advisor, Asian-Pacific Economic Affairs, The Asia Foundation.

Joel L. Fleishman is Professor of Law and Public Policy Studies and Vice-President, Duke University, where in addition to his professorship he has held many administrative posts. He has degrees, including the JD, from the University of North Carolina and a Master of Laws from Yale Law School. He has been Director, Institute of Policy Sciences and Public Affairs; Chairman, Department of Public Policy Studies; and Vice Chancellor for Education and Research in Public Policy at Duke University. From 1961 to 1967, he served as legal assistant to Governor Terry Sanford of North Carolina.

Richard D. Lambert is Director of The National Foreign Language Center at Johns Hopkins University. He is emeritus Professor of Sociology at the University of Pennsylvania, where he served as Chairman of the South Asia Regional Studies Department (and as Dean of Academic Planning, Continuing Education, and Development. He is past president of the Association of Asian Studies and of the American Academy of Political Science, whose *Annals* he has edited for 10 years. He has published extensively on international studies and on language and area studies. His books on this topic include *Language and Area Studies Review; Beyond Growth: The Next Stage in Language and Area Studies; Points of Leverage;* and *International Studies and the Undergraduate.*

J. Hillis Miller is Distinguished Professor of English and Comparative Literature at the University of California, Irvine. He received his doctorate from Harvard University and has held professorships at Johns Hopkins University and Yale University, where he was Frederick W. Hilles Professor of English and Professor of Comparative Literature. In 1986 he was president of the Modern Language Association. He has served as editor or on the advisory board of many journals and has lectured widely at home and abroad. His books include *Charles Dickens: The World of his Novels; Thomas Hardy: Distance and Desire; The Linguistic Moment;* and *The Ethics of Reading.* He has been a member of the American Academy of Arts and Sciences since 1970.

John R. Searle is Professor of Philosophy, University of California, Berkeley. He attended the University of Wisconsin, where he was awarded a Rhodes Scholarship to Oxford in his Junior year. He received his B.A., M.A., and D.Phil. degrees from Oxford. He was a lecturer at Oxford and has held visiting professorships in the United States, England, Canada, Norway, Germany, Italy, and Brazil. His books include *Speech Acts, Expression and Meaning; Intentionality;* and *Minds, Brains and Science.* In 1984 he was the Reith Lecturer on BBC, and he has appeared frequently on U.S. public television. In 1989 he was President of the American Philosophical Association. He has been a member of the American Academy of Arts and Sciences since 1977.

Charles Tilly is Distinguished Professor of Sociology and History and Director of the Center for Studies of Social Change at the New School for Social Research. He received his doctorate from Harvard University. He was professor of History, professor of Sociology, and Theodore M. Newcomb Professor of Social Science at the University of Michigan. He also has been associated with several universities in France, including the Ecole des Hautes Etudes en Sciences Sociales and University of Paris I and VII. He is a member of the National Academy of Sciences and the American Academy of Arts and Sciences.

Ralph H. Turner is Professor of Sociology, University of California, Los Angeles. His doctorate is in sociology from the University of Chicago. He has served as editor of the *Annual Review of Sociology* since 1980, and has been president of the American Sociological Association and vice-president of the International Sociological Association. His publications have been on collective behavior; social aspects of disaster, especially earthquakes; theory of social roles; and sociological theory and method. He is a member of the American Academy of Arts and Sciences.